D0486086

BEFORE THE WIND

BEFORE THE WIND

TRUE STORIES ABOUT SAILING

DAVID GOWDEY

International Marine
Camden, Maine

International Marine/
Ragged Mountain Press

A Division of The McGraw·Hill Companies

12 13 14 15 16 DOC/DOC 0 9 8 7 6

Copyright © 1994 David Gowdey

All rights reserved. The publisher takes no responsibility for the use of any of the materials or methods described in this book, nor for the products thereof. The name "International Marine" and the International Marine logo are trademarks of McGraw-Hill, Inc. Printed in the United States of America.

Library of Congress Cataloging-in-Publication Data
Gowdey, David, 1951–
Before the wind : true stories about sailing / David Gowdey.
p.   cm.
Originally published: Toronto : Macmillan Canada, 1992.
ISBN 0-07-023756-5
1. Sailing. 2. Sailboat racing. I. Title.
GV811.G67 1994
797.1'24—dc20   93-47922
                                       CIP

Questions regarding the content of this book should be addressed to:

International Marine
P.O. Box 220
Camden, ME 04843

Questions regarding the ordering of this book should be addressed to:

The McGraw-Hill Companies
Customer Service Department
P.O. Box 547
Blacklick, OH 43004
Retail Customers: 1-800-262-4729
Bookstores: 1-800-722-4726

Before the Wind is printed on recycled paper containing a minimum of 50% total recycled paper with 10% postconsumer de-inked fiber.

Cover design by Tania Craan
Cover photograph by Benjamin Mendlowitz

Page 101, *Reading the Weather*, Grumman Allied Industries, 1965.

Page 115, quote from *The Mirror of the Sea* by Joseph Conrad, London, 1906.

Page 179, quote from *The Schooner Flight* by Desmond Walcott, from *The Collected Poems of Desmond Walcott*, Farrar, Straus and Giroux, New York.

Contents

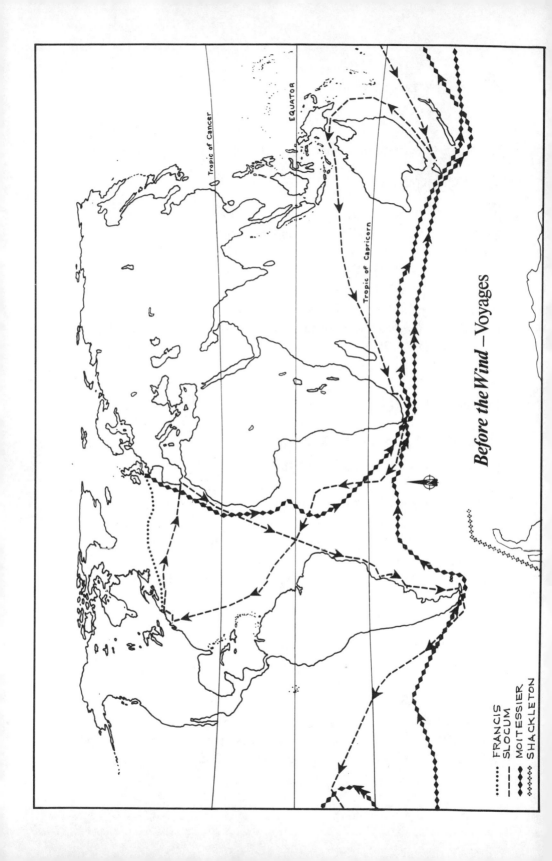

Before the Wind — Voyages

FRANCIS
SLOCUM
MOITESSIER
SHACKLETON

INTRODUCTION

DAVID GOWDEY

Our imaginations are piqued by space-travel, but the sea is our ancestral frontier. A nearby watercourse has always meant access to the world beyond. For early man, travel by land across any distance presented huge difficulties: deserts, ice-fields, marshes, mountain ranges: above all, vast, impenetrable forests. For centuries water was the only practical means of exploration, and some sense of this remains with us.

As the moon tugs on the oceans, the oceans act on us, drawing us toward them. To go to sea is to escape in the best sense, to flee trivial routine for something more lasting. The sea calls in a different voice to each of us, with a message we all understand: there's something beyond what we know, and we can reach it.

The first vessels were rafts fashioned from bundles of buoyant reeds. Instead of a bulky wooden superstructure, the reeds simply floated on the surface, allowing the sea to rush through while keeping the adventurers, if not dry, at least afloat. Thor Heyerdahl and others have convincingly shown that most of the first knowledge about our planet came from sailors.

From trial and error, basic lore about prevailing winds and currents evolved all over the world. The discovery of these rivers through the oceans took place thousands of years before Columbus. There is good evidence that the peoples who emerged in the Pacific after the last ice age were the first to put sailing craft to full use, travelling between islands that had been connected before the ice retreated and ocean levels rose. Rafts and boats represented the cutting edge of technology in their day, able to make long voyages as far as Egypt and Mesopotamia, where the first written cultures developed.

The northern caravel sea lane across the Pacific was discovered by resourceful South American tribes looking for a safe

1

island haven away from their enemies: when the Spaniards arrived in Peru they were given expert directions by Incas on how to reach islands in the Pacific thousands of miles away. The northern Kiro current that turns from the Philippines to run back to the coast of British Columbia may well have been a pathway for migration to the Americas, an arduous trip, but no more demanding than the tundra route between Siberia and Alaska.

Early voyages had to follow the prevailing winds and currents, but eventually sails were perfected that allowed ships like the early dhows to tack at a sharp angle into the wind. From this technology came movements into previously uncharted areas. The Phoenicians sailed as far as Britain, establishing a trade route in the early Bronze Age. In his book *Critical Path* Buckminster Fuller writes that the development of tacking, allowing travel by sea against prevailing currents, had an additional effect:

> Out of this remarkable skill came a new phase of "world" seafarers. No longer subject to the vagaries of the elements, they could make headway against them.
>
> After many thousands of years eastbound man became westbound. The former gave rise to the Eastern philosophy of "acceptance," which still persists. The latter was a new development and fundamentally altered humanity's thinking. To the sailor, God seems to be the prevailing winds and currents that carry one in a particular direction. To go against the wind or current, to "beat to windward," is therefore a deliberate act against Him. Here began a concept of man being contrary to his God.

Sailing puts us back in touch with the most basic forces on earth. On shore it's easy to forget, for we're assailed every moment with questions. The world closes in, demanding answers we don't have readily at hand, in a language foreign to our true natures. But when we are near the sea, as Robert Frost once wrote, we turn our backs on the land. We look to the horizon, to a chance to leave behind what we don't feel is part of us, to seek out something more authentic. When we depart, the land drops out of sight, and with it goes the complexity that we take so much for granted.

Writer and yachtsman Ernest K. Gann describes the great relief that follows:

> As soon as [the sailor] realizes that whatever he wants is not to be had, and moreover that even if it was available he could not use it, he loses the pox of desire . . . To observe human beings without pressing desire is to rediscover mankind, and is at times so encouraging that one is not ashamed to walk on two legs.

John F. Kennedy, speaking at Newport on the eve of the 1962 America's Cup races, had a further explanation:

> I really don't know why it is that all of us are so committed to the sea, except I think it's because in addition to the fact that the sea changes, and the light changes, and ships change, it's because we all came from the sea. All of us have in our veins the exact same percentage of salt in our blood that exists in the ocean, and therefore we have salt in our blood, in our sweat, in our tears. We are tied to the ocean. And when we go back to the sea – whether it is to sail or to watch it – we are going back from whence we came.

Today most inlanders' first glimpse of the sailing world comes through the expanding coverage of the America's Cup. Ted Turner's raucous win in 1977 upset the old guard at Newport, and Dennis Conner's drive to success has ushered in a brassy new era of massive corporate sponsorship. The races offer a firm test of innovative design and grace under pressure, as well as a showplace for all the arrogance and skulduggery the rich are currently willing to display. To many sailors the obsession with winning that characterizes racing seems out of place at sea, a refusal to let go of shorebound values. The graciousness shown by Sir Thomas Lipton while losing year after year made

him hugely popular with the public; I wonder if he'd be welcomed in the same spirit today.

But despite the often farcical arguments and the vast expense
the races pull hard on our emotions. It's partly tradition, partly
the beauty of the ships, partly our willingness to see it as a
symbol of national vigour. The great Lunenburg schooner
Bluenose, Canada's "ship on the dime," sailed a lovely course as a
racer and never had to appeal to the committee room for a win.
The series she dominated from 1921 to 1938 was open only to
actual saltbankers: anything designed solely for racing was
excluded, unless somehow the newcomer was able to prove a
worthy working vessel. Captain Angus Walters, the *Bluenose*'s
skipper, called the American challengers "a bit tender-sided,"
allowing that while they might be fast, they wouldn't hold up in
a stiff wind. Bluenose not only beat all comers but for many
years held the port record for a single day's fishing catch.

Sea travel makes a writer out of many a deckhand, and it
sometimes seems as if every singlehanded sailor in history has
published day-by-day memoirs. Out of the wealth of material
I've tried to collect stories that view not only life at sea but life
from the vantage point of the sea. I wanted to find pieces that
would be meaningful not just to sailors but to those who've
never been to sea. Stories like Stephen Thomas's South Seas
apprenticeship, or Ernest Shackleton's voyage up from the Antarctic, or Bernard Moitessier's abandonment of a round-the-
world race to continue farther on his own quest, deal with the
most basic themes we know. The sea *is* the world, three-
quarters of it, and what men and women experience there is
elemental.

1

Casting Off

Only once he failed to seize the cabin-door handle at the first grab. He waited a little, tried again, and again failed. His weight was growing heavier on my arm. He sighed slowly.

"D—n that handle!"

Without letting go his hold of me he turned about, his face lit up bright as day by the full moon.

"I wish she were out at sea," he growled, savagely.

"Yes, sir."

I felt the need to say something, because he hung on to me as if lost, breathing heavily.

"Ports are no good – ships rot, men go to the devil!"

I kept still, and after a while he repeated with a sigh:

"I wish she were at sea out of this."

Joseph Conrad
The Mirror of the Sea

I can assure you that I am eminently respectable, but find other respectable people tiresome.

From a letter to Jack London,
responding to his advertisement
for a crew

Working on a Dream

Ann Davison

Three years before her solo voyage across the Atlantic, Ann Davison began a sailing apprenticeship in a small boatyard near Portsmouth, England.

The only way to live is to have a dream green and growing in your life – anything else is just existing and a waste of breath. My dreams don't run on mink–coat–and–diamond lines – not that I have anything against mink coats and diamonds, but they aren't much use on an island, or in an airplane, or in a boat, and those are the sort of lines my dreams run along. Rugged stuff. Adventure, some people call it, or romance, or when they are really frustrated, escapism. If anyone asked me and I was unguarded enough to reply, I would call it the pursuit of beauty, or truth, and if I was honest I would admit it was largely curiosity, the urge to find out the why, the what, and the how at first hand, without simply taking someone else's word for it.

Most of my dreams have come true at one time or another, so adventure and I are old buddies. We have had some rare capers together, good, bad, exciting, interesting, and, on occasion, terrible, but never at any time have they been dull. I know by now that the glitter of romance as seen from afar often turns out to be pretty shoddy at close quarters, and what appears to be a romantic life is invariably an uncomfortable one; but I know, too, that the values in such living are usually sound. They have to be, or you don't survive. And occasionally you are rewarded by an insight into living so splendid, so wholly magnificent, you can be satisfied with nothing less ever after, so that you go on hoping and searching for another glimpse for the rest of your life.

The dream-boat business came up three years before I actually set out, because I had a life going spare and wanted to use it;

and the notion of sailing a small boat about the world appealed because it offered freedom, independence, travel, and a home into the bargain. It represented a variety of interests in the actual management and navigation of the ship, all fairly unknown activities to me, and it was necessary at the time for me to acquire new interests and so a new meaning in life; also it would surely provide unlimited copy with which to feed the type-writer and, incidentally, me, for I had degenerated into a writer of sorts through the years. The fact I knew nothing about boats, very little about sailing, and was terrified of the sea was no deterrent to a full-scale production of a dream. I could learn, and with knowledge some of the fears would vanish.

The decision to sail the Atlantic instead of groping around the coast as a shakedown cruise was not quite so crazy as it seems, for ships, like airplanes, are only likely to get into real trouble near land, which was one factor I knew irrefutably. Moreover, I reckoned I would know by the time I reached America whether I liked the life or not, and either way there ought to be a story in it. After all, no other woman had sailed the Atlantic single-handed, or even, so far as I knew, attempted to do so, which fact did not influence me in the least, though it turned out to be a useful stick with which to goad enthusiasm in others. Enthusi-asm in others is a primary necessity when undertaking an enter-prise one knows very little about.

The venture had to remain at the dream stage for a couple of years from its inception because I was starting life again from scratch with no more than the clothes I stood up in and with a fair pack of wolves howling at the door. To settle the wolves was the first consideration; money had to be made in order to feed them, and without capital or skill the quickest way to make any seemed to me to write a book. Just a hunch I had. However, this would not have been possible without the extraordinary gener-osity of two of the kindest people I know, who not only threw open their home to me, but, more important even than that, gave unstintingly their understanding and unfailing moral sup-port. Whatever their own private doubts may have been, they never once showed them to me. Never once did they ask, as they might well have done, "What if the book is a flop?" You take in a stray cat and it doesn't catch the mice. But their attitude was always to talk hopefully of the prospects "when the book comes out" as if its success was a foregone conclusion, though they could have had no possible grounds for such a belief.

As a matter of fact I wrote two books, writing the second whilst the first was gestating at the publishers, apparently unable to break off the habit; and without setting the world on fire, they did for me all I had hoped and gambled on. To drop the wolf motif, creditors were paid off, and a little was left over for dream money. But dreams like wolves (how did they get in again?) have to be fed, so in between books or stubborn chapters I went in search of boatlore against the time I owned one of my own. I even took a job as a hand in a boatyard for some months.

It was a small primitive yard on the south coast, unpretentious and unconventional, otherwise I should never have got the job, women in the boating industry being as popular as Beethoven at a jam session. It was tucked away at the end of an obscure mud creek where the tide used to creep in and out apologetically as if sorry to disturb. Plover spun over the nearby fields, curlew called from the saltings, wild duck paddled by the shore, and the whole setting was so rural it might have been a hundred miles from the sea, which was around the corner and way out of sight. The yard was so far from the nearest branch of civilization only the keenest boating enthusiast could ever find it, the postman rarely, and the newspaperman never.

The owner, Jake, was tall, dark, and bearded, stern and withdrawn, given to sudden flashes of disarming affability. He could build a boat, renovate a wreck, a radio, or an engine with equal facility and consummate skill. He wrote intelligent articles for the technical press and novels on the side. He once remarked after a long silence and apropos of nothing at all, "You talk about imagination, but no one has anything on the Lord."

His wife, Carol, was small and vital with the beauty of an eighteenth-century miniature. She ought to have worn a pompadour and patches, but instead wore pastel-coloured slacks and multicoloured scarves and lived at the run as though time was too scarce for walking. She was talented and versatile, equally at home splitting logs with a giant axe, making elegant clothes from her own designs, weaving mats on her patent loom, or carving doll's furniture out of scrap wood in the carpenter's shop. The doll's furniture was for their daughter, Susan, aged five, a prodigy who could, and would, read anything. "Is the crisis over?" she would inquire from behind a formidably political paper. She crawled under the boat where I was lying flat on my back learning the boating business from the bottom up – and just how much bottom there is to a thirty-foot boat has to be scraped to be appreciated – to terrify me with a string of strangely inconsequential questions: "Are you rich? Are you Spanish? Have you ever laid a baby?" The last no doubt inspired by the cackling of the hens, who enthusiastically used the entire boatyard as a nesting box, but the others came from heaven knows what recesses of a fertile mind.

The yard employed one real hand, a red-haired, red-bearded Canadian Jack-of-all-Trades, known as Vancouver. He lived in a sheet-iron shack he had built himself "back up in the bush," in other words amongst six trees at the end of a field, and bought ready-sliced bread because, as he said, it was one less chore to do. He worked with incredible speed and sang at his work, rarely stopping to give an order or make a remark, as he usually knew a song to suit. "It looks like rain in Cherry Blossom Lane," he would carol when the clouds came over. "We had better get the covers on this old hooker, tra-la." I like to sing at my work too, and if I happened to strike up first and he approved my choice we would harmonize; otherwise he would pull out all the stops and sing me down.

In a brief non-operatic moment he once told me to make a set of wedges to slip under the ribs taking the engine bearers in a cruiser we were building out of a lifeboat hull. I asked him how, not unreasonably I thought, to which he testily replied, "Ef I'd the time to show you I could make 'em myself." When I eventually produced the wedges after an unconscionable tussle in the carpenter's shop, he said philosophically, "Guess she don't fit so good, but what the heck – I ain't a boat builder and you ain't a boat builder's mate, so what kin they expect from a coupla amachewers?"

As a matter of fact both Vancouver and Jake were very patient with my shortcomings as a boatyard hand, but neither were prepared to spend time on instruction. I asked Jake where the water-line was to come on a boat I was painting, but he simply looked sardonic as only a bearded man can and said, "Work it out for yourself." It is as good a way as any, learning by the old-fashioned method of trial and error, soaking up such knowledge gained by a sort of osmosis, provided you have the time and can stand the knocks.

Most of the boats in the yard were old tore-outs like the one I lived in, but as it was hoped they would eventually become someone's pride and joy, they were scraped and burnt off, sanded down, stopped and cemented, painted and varnished until their own builders would not have known them. Apart from the crane on what Vancouver was pleased to call the dock, there were no mechanical aids, and all the work was done by hand, the hard, bruising, and basic way. We chipped and chiselled, drilled and bored. We lined up for engine installations; we steamed ribs and riveted them in. Occasionally we even got on the water, which was supposed to be our natural element, seeing we were all so wild about boats we had to work amongst them.

The most memorable of these brief brushes with Neptune was when the *Golden Fleece* was brought over from Portsmouth, entailing contact with some twelve miles of open water. Jake had a backache that day, so Vancouver was sent off to do the fetching and I was promoted to mate. Vancouver prepared for the voyage – it was a blazing hot day – by putting on oilskins, sou'wester, and sea boots. Carol was going to drive us to Portsmouth and she put on some gaily coloured scarves, and at the last moment Jake decided to come too, and put on a yachting cap. "I can't do anything," he agonized, "I'll simply sit and direct." As befits a master-mind.

We boarded the *Fleece* at her moorings in one of Portsmouth's more humble aquatic back alleys as the tide was sweeping in. The partial conversion of the boat included a cabin, and the engine room opened out directly onto the large cockpit. She was much hung about with gear and tarpaulins, and "For Sale" was written in large orange letters on the port bow. By the time the tide was on its way out we were still trying to start the engine. Jake ceased directing and said, "We can forget about going today." But Vancouver, that staunch individualist, simply removed his oilskins and swung the motor again, whereon it started. Jake, forgetting his backache, immediately sprang forward and cast off, and Vancouver, with a masterly grasp of events, leapt to the tiller.

Apart from running aground, and having the engine, obviously in a touchy condition, stop a few times, so that there were moments when we might almost have been classified as a harbour hazard, we cleared Portsmouth without incident.

Outside the harbour there was a pleasant quartering breeze. The day was bright and sunny. Jake pointed out the Nab Tower, the Isle of Wight, the *Queen Mary*, and one or two other local landmarks, whilst the *Fleece*, with her considerable top hamper, rolled along with joyous abandon. For a time we felt very gay and seagoing. Then an aircraft came screaming toward us at no height and Jake looked at it thoughtfully. "Ah yes, target area, I'd forgotten." Simultaneously Vancouver and I discovered we had the sea to ourselves and exclaimed, "Here?" with some urgency. Jake said, "We'll find that out." The plane roared over our heads, dived at the shore, climbed up on its tail, and came around with the evident intention of repeating the performance ad lib. We pressed on uncomfortably, hoping we did not resemble a target too much.

As the entrance to the harbour leading to our home creek drew abeam, Jake pointed to a small white speck on the horizon ahead. "We go around that buoy," he directed. "We do not," said Vancouver, making to turn in, and a brisk interchange followed as to times, tides, banks, and depths, which Vancouver closed by saying, "We ain't got the gas anyhow." Jake then decided to put the small amount of gas remaining in the spare can into the tank. My part in this operation consisted of assuming a Yogi attitude in the forepeak, juggling with the valves and inhaling petrol vapour whilst Jake filled the tank from deck. The motion was awful. My head was spinning as I tottered back to the cockpit to tell the others I was just out in time, ha ha, a few minutes more and I would have been sick.

Then the engine stopped. Without way on, and as if she had been waiting for this moment, the *Golden Fleece* cast decorum to the winds and indulged in an exhibition of free aquabatics that would have won her first prize anywhere in any company. This was her day out!

Frantic attempts to restore the engine to life were unavailing and in desperation Vancouver rigged a jury mast with the boat hook, but the tarpaulin he proposed using in lieu of a sail refused to be detached from the warps and woosies with which it was entangled on the cabin roof. I could not help him. I was sitting in the cockpit, transfixed, albeit an unwilling spectator, incapable of movement, and deaf to any appeals to my better nature, for I had none, nor any feelings to spare for my fellow men, being immobilized by a great personal discomfort. Thwarted in his attempt to rig a steadying sail, Vancouver divested himself of his oilskins, sou'wester, and sea boots and returned to the starting handle with a true cave-dweller's approach to action. He did not so much swing that engine as wring its neck. He tore off the carburetor, wrenched it to pieces, reassembled it, and flung it back in place, then proceeded to strangle the engine again. His face was purple and running with sweat. For some reason he appeared to be working against time.

Meantime, the *Fleece* fought back with every trick she knew.

Jake leant against the cockpit with a faraway look in his eyes.

"A little cottage," he murmured, "a little ivy-covered cottage."

"Chickens," I suggested faintly.

"Chickens," he assented, turning a most horrific colour, and adding with commendable composure, "Excuse me – I am going to be sick."

Vancouver erupted from the engine room, flung himself flat on the cockpit floor, and closed his eyes.

The *Fleece* had won hands down.

Jake recovered first; he looked sadly at the prone figure and said, "If we threw him over the side now, he would never know or care," then heroically took his aching back into the engine room. In a few moments, surprisingly, the engine started.

Vancouver leapt to life and the tiller. The engine stopped. He dropped back inert on deck. It started again. He sprang to the helm. It stopped and he dropped. Again it started and again he jumped to the tiller. It was quite fascinating. This time the engine kept on going and he turned for the harbour entrance flat out, unheeding of buoys, banks, bars, or Jake's entreaties to watch out. Spotting a plug behaving in a rather unusual manner – it appeared to be boiling – I mentioned it, just as a matter of interest, to Vancouver, who crouched over the tiller and hissed, "For Chrissake don't tell him; he'll wanna fix it."

Then a gusty altercation broke out as we approached the bar. It was low water and Jake maintained we would not make it. But Vancouver said, "We will," in a tone implying he was of a mind to carry the boat across if necessary. With the motor hacking and coughing, and a few inches to spare, we cleared the bar and ploughed up our home creek in the merest trickle of water until eventually the *Fleece* slid to a standstill about a mile from the yard in a valley of mud.

Silently Jake threw out the anchor, jumped over the side, and waded to the shore. Jake was a tall man, and noting where the mud came to on his boots Vancouver and I agreed it was not for us and decided to walk back to the yard along the channel in the remaining water. When it reached the seat of my pants I stopped worrying about getting wet.

Then we met a man grovelling in the mud of his own free will. "Saaaaay," said Vancouver, "cockles. They're mighty nice t' eat." So we went on a cockle hunt and, having no other container, used Vancouver's sou'wester as a basket.

Jake was prone and brooding over a resurgence of backache when we finally got back to the yard with a hatful of trophies. He looked at me pretty straightly. "And you," he grated, "said you wanted to sail the Atlantic."

from *My Ship Is So Small*,
William Sloane Associates, Inc., London, 1956.

Naming a Sloop

Buckminster Fuller

Of all the designs
Thus far formulated by humans
None have been
As adequately anticipatory
Of the probable reoccurrences
Of yesterday's experiences –
Positive and negative,
Large and small,
Frequent and infrequent,
Sudden and slow –
And therefore as
Progressively comprehensive
Complexedly adequate,
Economically exquisite,
Powerfully eloquent
And regeneratively reinspiring
To further evolutionary perfection
As is
The sailing ship.

It is visually obvious
Even to the inexperienced viewer
That the sailing ship is designed
To cope with nature's
Most formidably hostile
Environmental conditions
For human survival,
Those existing at the interface
Of the ocean's and the atmosphere's
Ofttimes tumultuous ferocity,
Where, for long and most often,

Of all places around Earth
An unprepared, ill-equipped humanity
Usually perished.

For it was the many lethal experiences
With those myriad
Of awesomely demanding conditions
Witnessed by a few fortunate survivors
Which progressively invoked
Man's subjective discovery
And objective invention
Of general engineering principles
As well as the foundations of mathematics
From which in turn he evolved
Not only competent naval architecture
But such other mathematical essentials as
Chronometers, compasses, charts
Spherical trigonometry, sextants
And celestial navigation,
And thereby derived
Instrumentally guidable safe passaging
Of multi-tonned vessels
Scudding along under full sail
Over the rocks and shoals permeated
Great ocean waters
Under the invisible conditions
Of night, fog and high seas.

And sailing ships
Unlike bulldozers
Do no damage to the sea, land or sky
While employing the windpower
Without any depletion
Of the vast wealth of universal energy.

And because the sailing ship's beauty
Is the unpremeditated consequence
Of omni-integrity in designing

Both its comprehensively anticipatory performance as a ship
As well as the technology of its building,
That functional beauty has inspired
The high-seas sailorman,
Voyaging safely within its womblike hold,
Not only reproductively to proliferate
The successful prototype designs
But also spontaneously to identify
Sailing ships
As females.

Three quarters of our planet
Is covered by water.
And in developing the ability
To live at sea
And thereby to integrate
The world-around occurring
But very unevenly distributed
Gamut of physical resources and knowledge,
And thus ultimately to make all resources
Available to the integrated production
And distributive service of all humanity
(Despite the world-around recurrent formidable conditions),
Humanity has manifested
Its greatest comprehensively anticipatory
Scientific designing effectiveness
In the high-seas sailing ship
The by-products of which have been
His establishment of a science-founded,
World-embracing,
Scientifically laboratoried,
Search and research navigated,
Speed of light intercommunicated,
Industrial mass-production complex –
Out of which, in turn,
Has come, evolutionarily,
Humanity's mastery of sky and interplanetary travel

And its biochemical conquest
Of physiological disorders
Of the human organism
And possibly soon to come
The adequate physical sustenance of all mankind.

Key to humanity's scientific discoveries,
Technical inventions,
Design conceptioning
And production realizations
Has been a phenomenon
Transcendental to humanity's
Self-disciplined
Objective concentrations of thought
And deliberate acts –
A phenomenon transcendental to humanity's
Consciously disciplined inventive capabilities.

That key is the first
And utterly unpremeditated event
In all discovery, invention and art.
It is humanity's *intuitive* awareness
Of having come unwittingly upon
A hereto unknown truth,
A lucidly conceptual,
Sublimely harmonic,
Regenerative relationship
Of a priori Universe –
An eternal principle –
And then moments later
A second *intuitive* awareness
Regarding what the conceiving individual human
Must do at once
To capture the awareness of
And secure the usefulness of
That eternally reliable generalized principle
For all humanity
For now and henceforth.

Again and again,
Step by step,
Intuition opens the doors
That lead to man's designing
Of more advantageous rearrangements
Of the physical complex of events
Which we speak of as the environment,
Whose evolutionary transition ever leads
Toward the physical and metaphysical success
Of all humanity.

And because its design
Permits humanity to live anywhere
Around our planet's watery mantle
And because this sailing craft
We are now to launch
Is the epitome of design competence –
As manifest at this moment
In the forever forwardly mounting and cresting wave
Of design capability –
We herewith give
To this world-around dwellable
High-seas sailing craft
The name – INTUITION.

from *Intuition*,
Doubleday, New York, 1972.

Slocum Sets Sail for the Azores

Joshua Slocum

Joshua Slocum was the first singlehanded sailor to circumnavigate the globe. He sailed from Yarmouth, Nova Scotia, in the summer of 1895; his voyage took three years and covered 46,000 miles. Eleven years later, at the age of 65, Slocum set sail from New England bound for South America, but was lost at sea in a gale.

In the fair land of Nova Scotia, a maritime province, there is a ridge called North Mountain, overlooking the Bay of Fundy on one side and the fertile Annapolis valley on the other. On the northern slope of the range grows the hardy spruce tree, well adapted for ship timbers, of which many vessels of all classes have been built. The people of this coast, hardy, robust, and strong, are disposed to compete in the world's commerce, and it is nothing against the master mariner if the birthplace mentioned on his certificate be Nova Scotia.

I was born in a cold spot, on coldest North Mountain, on a cold February 20, though I am a citizen of the United States, a naturalized Yankee, if it may be said that Nova Scotians are not Yankees in the truest sense of the word. On both sides my family were sailors, and if any Slocum should be found not seafaring, he will show at least an inclination to whittle models of boats and contemplate voyages. My father was the sort of man who, if wrecked on a desolate island, would find his way home if he had a jack-knife and could find a tree. He was a good judge of a boat, but the old clay farm which some calamity made his was an anchor to him. He was not afraid of a capful of wind, and he never took a back seat at a camp-meeting or a good, old-fashioned revival.

As for myself, the wonderful sea charmed me from the first. At the age of eight I had already been afloat along with other boys on the bay, with chances greatly in favour of being drowned. When a lad I filled the important post of cook on a fishing schooner; but I was not long in the galley, for the crew mutinied at the appearance of my first duff and "chucked me out" before I had a chance to shine as a culinary artist. The next step toward the goal of happiness found me before the mast in a full-rigged ship bound on a foreign voyage. Thus I came "over the bows," and not in through the cabin windows, to the command of a ship.

My best command was that of the magnificent ship *Northern Light*, of which I was part-owner. I had a right to be proud of her, for at that time – in the eighties – she was the finest American sailing-vessel afloat. Afterward I owned and sailed the *Aquidneck*, a little bark which of all man's handiwork seemed to me the nearest to perfection of beauty, and which in speed, when the wind blew, asked no favours of steamers. I had been nearly twenty years a shipmaster when I quit her deck on the coast of Brazil, where she was wrecked. My home voyage to New York with my family was made in the canoe *Liberdade*, without accident.

My voyages were all foreign. I sailed as freighter and trader principally to China, Australia, and Japan, and among the Spice Islands. Mine was not the sort of life to make one long to coil up one's ropes on land, the customs and ways of which I had finally almost forgotten. And so when times for freighters got bad, as at last they did, and I tried to quit the sea, what was there for an old sailor to do? I was born in the breezes, and I had studied the sea as perhaps few men have studied it, neglecting all else. Next in attractiveness, after seafaring, came ship-building. I longed to be master in both professions, and in a small way, in time, I accomplished my desire. From the decks of stout ships in the worst gales I had made calculations as to the size and sort of ship safest for all weather and all seas. Thus the voyage which I am now to narrate was a natural outcome not only of my love of adventure, but of my lifelong experience.

One midwinter day of 1892, in Boston, where I had been cast up from old ocean, so to speak, a year or two before, I was cogitating whether I should apply for a command, and again eat my bread and butter on the sea, or go to work at the shipyard, when I met an old acquaintance, a whaling-captain, who said: "Come to Fairhaven and I'll give you a ship. But," he added, "she wants some repairs." The captain's terms, when fully explained, were more than satisfactory to me. They included all the assistance I would require to fit the craft for sea. I was only too glad to accept, for I had already found out that I could not obtain work in the shipyard without first paying fifty dollars to a society, and as for a ship to command – there were not enough ships to go round. Nearly all our tall vessels had been cut down for coal-barges and were being ignominiously towed by the nose from port to port, while many worthy captains addressed themselves to Sailors' Snug Harbour.

The next day I landed at Fairhaven, opposite New Bedford, and found that my friend had something of a joke on me. For seven years the joke had been on him. The "ship" proved to be a very antiquated sloop called the *Spray*, which the neighbours declared had been built in the year 1. She was affectionately propped up in a field, some distance from salt water, and was covered with canvas. The people of Fairhaven, I hardly need say, are thrifty and observant. For seven years they had asked, "I wonder what Captain Eben Pierce is going to do with the old *Spray*?" The day I appeared there was a buzz at the gossip exchange: at last some one had come and was actually at work on the old *Spray*. "Breaking her up, I s'pose?" "No; going to rebuild her." Great was the amazement. "Will it pay?" was the question which for a year or more I answered by declaring that I would make it pay.

My axe felled a stout oak-tree nearby for a keel, and Farmer Howard, for a small sum of money, hauled in this and enough timbers for the frame of the new vessel. I rigged a steam-box and a pot for a boiler. The timbers for ribs, being straight saplings, were dressed and steamed till supple, and then bent over a log, where they were secured till set. Something tangible appeared every day to show for my labour, and the neighbours made the work sociable. It was a great day in the *Spray* shipyard when her new stem was set up and fastened to the new keel. Whaling-captains came from far to survey it. With one voice they pronounced it "A1," and in their opinion "fit to smash ice." The oldest captain shook my hand warmly when the breast-hooks were put in, declaring that he could see no reason why the *Spray* should not "cut in the bow-head" yet off the coast of Greenland. The much-esteemed stem-piece was from the butt of the smartest kind of a pasture oak. It afterward split a coral patch in two at the Keeling Islands and did not receive a blemish. Better timber for a ship than pasture white oak never grew. The breast-hooks, as well as all the ribs, were of this wood and were steamed and bent into shape as required. It was hard upon March when I began work in earnest; the weather was cold; still, there were plenty of inspectors to back me with advice. When a whaling-captain hove in sight, I just rested on my adze awhile and "gammed" with him.

New Bedford, the home of whaling-captains, is connected with Fairhaven by a bridge, and the walking is good. They never "worked along up" to the shipyard too often for me. It was the charming tales about arctic whaling that inspired me to put a double set of breast-hooks in the *Spray*, that she might shunt ice.

The season came quickly while I worked. Hardly were the ribs of the sloop up before apple-trees were in bloom. Then the daisies and the cherries came soon after. Close by the place where the old *Spray* had now dissolved rested the ashes of John Cook, a revered Pilgrim father, so the new *Spray* rose from hallowed ground. From the deck of the new craft I could put out my hand and pick cherries that grew over the little grave. The planks for the new vessel, which I soon came to put on, were of Georgia pine an inch and a half thick. The operation of putting them on was tedious, but, when on, the caulking was easy. The outward edges stood slightly open to receive the caulking, but the inner edges were so close that I could not see daylight between them. All the butts were fastened by through bolts, with screw-nuts tightening them to the timbers, so that there would be no complaint from them. Many bolts with screw-nuts were used in other parts of the construction, in all about a thousand. It was my purpose to make my vessel stout and strong.

Now, it is a law in Lloyd's that the *Jane* repaired all out of the old until she is entirely new is still the *Jane*. The *Spray* changed her being so gradually that it was hard to say at what point the old died or the new took birth, and it was no matter. The bulwarks I built up of white-oak stanchions fourteen inches high, and covered with seven-eighth-inch white pine. These stanchions, mortised through a two-inch covering-board, I caulked with thin cedar wedges. They have remained perfectly tight ever since. The deck I made of one-and-a-half-inch by three-inch white pine spiked to beams, six by six inches, of yellow or Georgia pine, placed three feet apart. The deck-inclosures were one over the aperture of the main hatch, six feet by six, for a cooking-galley, and a trunk farther aft, about ten feet by twelve, for a cabin. Both of these rose about three feet above the deck and were sunk sufficiently into the hold to afford head-room. In the spaces along the sides of the cabin, under the deck, I arranged a berth to sleep in and shelves for small storage, not forgetting a place for the medicine-chest. In the midship hold, that is, the space between cabin and galley, under the deck, was room for provision of water, salt beef, etc., ample for many months.

The hull of my vessel being now put together as strongly as wood and iron could make her, and the various rooms partitioned off, I set about "caulking ship." Grave fears were entertained by some that at this point I should fail. I myself gave some thought to the advisability of a "professional caulker." The very first blow I struck on the cotton with the caulking-iron, which I thought was right, many others thought wrong. "It'll crawl!" cried a man from Marion, passing with a basket of clams on his back. "It'll crawl!" cried another from West Island, when he saw me driving cotton into the seams. Bruno simply wagged his tail. Even Mr. Ben, a noted authority on whaling-ships, whose mind, however, was said to totter, asked rather confidently if I did not think "it would crawl." "How fast will it crawl?" cried my old captain friend, who had been towed by many a lively sperm-whale. "Tell us how fast," cried he, "that we may get into port in time." However, I drove a thread of oakum on top of the cotton, as from the first I had intended to do. And Bruno again wagged his tail. The cotton never "crawled."

When the caulking was finished, two coats of copper paint were slapped on the bottom, two of white lead on the topsides and bulwarks. The rudder was then shipped and painted, and on the following day the *Spray* was launched. As she rode at her ancient, rust-eaten anchor, she sat on the water like a swan.

The *Spray*'s dimensions were, when finished, thirty-six feet nine inches long, over all, fourteen feet two inches wide, and four feet two inches deep in the hold, her tonnage being nine tons net and twelve and seventy-one hundredths tons gross.

Then the mast, a smart New Hampshire spruce, was fitted, and likewise all the small appurtenances necessary for a short cruise. Sails were bent, and away she flew with my friend Captain Pierce and me, across Buzzard's Bay on a trial-trip all right. The only thing that now worried my friends along the beach was, "Will she pay?" The cost of my new vessel was $553.62 for materials and thirteen months of my own labour. I was several months more than that at Fairhaven, for I got work now and then on an occasional whale-ship fitting farther down the harbour, and that kept me the overtime.

I spent a season in my new craft fishing on the coast, only to find that I had not the cunning properly to bait a hook. But at last the time arrived to weigh anchor and get to sea in earnest. I had resolved on a voyage around the world, and as the wind on the morning of April 24, 1895, was fair, at noon I weighed anchor, set sail, and filled away from Boston, where the *Spray* had been moored snugly all winter. The twelve-o'clock whistles were blowing just as the sloop shot ahead under full sail. A short board was made up the harbour on the port tack, then coming about she stood seaward, with her boom well off to port, and swung past the ferries with lively heels. A photographer on the outer pier at East Boston got a picture of her as she swept by, her flag at the peak throwing its folds clear. A thrilling pulse beat high in me. My step was light on deck in the crisp air. I felt that there could be no turning back, and that I was engaging in an adventure the meaning of which I thoroughly understood. I had taken little advice from any one, for I had a right to my own opinions in matters pertaining to the sea. That the best of sailors might do worse than even I alone was borne in upon me not a league from Boston docks, where a great steamship, fully manned, officered, and piloted, lay stranded and broken. This was the *Venetian*. She was broken completely in two over a ledge. So in the first hour of my lone voyage I had proof that the *Spray* could at least do better than this full-handed steamship, for I was already farther on my voyage than she. "Take warning, *Spray*, and have a care," I uttered aloud to my bark, passing fairylike silently down the bay.

The wind freshened, and the *Spray* rounded Deer Island light, going at the rate of seven knots. Passing it, she squared away direct for Gloucester, where she was to procure some fishermen's stores. Waves dancing joyously across Massachusetts Bay met the sloop coming out, to dash themselves instantly into myriads of sparkling gems that hung about her breast at every surge. The day was perfect, the sunlight clear and strong. Every particle of water thrown into the air became a gem, and the *Spray*, making good her name as she dashed ahead, snatched necklace after necklace from the sea, and as often threw them away. We have all seen miniature rainbows about a ship's prow, but the *Spray* flung out a bow of her own that day such as I had never seen before. Her good angel had embarked on the voyage; I so read it in the sea.

Bold Nahant was soon abeam, then Marblehead was put astern. Other vessels were outward bound, but none of them passed the *Spray* flying along on her course. I heard the clanking of the dismal bell on Norman's Woe as we went by; and the reef where the schooner *Hesperus* struck I passed close aboard. The "bones" of a wreck tossed up lay bleaching on the shore abreast. The wind still freshening, I settled the throat of the mainsail to ease the sloop's helm, for I could hardly hold her before it with the whole mainsail set. A schooner ahead of me lowered all sail and ran into port under bare poles, the wind being fair. As the *Spray* brushed by the stranger, I saw that some of his sails were gone, and much broken canvas hung in his rigging from the effects of a squall.

I made for the cove, a lovely branch of Gloucester's fine harbour, again to look the *Spray* over and again to weigh the voyage, and my feelings, and all that. The bay was feather-white as my little vessel tore in, smothered in foam. It was my first experience of coming into port alone, with a craft of any size, and in among shipping. Old fishermen ran down to the wharf for which the *Spray* was heading, apparently intent upon braining herself there. I hardly know how a calamity was averted, but with my heart in my mouth, almost, I let go the wheel, stepped quickly forward, and downed the jib. The sloop naturally rounded in the wind and, just ranging ahead, laid her cheek against a mooring-pile at the windward corner of the wharf, so quietly, after all, that she would not have broken an egg. Very leisurely I passed a rope around the post, and she was moored. Then a cheer went up from the little crowd on the wharf. "You couldn't 'a' done it better," cried an old skipper, "if you weighed a ton!" Now, my weight was rather less than the fifteenth part of a ton, but I said nothing, only putting on a look of careless indifference to say for me, "Oh, that's nothing"; for some of the ablest sailors in the world were looking at me, and my wish was not to appear green, for I had a mind to stay in Gloucester several days. Had I uttered a word it surely would have betrayed me, for I was still quite nervous and short of breath.

The weather was mild on the day of my departure from Gloucester. On the point ahead, as the *Spray* stood out of the cove, was a lively picture, for the front of a tall factory was a flutter of handkerchiefs and caps. Pretty faces peered out of the windows from the top to the bottom of the building, all smiling *bon voyage*. Some hailed me to know where away and why alone. Why? When I made as if to stand in, a hundred pairs of arms reached out, and said come, but the shore was dangerous! The sloop worked out of the bay against a light southwest wind, and about noon squared away off Eastern Point, receiving at the same time a hearty salute – the last of many kindnesses to her at Gloucester.

The wind freshened off the point, and skipping along smoothly the *Spray* was soon off Thatcher's Island lights. Thence shaping her course east, by compass, to go north of Cashes Ledge and the Amen Rocks, I sat and considered the matter all over again and asked myself once more whether it were best to sail beyond the ledge and rocks at all. I had only said that I would sail round the world in the *Spray*, "dangers of the sea excepted," but I must have said it very much in earnest. The "charter–party" with myself seemed to bind me, and so I sailed on.

The *Spray*, heading east, stretched along the coast among many islands and over a tranquil sea. At evening of this day, May 10, she came up with a considerable island, which I shall always think of as the Island of Frogs, for the *Spray* was charmed by a million voices. From the Island of Frogs we made for the Island of Birds, called Gannet Island, and sometimes Gannet Rock, whereon is a bright, intermittent light, which flashed fitfully across the *Spray*'s deck as she coasted along under its light and shade. Thence shaping a course for Briar's Island, I came among vessels the following afternoon on the western fishing-grounds, and after speaking to a fisherman at anchor, who gave me a wrong course, the *Spray* sailed directly over the southwest ledge through the worst tide-race in the Bay of Fundy, and got into Westport harbour in Nova Scotia, where I had spent eight years of my life as a lad.

I now stowed all my goods securely, for the boisterous Atlantic was before me, and I sent the topmast down, knowing that the *Spray* would be the wholesomer with it on deck. Then I gave the lanyards a pull and hitched them afresh and saw that the gammon was secure, also that the boat was lashed, for even in summer one may meet with bad weather in the crossing.

In fact, many weeks of bad weather had prevailed. On July 1, however, after a rude gale, the wind came out nor'west and clear, propitious for a good run. On the following day, the head sea having gone down, I sailed from Yarmouth, and let go my last hold on America. The log of my first day on the Atlantic in the *Spray* reads briefly: "9:30 a.m. sailed from Yarmouth. 4:30 p.m. passed Cape Sable; distance, three cables from the land. The sloop making eight knots. Fresh breeze N.W." Before the sun went down I was taking my supper of strawberries and tea in smooth water under the lee of the east-coast land, along which the *Spray* was now leisurely skirting.

At noon on July 3 Ironbound Island was abeam. The *Spray* was again at her best. A large schooner came out of Liverpool, Nova Scotia, this morning, steering eastward. The *Spray* put her hull down astern in five hours. At 6:45 p.m. I was in close under Chebucto Head light, near Halifax Harbour. I set my flag and squared away, taking my departure from George's Island before dark to sail east of Sable Island. There are many beacon lights along the coast. Sambro, the Rock of Lamentations, carries a noble light, which, however, the liner *Atlantic*, on the night of her terrible disaster, did not see. I watched light after light sink astern as I sailed into the unbounded sea, till Sambro, the last of them all, was below the horizon. The *Spray* was then alone, and sailing on, she held her course. July 4, at 6 a.m., I put in double reefs, and at 8:30 a.m. turned out all reefs. At 9:40 p.m. I raised the sheen only of the light on the west end of Sable Island, which may also be called the Island of Tragedies.

The fog, which till this moment had held off, now lowered over the sea like a pall. I was in a world of fog, shut off from the universe. I did not see any more of the light. By the lead, which I cast often, I found that a little after midnight I was passing the east point of the island, and should soon be clear of dangers of land and shoals. The wind was holding free, though it was from the foggy point, south-southwest. It is said that within a few years Sable Island has been reduced from forty miles in length to twenty, and that of three lighthouses built on it since 1880, two have been washed away and the third will soon be engulfed.

On the evening of July 5 the *Spray*, after having steered all day over a lumpy sea, took it into her head to go without the helmsman's aid. I had been steering southeast by south, but the wind hauling forward a bit, she dropped into a smooth lane, heading southeast, and making about eight knots, her very best work. I crowded on sail to cross the track of the liners without loss of time and to reach as soon as possible the friendly Gulf Stream. The fog lifting before night, I was afforded a look at the sun just as it was touching the sea. I watched it go down and out of sight. Then I turned my face eastward, and there, apparently at the very end of the bowsprit, was the smiling full moon rising out of the sea. Neptune himself coming over the bows could not have startled me more. "Good evening, sir," I cried; "I'm glad to see you." Many a long talk since then I have had with the man in the moon; he had my confidence on the voyage.

About midnight the fog shut down again denser than ever before. One could almost "stand on it." It continued so for a number of days, the wind increasing to a gale. The waves rose high, but I had a good ship. Still, in the dismal fog I felt myself drifting into loneliness, an insect on a straw in the midst of the elements. I lashed the helm, and my vessel held her course, and while she sailed I slept.

During these days a feeling of awe crept over me. My memory worked with startling power. The ominous, the insignificant, the great, the small, the wonderful, the commonplace all appeared before my mental vision in magical succession. Pages of my history were recalled which had been so long forgotten that they seemed to belong to a previous existence. I heard all the voices of the past laughing, crying, telling what I had heard them tell in many corners of the earth.

The loneliness of my state wore off when the gale was high and I found much work to do. When fine weather returned, then came the sense of solitude, which I could not shake off. I used my voice often, at first giving some order about the affairs of the ship, for I had been told that from disuse I would lose my speech. At the meridian altitude of the sun I called aloud, "Eight bells," after the custom on a ship at sea. Again from my cabin I cried to an imaginary man at the helm, "How does she head, there?" and again, "Is she on her course?" But getting no reply, I was reminded the more palpably of my condition. My voice sounded hollow on the empty air, and I dropped the practice. However, it was not long before the thought came to me that when I was a lad I used to sing: why not try that now, where it would disturb no one? My musical talent had never bred envy in others, but out on the Atlantic, to realize what it meant, you should have heard me sing. You should have seen the porpoises leap when I pitched my voice for the waves and the sea and all that was in it. Old turtles, with large eyes, poked their heads up out of the sea as I sang "Johnny Boker," and "We'll Pay Darby Doyl for his Boots," and the like. But the porpoises were, on the whole, vastly more appreciative than the turtles; they jumped a deal higher. One day when I was humming a favourite chant, I think it was "Babylon's a-Fallin'," a porpoise jumped higher than the bowsprit. Had the *Spray* been going a little faster she would have scooped him in. The sea-birds sailed around rather shy.

July 10, eight days at sea, the *Spray* was twelve hundred miles east of Cape Sable. One hundred and fifty miles a day for so small a vessel must be considered good sailing. It was the greatest run the *Spray* ever made before or since in so few days. On the evening of July 14, in better humour than ever before, all hands cried, "Sail ho!" The sail was a barkantine, three points on the weather bow, hull down. Then came the night. My ship was sailing along now without attention to the helm. The wind was south; she was heading east. Her sails were trimmed like the sails of the nautilus. They drew steadily all night. I went frequently on deck, but found all well.

A merry breeze kept on from the south. Early in the morning of the 15th the *Spray* was close aboard the stranger, which proved to be *La Vaguisa* of Vigo, twenty-three days from Phila-

delphia, bound for Vigo. A lookout from his masthead had
spied the *Spray* the evening before. The captain, when I came
near enough, threw a line to me and sent a bottle of wine across
slung by the neck, and very good wine it was. He also sent his
card, which bore the name of Juan Gantes. I think he was a good
man, as Spaniards go. But when I asked him to report me "all
well" (the *Spray* passing him in a lively manner), he hauled his
shoulders much above his head; and when his mate, who knew
of my expedition, told him that I was alone, he crossed himself
and made for his cabin. I did not see him again. By sundown he
was as far astern as he had been ahead the evening before.

There was now less and less monotony. On July 16 the wind
was northwest and clear, the sea smooth, and a large bark, hull
down, came in sight on the lee bow, and at 2:30 p.m. I spoke the
stranger. She was the bark *Java* of Glasgow, from Peru for
Queenstown for orders. Her old captain was bearish, but I met a
bear once in Alaska that looked pleasanter. At least, the bear
seemed pleased to meet me, but this grizzly old man! Well, I
suppose my hail disturbed his siesta, and my little sloop passing
his great ship had somewhat the effect on him that a red rag has
upon a bull. I had the advantage over heavy ships, by long odds,
in the light winds of this and the two previous days. The wind
was light; his ship was heavy and foul, making poor headway,
while the *Spray*, with a great mainsail bellying even to light
winds, was just skipping along as nimbly as one could wish.
"How long has it been calm about here?" roared the captain of
the *Java*, as I came within hail of him. "Dunno, cap'n," I shouted
back as loud as I could bawl. "I haven't been here long." At this
the mate on the forecastle wore a broad grin. "I left Cape Sable
fourteen days ago," I added. (I was now well across toward the
Azores.) "Mate," he roared to his chief officer, "Mate, come
here and listen to the Yankee's yarn. Haul down the flag, mate,
haul down the flag!" In the best of humour, after all, the *Java*
surrendered to the *Spray*.

The acute pain of solitude expected at first never returned. I
had penetrated a mystery, and, by the way, I had sailed through a
fog. I had met Neptune in his wrath, but he found that I had not

treated him with contempt, and so he suffered me to go on and explore.

In the log for July 18 there is this entry: "Fine weather, wind south-southwest. Porpoises gamboling all about. The S.S. *Olympia* passed at 11:30 a.m., long. W. 34° 50'."

"It lacks now three minutes of the half-hour," shouted the captain, as he gave me the longitude and the time. I admired the businesslike air of the *Olympia*; but I have the feeling still that the captain was just a little too precise in his reckoning. That may be all well enough, however, where there is plenty of sea-room. But over-confidence, I believe, was the cause of the disaster to the liner *Atlantic*, and many more like her. The captain knew too well where he was. There were no porpoises at all skipping along with the *Olympia*! Porpoises always prefer sailing ships. The captain was a young man, I observed, and had before him, I hope, a good record.

Land ho! On the morning of July 19 a mystic dome like a mountain of silver stood alone in the sea ahead. Although the land was completely hidden by the white, glistening haze that shone in the sun like polished silver, I felt quite sure that it was Flores Island. At half-past four p.m. it was abeam. The haze in the meantime had disappeared. Flores is one hundred and seventy-four miles from Fayal, and although it is a high island, it remained many years undiscovered after the principal group of the islands had been colonized.

Early on the morning of July 20 I saw Pico looming above the clouds on the starboard bow. Lower lands burst forth as the sun burned away the morning fog, and island after island came into view. As I approached nearer, cultivated fields appeared, "and oh, how green the corn!" Only those who have seen the Azores from the deck of a vessel realize the beauty of the mid-ocean picture.

At 4:30 p.m. I cast anchor at Fayal, exactly eighteen days from Cape Sable. The American consul, in a smart boat, came alongside before the *Spray* reached the breakwater, and a young naval officer, who feared for the safety of my vessel, boarded, and offered his services as pilot. The youngster, I have no good reason to doubt, could have handled a man-of-war, but the *Spray* was too small for the amount of uniform he wore. However, after fouling all the craft in port and sinking a lighter, she was moored without much damage to herself. This wonderful pilot expected a "gratification," I understood, but whether for the reason that his government, and not I, would have to pay the cost of raising the lighter, or because he did not sink the *Spray*, I could never make out. But I forgive him.

It was the season for fruit when I arrived at the Azores, and there was soon more of all kinds of it put on board than I knew what to do with. Islanders are always the kindest people in the world, and I met none anywhere kinder than the good hearts of this place. The people of the Azores are not a very rich community. The burden of taxes is heavy, with scant privileges in return, the air they breathe being about the only thing that is not taxed. The mother-country does not even allow them a port of entry for a foreign mail service. A packet passing never so close with mails for Horta must deliver them first in Lisbon, ostensibly to be fumigated, but really for the tariff of the packet. My own letters posted at Horta reached the United States six days behind my letter from Gibraltar, mailed thirteen days later.

The day after my arrival at Horta was the feast of a great saint. Boats loaded with people came from other islands to celebrate at Horta, the capital, or Jerusalem, of the Azores. The deck of the *Spray* was crowded from morning till night with men, women, and children. On the day after the feast a kind-hearted native harnessed a team and drove me a day over the beautiful roads all about Fayal, "because," said he, in broken English, "when I was in America and couldn't speak a word of English, I found it hard till I met some one who seemed to have time to listen to my story, and I promised my good saint then that if ever a stranger came to my country I would try to make him happy." Unfortunately this gentleman brought along an interpreter, that I might "learn more of the country." The fellow was nearly the death of me, talking of ships and voyages, and of the boats he had steered, the last thing in the world I wished to hear. He had sailed out of New Bedford, so he said, for "that Joe Wing they call 'John.'" My friend and host found hardly a chance to edge in a word. Before we parted my host dined me with a cheer that would have gladdened the heart of a prince, but he was quite alone in his house. "My wife and children all rest there," said he pointing to the churchyard across the way. "I moved to this house from far off," he added, "to be near the spot, where I pray every morning."

I remained four days at Fayal, and that was two days more than I had intended to stay. It was the kindness of the islanders and their touching simplicity which detained me. A damsel, as innocent as an angel, came alongside one day and said she would embark on the *Spray* if I would land her at Lisbon. She could cook flying-fish, she thought, but her forte was dressing bacalhao. Her brother Antonio, who served as interpreter, hinted that, anyhow, he would like to make the trip. Antonio's heart went out to one John Wilson, and he was ready to sail for America by way of the two capes to meet his friend. "Do you know John Wilson of Boston," he cried. "I knew a John Wilson," I said, "but not of Boston." "He had one daughter and one son," said Antonio, by way of identifying his friend. If this reaches the right John Wilson, I am told to say that "Antonio of Pico remembers him."

from *Sailing Alone Around the World,*
Century Company, New York, 1900.

STEERAGE SCENES

ROBERT LOUIS STEVENSON

In 1879, Robert Louis Stevenson fell in love with an American woman he'd met in France. Tubercular and low on funds, he boarded an emigrant ship to cross the Atlantic, then travelled across the continent by train to meet her in California. They married, and two years later he returned to Scotland to publish *Treasure Island*, assuring his lasting success.

Our companion (Steerage No. 2 and 3) was a favourite resort. Down one flight of stairs there was a comparatively large open space, the centre occupied by a hatchway, which made a convenient seat for about twenty persons, while barrels, coils of rope, and the carpenter's bench afforded perches for perhaps as many more. The canteen, or steerage bar, was on one side of the stair; on the other, a no less attractive spot, the cabin of the indefatigable interpreter. I have seen people packed into this space like herrings in a barrel, and many merry evenings prolonged there until five bells, when the lights were ruthlessly extinguished and all must go to roost.

It had been rumoured since Friday that there was a fiddler aboard, who lay sick and unmelodious in Steerage No. 1; and on the Monday forenoon, as I came down the companion, I was saluted by something in Strathspey time. A white-faced Orpheus was cheerily playing to an audience of white-faced women. It was as much as he could do to play, and some of his hearers were scarce able to sit; yet they had crawled from their bunks at the first experimental flourish, and found better than medicine in the music. Some of the heaviest heads began to nod in time, and a degree of animation looked from some of the palest eyes. Humanly speaking, it is a more important matter to play the fiddle, even badly, than to write huge works upon recondite subjects. What could Mr. Darwin have done for these sick women? But this fellow scraped away; and the world was positively a better place for all who heard him. We have yet to understand the economical value of these mere accomplishments. I told the fiddler he was a happy man, carrying happiness about with him in his fiddle-case, and he seemed alive to the fact.

"It is a privilege," I said. He thought a while upon the word, turning it over in his Scots head, and then answered with conviction, "Yes, a privilege."

That night I was summoned by "Merrily Danced The Quaker's Wife" into the companion of Steerage No. 4 and 5. This was, properly speaking, but a strip across a deck-house, lit by a sickly lantern which swung to and fro with the motion of the ship. Through the open slide-door we had a glimpse of a grey night sea, with patches of phosphorescent foam flying, swift as birds, into the wake, and the horizon rising and falling as the vessel rolled to the wind. In the centre the companion ladder plunged down sheerly like an open pit. Below, on the first landing, and lighted by another lamp, lads and lasses danced, not more than three at a time for lack of space, in jigs and reels and hornpipes. Above, on either side, there was a recess railed with iron, perhaps two feet wide and four long, which stood for orchestra and seats of honour. In the one balcony five slatternly Irish lasses sat woven in a comely group. In the other was posted Orpheus; his body, which was convulsively in motion, forming an odd contrast to his somnolent, imperturbable Scots face. His brother, a dark man with a vehement, interested countenance, who made a god of the fiddler, sat by with open mouth, drinking in the general admiration and throwing out remarks to kindle it. "That's a bonny hornpipe now," he would say, "it's a great favourite with performers; they dance the sand dance to it." And he expounded the sand dance. Then suddenly it would be a long "Hush!" with uplifted finger and glowing, supplicating eyes; "he's going to play 'Auld Robin Grey' on one string!" And throughout this excruciating movement, – "On one string, that's on one string!" he kept crying.

I would have given something myself that it had been on none; but the hearers were much awed. I called for a tune or two, and thus introduced myself to the notice of the brother, who directed his talk to me for some little while, keeping, I need hardly mention, true to his topic, like the seamen to the star. "He's grand of it," he said confidentially. "His master was a music-hall man." Indeed the music-hall man had left his mark, for our fiddler was ignorant of many of our best old airs; "Logie o' Buchan," for instance, he only knew as a quick, jigging figure in a set of quadrilles, and had never heard it called by name. Perhaps, after all, the brother was the more interesting performer of the two. I have spoken with him afterwards repeatedly, and found him always the same quick, fiery bit of a man, not without brains; but he never showed to such advantage as when he was thus squiring the fiddler into public note. There is nothing more becoming than a genuine admiration; and it shares this with love, that it does not become contemptible although misplaced.

The dancing was but feebly carried on. The space was almost impracticably small; and the Irish wenches combined the extreme of bashfulness about this innocent display with a surprising impudence and roughness of address. Most often, either the fiddle lifted up its voice unheeded, or only a couple of lads would be footing it and snapping fingers on the landing. And such was the eagerness of the brother to display all the acquirements of his idol, and such the sleepy indifference of the performer, that the tune would as often as not be changed, and the hornpipe expire into a ballad before the dancers had cut half a dozen shuffles.

In the meantime, however, the audience had been growing more and more numerous every moment; there was hardly standing-room round the top of the companion; and the strange instinct of the race moved some of the newcomers to close both the doors, so that the atmosphere grew insupportable. It was a good place, as the saying is, to leave.

The wind hauled ahead with a head sea. By ten at night heavy sprays were flying and drumming over the forecastle; the companion of Steerage No. 1 had to be closed and the door of communication through the second cabin thrown open. Either from the convenience of the opportunity, or because we had already a number of acquaintances in that part of the ship, Mr. Jones and I paid it a late visit. Steerage No. 1 is shaped like an isosceles triangle, the sides opposite the equal angles bulging outward with the contour of the ship. It is lined with eight pens of sixteen bunks apiece, four bunks below and four above on either side. At night the place is lit with two lanterns, one to each table. As the ship beat on her way among the rough billows, the light passed through violent phases of change and was thrown to and fro and up and down with startling swiftness. You were tempted to wonder, as you looked, how so thin a glimmer could control and disperse such solid blackness.

When Jones and I entered we found a little company of our acquaintances seated together at the triangular foremost table. A more forlorn party, in more dismal circumstances, it would be hard to imagine. The motion here in the ship's nose was very violent; the uproar of the sea often overpoweringly loud. The yellow flicker of the lantern spun round and round and tossed the shadows in masses. The air was hot, but it struck a chill from its foetor. From all round in the dark bunks the scarcely human noises of the sick joined into a kind of farmyard chorus. In the midst, these five friends of mine were keeping up what heart they could in company. Singing was their refuge from discomfortable thoughts and sensations. One piped, in feeble tones, "O Why Left I My Hame?" which seemed a pertinent question in the circumstances. Another, from the invisible horrors of a pen where he lay dog-sick upon the upper shelf, found courage, in a blink of his sufferings, to give us several verses of the "Death of Nelson"; and it was odd and eerie to hear the chorus breathe feebly from all sorts of dark corners, and "this day had done his dooty" rise and fall and be taken up again in this dim inferno, to an accompaniment of plunging, hollow-sounding bows and the rattling spray-showers overhead.

All seemed unfit for conversation; a certain dizziness had interrupted the activity of their minds; and except to sing they were tongue-tied. There was present, however, one tall, power-ful fellow of doubtful nationality, being neither quite Scotsman nor altogether Irish, but of surprising clearness of conviction on the highest problems. He had gone nearly beside himself on the Sunday, because of a general backwardness to endorse his defi-nition of mind as "a living, thinking substance which cannot be felt, heard, or seen" – nor, I presume, although he failed to mention it, smelt. Now he came forward in a pause with another contribution to our culture.

"Just by way of change," said he, "I'll ask you a Scripture riddle. There's profit in them too," he added ungrammatically.

This was the riddle –

C and P
Did agree
To cut down C;
But C and P
Could not agree
Without the leave of G.
All the people cried to see
The crueltie
Of C and P.

Harsh are the words of Mercury after the songs of Apollo! We were a long time over the problem, shaking our heads and gloomily wondering how a man could be such a fool; but at length he put us out of suspense and divulged the fact that C and P stood for Caiaphas and Pontius Pilate.

I think it must have been the riddle that settled us; but the motion and the close air likewise hurried our departure. We had not been gone long, we heard next morning, ere two or even three out of the five fell sick. We thought it little wonder on the whole, for the sea kept contrary all night. I now made my bed upon the second cabin floor, where, although I ran the risk of being stepped upon, I had a free current of air, more or less vitiated indeed, and running only from steerage to steerage, but at least not stagnant; and from this couch, as well as the usual sounds of a rough night at sea, the hateful coughing and retching of the sick and the sobs of the children, I heard a man run wild with terror beseeching his friend for encouragement. "The ship's going down!" he cried with a thrill of agony. "The ship's going down!" he repeated, now in a blank whisper, now with his voice rising toward a sob; and his friend might reassure him, reason with him, joke at him – all was in vain, and the old cry came back, "The ship's going down!" There was something panicky and catching in the emotion of his tones; and I saw in a clear flash what an involved and hideous tragedy was a disaster to an emigrant ship. If this whole parishful of people came no more to land, into how many houses would the newspaper carry woe, and what a great part of the web of our corporate human life would be rent across for ever!

The next morning when I came on deck I found a new world indeed. The wind was fair; the sun mounted into a cloudless heaven; through great dark blue seas the ship cut a swath of curded foam. The horizon was dotted all day with companionable sails, and the sun shone pleasantly on the long, heaving deck.

We had many fine-weather diversions to beguile the time. There was a single chess-board and a single pack of cards. Sometimes as many as twenty of us would be playing dominoes for love. Feats of dexterity, puzzles for the intelligence, some arithmetical, some of the same order as the old problem of the fox and the goose and cabbage, were always welcome; and the latter, I observed, more popular as well as more conspicuously well done than the former. We had a regular daily competition to guess the vessel's progress; and twelve o'clock, when the result was published in the wheelhouse, came to be a moment of considerable interest. But the interest was unmixed. Not a bet was laid upon our guesses. From the Clyde to Sandy Hook I never heard a wager offered or taken. We had, besides, romps in plenty. Puss in the Corner, which we had rebaptised, in more manly style, Devil and Four Corners, was my own favourite game; but there were many who preferred another, the humour of which was to box a person's ears until he found out who had cuffed him.

This Tuesday morning we were all delighted with the change of weather, and in the highest possible spirits. We got in a cluster like bees, sitting between each other's feet under lee of the deck-houses. Stories and laughter went around. The children climbed about the shrouds. White faces appeared for the first time and began to take on colour from the wind. I was kept hard at work making cigarettes for one amateur after another, and my less than moderate skill was heartily admired. Lastly, down sat the fiddler in our midst and began to discourse his reels, and jigs, and ballads, with now and then a voice or two to take up the air and throw in the interest of human speech.

Through this merry and good-hearted scene there came three cabin passengers, a gentleman and two young ladies, picking their way with little gracious titters of indulgence, and a Lady-Bountiful air about nothing, which galled me to the quick. I have little of the radical in social questions, and have always nourished an idea that one person was as good as another. But I began to be troubled by this episode. It was astonishing what insults these people managed to convey by their presence. They seemed to throw their clothes in our faces. Their eyes searched us all over for tatters and incongruities. A laugh was ready at their lips; but they were too well-mannered to indulge it in our hearing. Wait a bit, till they were all back in the saloon, and then hear how wittily they would depict the manners of the steerage. We were in truth very innocently, cheerfully, and sensibly engaged, and there was no shadow of excuse for the swaying elegant superiority with which these damsels passed among us, or for the stiff and waggish glances of their squire. Not a word was said; only when they were gone Mackay sullenly damned their impudence under his breath; but we were all conscious of an icy influence and a dead break in the course of our enjoyment.

from *The Amateur Emigrant*,
Chatto and Windus, Edinburgh, 1895.

THE PSYCHOLOGICAL SITUATION AT SEA

MICHAEL STADLER

When one reads sensationalized magazine articles with headings like "Female Crew Members Murder Skipper" or "Mutiny on Yacht – Two People Killed," one wonders how it is possible for such quintessential extremes of human nature to surface in the realms of a leisure sport. Why do we not hear of such things happening in motorcycling or ice-dancing? What is so special about the situation on board a yacht on a long cruise?

Generally speaking, we grow up and develop in a world on land. When we go to sea we are "socialized" for a second time. The yachtsman finds himself for a long period of time in extremely cramped conditions with no personal privacy and no possibility of escape. He is part of a group which has a fixed formal structure that does not necessarily coincide with its psychological structure. The change from life on land to life at sea entails special problems which will be discussed below. It might serve to shed some light on the matter if we analyze an incident which enthralled yachtsmen in 1982/3.

The *Apollonia* Case

In the summer of 1981 two men meet in Pasito Blanco on Gran Canaria: one is Herbert Klein, a German businessman who has opted out of his bourgeois existence in order to build a new life for himself with a yacht–chartering business in the Caribbean. To do this he has purchased the former flagship of the Bremen Sailing Club, the *Wappen von Bremen* and, after repair work and fitting out, has put to sea from Wesermundung in what is now the *Apollonia*. The other man, Paul Termann, was brought up in East Germany, trained as an electrician, and after moving to West Germany became a helicopter pilot in the army and later a chief engineer with the Federal Railway. He has invested his life savings in a round-the-world cruise with his girlfriend Dorothea.

Klein has little sailing experience, but he has the A-Schein (sailing certificate). For the stretch up to Gran Canaria, in addition to other crew, he has employed a skipper whom he dismisses along with the others on arrival in Gran Canaria. He has made several half-hearted attempts to learn the rudiments of navigation during this first stage. Termann has been sailing since he was ten years old. He possesses all the certificates and has travelled the first leg of his voyage on another boat as the navigator. Here in Gran Canaria his dream of sailing round the world is abruptly broken when he and his girlfriend are dismissed by the captain of the yacht *Orion* without their financial investment being returned.

The personalities of Klein and Termann, conditioned by their different histories, are dissimilar to say the least. Klein is regarded as a likeable person; he is amiable and fond of a joke. Carefree, frivolous, lacking in independence, seeking the good opinion of others, he both overestimates himself and is insecure at the same time. This characterization accords with the permanent holiday mood he has displayed since "dropping out." Diverse assessments of Termann on the other hand confirm that he was serious, reserved, civil, industrious, obliging, diligent, and helpful – almost Prussian qualities of character, which occasionally develop into an insistence bordering on pedantry.

After the paths of Klein and Termann meet in Gran Canaria they become friends when they both realize how much they need each other: Klein has a yacht but no experience, Termann can navigate but has no boat. They are joined by two further members of crew found through a newspaper advertisement, Michael and Dieter. The crew of six, then, initially comprises three groups of two – Klein and his girlfriend Gabrielle, Termann and his girlfriend Dorothea, and Michael and Dieter.

The members of the three groups have not been acquainted with one another beforehand, so when the lines are cast off for St. Vincent across the Atlantic the responsibilities on board are anything but clear and straightforward. As owner, Klein also claims the role of skipper, albeit somewhat half-heartedly. Before setting out, he says that he actually attaches no importance to it. Termann, who is the only one on board possessing the qualifications to command a vessel and as the most experienced sailor is entitled to this role, accepts Klein's leadership to begin with, since he believes in the assertive power of his professional expertise and navigational, technical, and practical skills.

No further role allocation takes place, but the frail hierarchy nevertheless begins to alter in the course of the trip. Klein begins increasingly to "parade" the fact that he is the captain while Termann expresses his criticism of the decision, remarking on the carelessness of the skipper more and more clearly. Termann insists on painstakingly accurate adherence to nautical practices and security measures. Klein is not at all particular about this, for after all they aren't on the *Gorch Fock*. While the boat is travelling at full speed with the trade winds, the crew amuse themselves by jumping into the water off the bow and pulling themselves back in again on lines lowered from the stern. When Termann objects to this behaviour on safety grounds, he is derided as a coward. Klein and the rest of the crew deliberately set out to annoy Termann by continually knotting the running gear against his advice.

In addition to the shifting tensions within the nautical hierarchy, a group structure has meanwhile also been developing among this odd assortment. Klein and his girlfriend, together with Michael and Dieter, form a subgroup. They converse amongst themselves most of the time; they share the same attitude toward sailing, looking upon the Atlantic crossing as a holiday cruise. They sit opposite the other two, Termann and Dorothea, poking fun at them. Neither of the two subgroups can manage without the other; neither group can withdraw from the other completely.

There are tensions between the groups which are sparked off by trivialities and which build up more and more in the course of the cruise. Offence is taken at insignificant details. The obvious thing to do had they been ashore, namely, to part company, is not possible here. Termann, for whom good seamanship and safety on board are the prime considerations, is constantly humiliated by Klein in front of the others. The social climate on board grows worse and worse with the tensions increasing to an unbearable level. The "stronger" group around Klein celebrates the half-way stage across the Atlantic with a bottle of champagne. Termann and his girlfriend are not invited to participate. The crew are completely broken apart. Not even a three-day storm rallies them. There is no longer any common purpose, no common goal, no standards, and no overall binding hierarchy.

The frustrations which Termann has had to endure since the beginning of the cruise, indeed, since beforehand on the *Orion*, have brought him to a mental state where in his present position, from which there is no possibility of escape, they can only manifest themselves in either complete self-effacement or extreme aggression.

What would under normal circumstances have been a trivial incident in this case lights the fuse to the powderkeg. At the start of the morning watch at 0800 Dorothea prepares breakfast for herself and Termann, leaving the dishes from the night before unwashed. Klein is furious about this and a violent exchange of words takes place, during which Termann announces that he is taking over command of the yacht and threatens to shoot Klein and his girlfriend. There are two guns on board; Termann and Klein each possess one. At gunpoint Termann forces Klein to hand over his weapon and demands that he write him a reference. Klein can at this moment only manage a grim smile in response to the provocation, and Termann takes over command of the yacht in true mutinous fashion.

Up until now Klein and the other members of his group have not realized the gravity of the situation; only now do they become fully aware of the danger they are in. It is clear that Termann's aggression has been accumulating from a vast number of lesser frustrations which were insignificant in themselves and which have not been considered important by the others. With the gun Termann is now the most powerful man on board.

For him, especially in front of his girlfriend, there is no going back.

For the group of four there is no way out. The socio-psychological situation is strained to breaking point; it will later be described by the survivors as having been a period of "psycho-terror." Termann is now quite composed in the formulation of his death threat to the ship's owner and his girlfriend: "You have only ten minutes left. I must first shoot the sun. Today, the thirteenth of December, is your day of reckoning."

Fear spreads throughout the boat; irrationality takes hold. Klein offers to do the shooting himself. Termann humiliates him by giving him the opportunity to do so. Klein has to admit that he cannot do it. For the first time Klein and Gabrielle realize the hopelessness of their situation. On her knees Gabrielle begs Termann to spare their lives. Meanwhile the others have gathered in the fo'c'sle preparing to tack, and Klein urges his group to take action. The plan is to overpower Termann. Klein takes an iron pump handle and strikes Termann over the head from behind while he is sitting at the chart table.

Termann reacts in blind rage and shoots at Michael and Gabrielle. Klein's girlfriend is killed. Dorothea points Klein out to Termann, who now has blood streaming down his face from the blows he has received. The third shot meets its mark and likewise proves fatal. With this Termann's aggression burns itself out. The corpses are thrown overboard. Termann composes an "accident" report of the incident and merely threatens to have Michael and Dieter killed if they let the truth be known about what has happened – a feeble gesture in view of the fact that he and Dorothea intended to appropriate the *Apollonia* for themselves.

What followed was a matter for the courts and may be looked up in the case reports. Termann was finally sentenced to life imprisonment for murder. His girlfriend received a three-year prison sentence for being an accessory. It was not only the court who were of the opinion that all this would never have happened on land.

From a socio-psychological point of view, several danger areas present themselves for investigation on the evidence of the above incident. These not only determine the psychological environment during Atlantic crossings but on shorter trips as well – confinement and isolation, the group-dynamic situation, the role and style of leadership, and the common causes of anxiety and aggression.

Social Distancing – the problems of living space on board

If the *Apollonia* drama could never have played itself out in the same way on land, what then are the specific conditions which can arise (but which are obviously not inevitable) on board a yacht?

In the first place, the "social density" on yachts is extremely high – there are often six to eight crew members living together for an extended period in 10 to 20 square metres per person. Elsewhere, similar spatial conditions are only to be found in overcrowded prisons. What is wrong with this is that everyone needs a certain amount of space to themselves, their own private area of responsibility, and the opportunity to withdraw from others. To begin with, we each have our own personal "buffer zone" around our bodies. The extent of this buffer zone, the boundaries of which no one will cross voluntarily, is naturally dependent on sex, degree of intimacy with the other person, and the nature of the situation. Invasion of the personal buffer zone is, of course, tolerated for a short while in certain situations – while waiting in large queues, in the cinema, and so forth. But if one observes, for instance, tables in restaurants or libraries filling up little by little, it is quite clear that people will always choose the greatest social distance possible in the given circumstances.

The ideal distance between people in the Western world is considered to be 1.2 m to 1.5 m. This naturally shrinks when common tasks demand a necessary proximity, but on yachts the extent of the social distance, of the body's buffer zone in partic-ular, is continually undercut due to the prevailing spatial condi-tions. Invasion of one's personal space has sometimes to be accepted for a considerable length of time.

There must be a place for each member of the crew on board which guarantees privacy and to which they can retreat when they feel like it. A sailor's bunk is naturally the most suitable spot. In the light of this, care must be taken that on longer cruises every member of the crew has his own bunk and that no one is allocated the emergency bunk which during the day doubles as the saloon seat. It is important that the private area of each crew member is respected, and thus preserved, by the rest of the crew. At all events, the absolute uppermost limit to the number of crew on a long-term cruise – and by a long-term cruise we mean being at sea for over a week – should be set by the number of fixed berths available. From the point of view of privacy, the space set aside on board for the individual acquires almost symbolic significance. The offer of a small locker, some place in which a few personal bits and pieces may be stored, will usually be gratefully appreciated by the crew.

Prolonged conditions of stress can make life unbearable, and stress through crowding can be reduced by taking the following measures:

1. Clear role allocation and hierarchy on board
2. Clearly structured conditions of interaction (who must be informed/consulted about what)
3. Good social interaction
4. Team spirit
5. Co-operative attitude and co-operative activity
6. Rational discussion of problems in place of emotional reaction
7. Awareness of stress through crowding (knowing something is going to happen is often enough to reduce one's susceptibility)
8. Closure of the bulkheads and passage ways from time to time to enable individuals or subgroups to withdraw
9. Telling yourself that a restricted situation also has advantages which are often sought after on land.

Traditionally the captain of the ship is given a cabin to himself (provided, of course, there is such a thing as a single cabin on

board). This is generally considered his due, regardless of his
actual needs. Other members of the crew seek to stake out their
territory in different ways. Individuals claim, more or less
overtly, the galley, fo'c'sle, sail bags, anchor system, radio system etc. for their own personal areas of responsibility. This kind
of territorial behaviour by human beings seems irrational even
if it does have deep roots in our evolutionary history. Generally
speaking, it is an expression of undefined or unstructured
power and authority relations on board.

Territorial behaviour may, in individual cases, take many different forms of expression. It can happen that a crew member
feels his territory is being invaded when someone else takes over
a job for which he has hitherto felt himself to be responsible.
Such "infringements" are always met with aggression,
although whether this takes an open or hidden form depends on
the position occupied by the aggressor in the order of rank on
board. Some people manage to swallow their anger, but this is
rare. Another instance of territorial encroachment can be seen if
the skipper constantly checks his watch leader's navigation.
This is an example of how the territories of the different role
players on board can overlap. The watch leaders are responsible
for navigation for the duration of their watch; the skipper,
however, is at all times responsible for what happens on board
over and above and including what the watch leaders do. Even
so, the skipper would do well only to check the navigation
when it seems necessary from the point of view of safety, and he
should do so as discreetly as possible. Watch leaders learn best
from their own mistakes, that is, when they have discovered the
errors in their navigation for themselves. For this reason the
skipper should only proffer criticism if it is requested. He
should also always be sparing with praise.

Territorial behaviour of the kind described above invariably
stirs up conflicts of authority and questions of competence. A
skipper who silently demonstrates in all his actions how capable
he is himself, and how incapable the others are, only succeeds in
promoting the slow but systematic growth of dissatisfaction on
board.

What gives the skipper his authority?

The skipper determines the "working atmosphere" on board. His personality, conduct, the way in which he issues instructions – in short, his style of leadership – play a crucial role in determining the attitude of his crew. The general mood might be one of frustration and reluctance, with each member of the crew preferring to go his own way and only grudgingly accepting the division of labour. In contrast, it may be that the group works together as a team, looking upon each task as a necessary step toward the achievement of a common objective and refusing to become downcast in difficult situations. Certainly the skipper of a yacht is no longer the "master over the life and death" of his crew that he used to be in the early days of seafaring, when he could uphold his authority by force of arms and was free to punish his crew in any way he saw fit. Nevertheless, the responsibility of the Captain as recorded in the International Regulations for Preventing Collisions at Sea(4) imposes special duties upon him and at the same time grants him special rights. This does not mean that the skipper cannot consult the watch leaders before he makes a decision or discuss plans for the cruise with his crew. But with the safety of the crew and the yacht at stake, final responsibility rests with the skipper, who must make his decisions clearly, unambiguously, promptly – and alone.

In the light of this it would seem sensible, in cases where several of the crew are taking part in an open-sea cruise for the first time, to discuss at a preliminary meeting not merely whether Beck's beer or Budweiser should be bought but also the special socio-psychological implications that arise from having a clear leadership structure on board a boat. A student group would find it difficult, for example, to reconcile themselves to the idea of Mr. X, someone who sat quietly in seminars contributing little to the discussion, suddenly assuming the role of skipper and being able self-assuredly to issue instructions to his fellows. Role conflicts of this kind arise because groups on land have a certain structure which accords with social hierarchy and in which emphasis is placed on communication skills. At sea the same group suddenly acquires a new formal structure because different skills and experience are required. These conflicts should be foreseen and openly discussed before a cruise. Otherwise the skipper's authority might only grudgingly be accepted, if at all, because neither he nor the rest of the crew are able to detach themselves from the group structure which operates ashore. It must be emphasized that while the idea of one person having formal authority is often regarded in a negative light on land (because there is seldom any call for leadership by a single person), at sea it can be the one factor that guarantees the safety and survival of the crew.

Almost anyone who has sailed in different crews believes he knows the personal qualities – besides seafaring and navigational skills – that make a good skipper. He distinguishes himself by his initiative, stamina, know-how, self-confidence, willingness to take responsibility, intelligence, sociability, and so on. He is not an excitable type but exudes calm and confidence. He has a good sense of judgment and is physically fit.

There are any number of good skippers who lack many of these qualities. Furthermore it is almost impossible to recognize many of these qualities beforehand on land, and the positive abilities that a skipper possesses may only come to the fore in times of crisis. However there are certain behavioural characteristics which are evident after only a short while at sea which distinguish good skippers:

- They are the most strict adherents to the group standards (eg: no smoking below deck, conscientious fulfilment of galley duty, observation of safety precautions).
- They do not sit aft in the cockpit issuing commands for the crew to carry out, but participate fully, helping with difficult manoeuvres.
- They do not take solitary decisions but, where possible, discuss in advance with the crew what is to be done, allowing them to choose from alternative courses of action or explaining the reasons behind a particular decision. When

decisions have to be made immediately under pressure, they discuss them with the crew afterwards.

- They do not undertake themselves all the difficult tasks which require a high degree of skill (harbour manoeuvres, sail changes, sextant measurements) but, as far as the situation permits, give the crew the opportunity to learn and, in time, to apply and develop their own skills.
- When a skipper issues instructions he must ensure that they are well thought out and not immediately subject to amendments; they should be clear and easily understood. If they contradict earlier instructions, this should be remarked. Furthermore, they should be directed at a specific person and the same person should not be given more than one set of instructions at a time ("Can you just clear the peak halyard and check the diesel?").
- Finally, a good skipper is one who gets to know the individual needs, interests, and problems of his crew and makes allowances for these in the division of labour onboard.

This list of behavioural characteristics, although incomplete, nevertheless demonstrates that it is perhaps less a question of the inherent personal qualities that single someone out for the role of skipper than certain codes of conduct which can be summed up under the heading "style of leadership" and which anyone can learn.

In a classic socio-psychological investigation three different styles of leadership – the authoritarian, the democratic, and the laissez-faire – were tried out in youth groups, each of which had a special task to fulfil. The authoritarian leader determined what and how things were to be done in every detail and only ever informed the group of the course of action one step at a time. He determined what each individual had to do and the group were left uninformed about future developments. Any praise or criticism was directed at individuals.

With the democratic style of leadership the method of approach was decided upon jointly through group discussions. Each step was planned jointly after the leader had put forward the various alternatives. The allocation of tasks was left up to the group. The group leader himself fitted in with the activities of the others. He praised and criticized individual actions, not individuals.

Finally, with the third group, all the decision making was left to the group itself. The leader did not participate at all and only offered his opinion when it was asked for. There was no praise or criticism.

The results of this investigation are very interesting and can give us valuable clues as to how to behave on board. Under the authoritarian style of leadership, a lot of aggression was apparent among the group members, especially against outsiders. Furthermore, both toadying and power-seeking behaviour were in evidence. There was relatively little sense of team spirit and as the pressure diminished the group fell apart. Group satisfaction was low even though the task was completed relatively quickly and efficiently.

Under the democratic style there proved to be more independent work motivation among the group members. The group held together more and was satisfied with its activity, although in purely numerical terms its performance was not as good as that of the authoritarian-led group. There were, however, more original ideas produced by this group.

Lastly, the laissez-faire group demonstrated the lowest work performance and the least team spirit. At times there was no group structure at all, making the pursuit of common group objectives correspondingly difficult.

If we compare these styles of leadership and their results with the behavioural characteristics of good skippers which were listed earlier, the democratic approach would seem to be the optimal style of leadership. There should, however, be the reservation that in certain circumstances the skipper should exercise greater authority since it may be that such action is necessary to retrieve a difficult situation.

Anarchistic laissez-faire leadership does not lend itself to seafaring. If we were to ask "Which member of the crew would you prefer to go on a pub crawl with?" it is highly likely that most of the votes would be for a different person than if we were to ask "Which member of the crew would you choose to help you to weather a storm?" Social psychologists have found that in groups, and even in institutions and communities, there are two different leadership roles which are fulfilled by different people. On the one hand there is the efficient type whose qualifications and track record are undisputed, while on the other hand there is the popular type who is most likely to act as confidant for social and emotional problems. We enjoy working with the former and enjoy the company of the latter.

One might think that the ideal skipper should combine both roles. However this is seldom the case because the types of behaviour determined by the different roles are, to a certain extent, mutually exclusive: a safety-conscious skipper who is concentrating on the task in hand may, in a moment of crisis, be unable to provide any social/emotional support. In practice it is most often the case that the two roles are split: the skipper being the most capable man onboard and another member of the crew being the most popular. As analysis of reports of long-term cruises shows, this kind of group-dynamic situation generally proves to be stable and satisfactory. It only becomes problematic if the common ground and mutual respect of the role holders breaks down, in which case their personal motives conflict and the development of subgroups is set in motion. This situation can give rise to unbearable tensions. For a well-balanced group structure it is thus necessary for the skipper to accept the fact that he is not the most important person on board in every respect.

from *The Psychology of Sailing*,
A and C Black (Publishers) Ltd., Huntingdon, 1983.

Rounding the Cape

Richard Henry Dana

In 1834 Richard Henry Dana was forced to leave Harvard as an undergraduate because of poor health, but shortly afterward he enlisted in the merchant marine and spent the next two years voyaging around Cape Horn to the California territory. D.H. Lawrence called his resulting account "a very great book."

The first day we passed at sea was the Sabbath. As we were just from port, and there was a great deal to be done on board, we were kept at work all day, and at night the watches were set and everything put into sea order. When we were called aft to be divided into watches, I had a good specimen of the manner of a sea captain. After the division had been made, he gave a short characteristic speech, walking the quarterdeck with a cigar in his mouth and dropping the words out between the puffs.

"Now, my men, we have begun a long voyage. If we get along well together, we shall have a comfortable time; if we don't, we shall have hell afloat. All you've got to do is to obey your orders and do your duty like men, then you'll fare well enough; if you don't, you'll fare hard enough, I can tell you. If we pull together, you'll find me a clever fellow; if we don't, you'll find me a bloody rascal. That's all I've got to say. Go below, the larboard watch!"

I being starboard, or second mate's watch, had the opportunity of keeping the first watch at sea. S., a young man, making, like myself, his first voyage, was in the same watch, and as he was the son of a professional man, and had been in a counting room in Boston, we found that we had many friends and topics in common. We talked these matters over: Boston, what our friends were probably doing, our voyage, etc., until he went to take his turn at the lookout and left me to myself.

I had now a fine time for reflection. I felt for the first time the perfect silence of the sea. The officer was walking the quarter-deck, where I had no right to go, one or two men were talking on the forecastle, whom I had little inclination to join, so that I was left open to the full impression of everything about me. However much I was affected by the beauty of the sea, the bright stars, and the clouds driven swiftly over them, I could not but remember that I was separating myself from all the social and intellectual enjoyments of life. Yet, strange as it may seem, I did then and afterward take pleasure in these reflections, hoping by them to prevent my becoming insensible to the value of what I was leaving.

But all my dreams were soon put to flight by an order from the officer to trim the yards, as the wind was getting ahead; and I could plainly see by the looks the sailors occasionally cast to windward, and by the dark clouds that were fast coming up, that we had bad weather to prepare for, and had heard the captain say he expected to be in the Gulf Stream by twelve o'clock. In a few minutes eight bells were struck, the watch called, and we went below.

I now began to feel the first discomforts of a sailor's life. The steerage in which I lived was filled with coils of rigging, spare sails, old junk, and ship stores, which had not been stowed away. Moreover, there had been no berths built for us to sleep in, and we were not allowed to drive nails to hang our clothes upon. The sea, too, had risen, the vessel was rolling heavily, and everything was pitched about in grand confusion. There was a complete "hurrah's nest," as the sailors say, "everything on top and nothing at hand." A large hawser had been coiled away upon my chest; my hats, boots, mattress, and blankets had all fetched away and gone over leeward, and were jammed and broken under the boxes and coils of rigging. To crown all, we were allowed no light to find anything with, and I was just beginning to feel strong symptoms of seasickness, and that listlessness and inactivity which accompany it.

Giving up all attempts to collect my things together, I lay down upon the sails, expecting every moment to hear the cry of "all hands ahoy," which the approaching storm would soon make necessary. I shortly heard the raindrops falling on deck, thick and fast, and the watch evidently had their hands full of work, for I could hear the loud and repeated orders of the mate, the trampling of feet, the creaking of blocks, and all the accompaniments of a coming storm. In a few minutes the slide of the hatch was thrown back, which let down the noise and tumult of the deck still louder, the loud cry of "All hands, ahoy! tumble up here and take in sail!" saluted our ears, and the hatch was quickly shut again.

When I got up on deck, a new scene and a new experience was before me. The little brig was close-hauled upon the wind, and lying over, as it then seemed to me, nearly upon her beam ends. The heavy head sea was beating against her bows with the noise and force almost of a sledge-hammer, and flying over the deck, drenching us completely through. The topsail halyards had been let go, and the great sails were filling out and backing against the masts with a noise like thunder. The wind was whistling through the rigging, loose ropes flying about; loud and, to me, unintelligible orders constantly given and rapidly executed, and the sailors "singing out" at the ropes in their hoarse and peculiar strains. In addition to all this, I had not got my "sea legs on," was dreadfully sick, with hardly strength enough to hold on to anything, and it was "pitch dark." This was my state when I was ordered aloft, for the first time, to reef topsails.

How I got along, I cannot now remember. I "laid out" on the yards and held on with all my strength. I could not have been of much service, for I remember having been sick several times before I left the topsail yard. Soon all was snug aloft, and we were again allowed to go below. This I did not consider much of a favour, for the confusion of everything below, and the inexpressible sickening smell caused by the shaking up of the bilge-water in the hold, made the steerage but an indifferent refuge from the cold wet decks.

I had often read of the nautical experiences of others, but I felt as though there could be none worse than mine; for in addition to every other evil, I could not but remember that this was only the first night of a two years' voyage. When we were on deck we were not much better off, for we were continually ordered about by the officer, who said that it was good for us to be in motion. Yet anything was better than the horrible state of things below. I remember very well going to the hatchway and putting my head down when I was oppressed by nausea, and always being relieved immediately. It was as good as an emetic.

This state of things continued for two days.

Wednesday, Aug. 20th. We had the watch on deck from four till eight, this morning. When we came on deck at four o'clock, we found things much changed for the better. The sea and wind had gone down, and the stars were out bright. I experienced a corresponding change in my feelings; yet continued extremely weak from my sickness. I stood in the waist on the weather side, watching the gradual breaking of the day, and the first streaks of the early light. Much has been said of the sunrise at sea; but it will not compare with the sunrise on shore. It wants the accompaniments of the songs of birds, the awakening hum of men, and the glancing of the first beams upon trees, hills, spires, and housetops, to give it life and spirit. But though the actual rise of the sun at sea is not so beautiful, yet nothing will compare with the early breaking of day upon the wide ocean.

There is something in the first grey streaks stretching along the eastern horizon and throwing an indistinct light upon the face of the deep, which combines with the boundlessness and unknown depth of the sea round you and gives one a feeling of loneliness, of dread, and of melancholy foreboding, which nothing else in nature can give. This gradually passes away as the light grows brighter, and when the sun comes up, the ordinary monotonous sea day begins.

From such reflections as these, I was aroused by the order from the officer, "Forward there! Rig the head pump!" I found that no time was allowed for daydreaming, but that we must "turn to" at the first light. Having called up the "idlers," namely carpenter, cook, steward, etc., and rigged the pump, we commenced washing down the decks. This operation, which is performed every morning at sea, takes nearly two hours; and I had hardly the strength enough to get through it.

After we had finished, swabbed down, and coiled up the rigging, I sat down on the spars, waiting for seven bells, which was the sign for breakfast. The officer, seeing my lazy posture, ordered me to slush the mainmast, from the royal masthead down. The vessel was then rolling a little, and I had taken no sustenance for three days, so that I felt tempted to tell him that I had rather wait till after breakfast; but I knew that I must "take the bull by the horns," and that if I showed any signs of want of spirit or of backwardness, I should be ruined at once. So I took my bucket of grease and climbed up to the royal masthead. Here the rocking of the vessel which increases the higher you go from the foot of the mast, which is the fulcrum of the lever, and the smell of the grease, which offended my fastidious senses, upset my stomach again, and I was not a little rejoiced when I got upon the comparative terra firma of the deck. In a few minutes seven bells were struck, the log hove, the watch called, and we went to breakfast.

Here I cannot but remember the advice of the cook, a simple-hearted African.

"Now," says he, "my lad, you are well cleaned out; you haven't got a drop of your 'long-shore swash aboard of you. You must begin on a new tack – pitch all your sweetmeats overboard, and turn to upon good hearty salt beef and seabread, and I'll promise you, you'll have your ribs well sheathed, and be as hearty as any of 'em, afore you are up to the Horn." This would be good advice to give passengers, when they speak of the little niceties which they have laid in, in case of seasickness.

I cannot describe the change which half a pound of cold salt beef and a biscuit or two produced in me. I was a new being. We had a watch below until noon, so that I had some time to myself; and getting a huge piece of strong, cold salt beef from the cook, I kept gnawing upon it until twelve o'clock. When we went on deck I felt somewhat like a man, and could begin to learn my sea duty with considerable spirit.

from *Two Years Before the Mast*,
Boston, 1840.

SONG OF THE SIRENS

ERNEST K. GANN

I

Man goes down to the sea in many ways, the least common of which is actually going to sea. Yet there are and always have been relatively few sailors. It is said we came from the sea, beginning as unicells; our sperm tastes of the sea, our tears are of salt water. As embryos we resemble fish, and the mammals of the oceans are our underdeveloped cousins. Noah rescued our species by putting to sea, and only at sea may the complete mixture of all the grand elements best be sensed and comprehended.

To all of the many theories there are counterarguments, sometimes scientific and sometimes quasi-religious. There is no true satisfaction in either the arguments or the theories, and the real key seems to have been lost or deliberately hidden somewhere in the beginning of man's time.

The hour of day seems to have little effect on the magnetic power of the sea. It makes no difference if you bring a vessel into port at three o'clock in the afternoon or three o'clock in the morning. It matters not if the sun is shining or if it is pouring rain. Someone, at least one human being, will appear and take your heaving line or just stand watching while the vessel is secured alongside the dock. Weather and time influence only the number of people so compelled, and the same silent supervision applies to any vessel departing, whether previous notice has been given or not. Whether it be Oslo or Nassau, Piraeus or Honolulu, Papeete or Curaçao, Travemünde, La Coruña, San Francisco, Stockholm, Balboa, Christiansø, or Milos – fair weather or foul, you may depend absolutely that at least one human being will be standing on the wharf in silent welcome or farewell.

Man seems to have an instinct for such moments.

The people who engage themselves in this activity are of every race and environment. They appear from nowhere and are known collectively as the "Dock Committee," though their numbers may vary from one to a thousand. No one can say where or when those who oblige themselves to greet a vessel at three o'clock in the morning, sleep. They never appear to have dressed in haste. No one is certain where those who wait patiently for hours until a vessel sails, work. People serving on Dock Committees seem to have no other business. Yet the committees are not composed of mere loungers or even retired mariners down for a nostalgic moment with the sea. There are women who stand as transfixed as any man; there are well-dressed businessmen, entire families, lovers, and the lonely. All behave in exactly the same way regardless of their geographical location. They watch in a kind of reverent silence, seldom moving, and when either the arrival or sailing has been completed they continue to hold their positions. Only their eyes move, hungrily, as if they fear missing the slightest detail of a vessel or her rig. They stare at those aboard, observing every activity in a manner which becomes infuriating until you meet their eyes and understand they are really not seeing you but themselves. For their eyes are glazed with the faraway and they are totally unconscious of their rudeness.

Probably those who come down to the wharves and harbours of the world are ultimately driven by a stronger force than may be discovered in science or religion. Perhaps they come because a ship is a tangible representation of their romantic dreaming, a mental indulgence shared in one fashion or another by all but beasts. The solitude of an empty sea viewed from shore is one thing: euphoric, or for dark brooding according to the will. The sea and a ship complement each other in the imagination, and the urge is to become as closely identified with both as may be possible. Thus people of Dock Committees will not stand back on the wharf, but will move to the very edge of it and sometimes in their eagerness nearly fall into the sea. And perhaps when a vessel arrives or leaves, the long-stifled dreams of the spectators respond accordingly, for sailings invariably create visible sadness, while arrivals provoke a certain excitement and cryptic joy. At such times a wharf is a place where these emotions can be shared with strangers.

Even sailors forget that the horizon observed from 10 feet above the water is a mere 3 1/2 miles away. To Dock Committees, and to others who linger on a lonely beach, the sea horizon has forever been limitless. Beyond it is adventure and romance, mystery, the swirling kingdoms of every man's imagination. These are essentials beyond the ocean horizon not to be found in daily life, neither in books, nor music, nor art in any form, and as modern existence becomes more and more protected those essentials become increasingly more difficult to enjoy.

So it could be that the members of Dock Committees are starving. Only by coming down to the sea can they suck up morsels of adventure, which is essential to full life.

II

Ever since the *Henrietta* I had been unable to regard any well-made sail with proper respect, for in that little Caribbean sloop I was shipmates with a sail so unique that it dominated life aboard. Bigelow, who would later serve as First Mate in the *Albatros*, had joined me in the *Henrietta* and had brought along his identical twin brother, whom for convenience I thought of as Bigelow number two. Both men were expert sailors and both were nearly hypnotized by the *Henrietta*'s unforgettable mainsail.

It was shaped like the ass of a hippopotamus and was approximately the same colour. It was riven with holes. The clew was tied to the boom with a piece of twine and the foot was made fast in the same careless fashion. The luff was very loosely held to the mast by a frayed lacing of thin sisal, and the head was hoisted by a length of the same stuff. The mast was supported by two rusty wire shrouds on either side which were led to deadeyes served by lanyards of withered and quite unidentifiable rope. When under way in the *Henrietta*, particularly when the Caribbean breeze became a fresh wind, we stared at this assembly in wonder, and in the absolute certainty that any moment it must all come tumbling down.

The *Henrietta* was a sloop of 38 feet overall and of orthodox design for small trading in the Caribbean. She was built by eye in the West Indian tradition with strict economy being uppermost in the minds of both builder and owner. I chartered her because she was the only boat in the harbour of Antigua which showed a trace of new paint. She was owned and sailed by a giant blue-black man with one of the world's most engaging smiles. His name was Coagli and when I told him of my intention to cruise the Antilles and that I would pay him as if he were transporting cargo, he urged me to hire a yacht from one of the several available at English Harbour. But I had ever been a poor sybarite and at length persuaded him that although my intentions might be eccentric they were at least legal. The *Henrietta*'s mainsail was wrapped around the boom sausage fashion, and later I wondered if I would have gone through with our bargain had it been entirely visible.

It was the *Henrietta*'s mainsail combined with the presence of the twin Bigelows that nearly transformed me into a teetotaler.

As so often happens in the Caribbean, the northerly winds turned chill and not one of us had brought any warm gear. Goose bumps peckled Coagli's mighty bare arms as he grinned and sang and leaned for hours against the mast. The staccato snapping of his shirttail in the wind was our anemometer, and when the tempo quickened whoever had the helm would automatically ease the sheet or come up a trifle into the wind. We made St. Kitts and Saba and in time came to anchor off Barbuda, which is an islet situated north and east of the principal Antilles.

We were by now deeply impressed by our shipmate Coagli. He was a sailor's sailor. When the winds had fallen so that ordinarily we would have been becalmed, we had seen him take up a wooden dipper and throw salt water at his pitiful mainsail until the whole of it was soaked. To our amazement the effect upon our speed was immediately noticeable. If we had been nearly stationary in the water we would begin to move, and if we had been merely lazing along with a whispering of water at the stem, then we would pick up a full half-knot or so and sometimes more without the slightest increase in wind. This condition would prevail as long as Coagli continued to toss water. When the sail dried, the *Henrietta* became lethargic again.

"The sail be thirsty," Coagli would announce and resume his water tossing. As if this eerie performance were not enough to make us question the laws of aerodynamics, Coagli would sometimes speak to the sail as if it were a living thing. He did not utter either well-formed or connected words but rather chanted sounds and syllables which he himself made no pretence of comprehending. All he knew, and all we could observe, was that his incantations worked. The sail and then the *Henrietta* responded exactly as if by voice commands he was controlling the power of an invisible sea serpent harnessed to our hull.

The more we studied the sail the worse it appeared. It had been stretched without mercy, several inches of the leech flapped uselessly no matter how we trimmed it, and the great bulbous area which presumably was the principal driving force of the sail was so low in relation to the remainder that it often plopped into the sea and collapsed. There was absolutely no scientific reason why the *Henrietta* should move in anything less than a gale, much less go dancing along like a racer in hot pursuit. Coagli had no explanation, but his inner pride became apparent when he said, "She jes go, that's all, she jes go! and go!"

All of the *Henrietta*'s ballast was inside and consisted of burlap sacks filled with sand and laid in the single hold. During the day if the wind made up and the cold spray doused us so that life aboard the *Henrietta* was as uncomfortable as Coagli had promised it would be, I would abandon masochism when my trick at the helm was done and slip down to the cargo hold. The sandbags were damp and hard from moisture and only a thin bar of twilight came through the hatch coaming, but at least there was no wind.

Here in company with a multitude of sand fleas we slept. Here also I found the gloomy atmosphere conducive to specialized thinking. Why should the *Henrietta* sail so sweetly when Coagli was at the helm and become so listless when either of the Bigelows or myself took charge? I had supposed that after the first day we would get on to her, for certainly a man who could sail one vessel could with some familiarization sail any other – but it wasn't working out that way. My arms ached from heaving on the hardwood tiller, and there had been times during this day's no-nonsense blow when I thought I should lose her altogether. The Bigelows, one after the other, were likewise sorely tried, and it was not until Coagli's turn that the *Henrietta* was tamed.

Coagli's innate sense of decency kept him from pointing out how remarkable was the change, but as I watched him leaning back and effortlessly mixing adjustments of tiller and sheet I listened ever more carefully to his calypso monologue with the mainsail. And in time I realized that he spoke in a rhythmic beat, a gush of syllables alternating with a silence as his tremendous chest swelled with air. Then he would exhale a singsong of syllables again and slap his bare feet against the deck while at the same time adjusting the mainsheet and matching it with minor movements of the tiller. Was it my imagination that suggested these actions corresponded with the heaving of the seas? Was there some mysterious accord between this blue-black genius and the ocean which enabled him to abide so much better with it and the wind than we could?

Because the *Henrietta* was totally dependent on her ability to sail, I had envisioned dreary delays waiting in some isolated port for more wind or less wind. I had therefore taken the precaution of stowing a modest-sized keg of rum alongside our water barrels, and in the evenings when all was secure I drew upon it. The rum was not of medal-winning calibre, but the colour was pleasing and the bouquet not objectionable. In body it could not compare with Bardinet, but it did have a certain integrity. Unfortunately my appreciation of it was a lonely affair, since both Bigelows were Quakers and members of Alcoholics Anonymous. Coagli would accept a dollop in his glass which he seemed to use as mouthwash. He would take a sip, roll it about his mouth, and when he thought I was not watching, spit it into the sea. I finally realized that his huge and sensitive heart had simply instructed him to keep me company.

I was brooding about our relative sailing abilities as we lay at anchor off Barbuda. There were fish frying over our charcoal brazier and in my hand, nearly finished, was my second rum of the evening. I sat beside the keg trying to concentrate on the West Indian sunset which emblazoned the sky behind the Bigelow brothers, yet the business of the mainsail would not leave my mind. The Bigelows were equally perplexed. Bigelow number one said, "Coagli, are you sure you haven't an engine hidden below that only works when you take the helm?"

Coagli simply laughed and in his embarrassment spent some time readjusting the fire beneath the fish.

Bigelow number one said, "Eventually we will find out that Coagli has a trained dolphin who lives aft of the rudder and gives a shove when the boss says go."

"There are people who are one with the sea," Bigelow number two stated in his firm way. "They are part fish and part oceanic bird and our friend is a little of both."

"We think and he feels," Bigelow number one said.

The rum was souring in my throat. Could it be that all of this time I had missed some sensual connection with the sea? I had thought myself in complete harmony with it always, whether it chose to exalt or humble me.

Suddenly a possible answer came to me, for the Bigelow twins were talking together as they often did in a way that phased out any other present company. At such times so alike was their tone, phrasing, and pronunciation it was quite impossible to tell when one fell silent and the other spoke. I closed my eyes and listened. Every audible factor of their speech was identical, and listening I realized they were thinking as one; they were a man talking to himself. I opened my eyes and saw them still side by side in silhouette against the sun. And each of their movements was identical. They moved as one.

The rum, I thought, has brought me single vision instead of double and I must not touch it again, lest the Bigelows melt away entirely. And then I thought, Here were two mature and stalwart men, each in himself an accomplished personality and yet they were as alike as waves of the ocean.

I remembered then how rich the sea was in unexplainable things and how the ancients had accepted them readily and decorated their charts with wonders they could not hope to comprehend. Never before had I questioned the phenomenon of the Bigelows, yet I realized now that it could not have been purely a matter of genetics. A kindred power enabled Coagli, who knew nothing whatever of coefficients, metracentric heights, or centres of effort, to sail his contradictory little sloop in a style far better than we could ever hope to achieve.

Suddenly I thought, A pox on this inferior rum! It had led me to inquiry instead of acceptance and thus stood me into the danger of losing my sailorman's peace.

In the *Henrietta* I learned that there are certain things of the sea we must accept – as is.

III

If the ship be on the starboard Tack, close hauled, her Head North, of course the Wind at E.N.E., the Water tolerably smooth, and it be thought necessary to put about, and stand on the larboard Tack, everything being ready before: the first Precaution is (as indeed it should be at all times in steering by the Wind), to have her so suited with Sail as nearly to steer herself, with little assistance from the Rudder; by which management her way will be more powerful through the Water; she will be brought to the wind with a small Helm – and probably not have any Stern-way through the whole Rotation . . .

These gospel words thunder from the chapter entitled "Tacking Expeditiously" which is included in a mighty and durable work known as *The Young Sea Officer's Sheet Anchor*. It is a splendid book of nautical wisdom by one Darcy Lever, Esq., who desired to make life easier for "the young Gentlemen of the Royal Navy, the Honourable East India Company [who] sometimes feel a diffidence in soliciting information; either from a fear of exposing their ignorance, or from an idea that such a request may be treated with ridicule."

In short it was intended to be a reference consulted in privacy, which I found it convenient to do. This jewel of maritime literature describes the intricacies of square-rigged sailing in rolling phrases to rival Gibbon. Reading it transports you back to 1819, the year its second edition was published, and as far as I could discover it is the only lucid treatment of the subject since that date. It saved me from making too many mistakes on the day the *Albatros* made her debut under square rig.

For the last moment of truth had come and my grandest folly was about to be exposed. Here was a ship of approximately 100 tons apparently ready in all respects for sea, and there just beyond the sheltering estuary a fine fresh wind was scuffling across San Francisco Bay. It was a Saturday and hence a union-proclaimed day of rest for Dickerhoff, who had grunted more ominously than usual on the night before and said he guessed he had done all he could do. I did not care to question him further as to the exact meaning of such a finality. Of course Dickerhoff knew very well that the Captain of this vessel had never commanded a square-rigger in his life, which may have been why, not wishing to witness disaster, he chose to stay home on this day.

To gain experience in a square rig of any size you must either be a foreign cadet (Japanese, Norwegian, Danish, Swedish, Spanish, Chilean, Portuguese, or German), or serve in the U.S. Coast Guard's *Eagle*. So I had to depend heavily on Lever's instructive companionship and upon Holcomb, whose nature being somewhat more tender than Dickerhoff's, caressed his dolphin-striker jaw and allowed as how there were enough menaces to navigation in the bay without turning me loose in a rig which at least looked complicated. To serve as crew I had

assembled a heterogeneous group of people who believed that
as I had managed to captain the *Albatros* all the way from Rotter-
dam without calamity, certainly an afternoon in the Bay should
be a lark. I did not bother telling them how little I knew during
a sort of rehearsal just before leaving the dock. It was easier
demonstrating what I did know. I lectured slowly and with
many repetitions, since I was aware that as soon as my supply of
book learning was exhausted we would be obliged to sail.

Holcomb seated himself on the taffrail and watched me with
a sort of bemused tolerance throughout the performance. I was
aware that he shook his head in dismay several times and rolled
one cigarette after another, possibly to keep his hands occupied
so he wouldn't surrender to impulse and clamp them over his
mouth.

I began by saying we could forget the mainsail, which
remained exactly as it had been when the *Albatros* was a
schooner and still functioned in the same way. Even those who
sailed very small boats understood it. But now on the foremast I
pointed out the four yards beginning at the highest, which was
the topgallant, being careful in my newly acquired snobbery to
pronounce it t'gallant. Captain Ahab might have been proud of
me, but out of the corner of my eye I noticed a slight twitching
about Holcomb's mouth as I explained that the t'gallant yard
slid up and down a metal track which had been welded to the
forward side of the mast in the German style.

Below the t'gallant was the upper topsail yard, which also
slid on a metal track when being hoisted or lowered. Below it
was the lower topsail yard, which was fixed in place vertically.
The lowest and obviously the largest was the forecourse yard,
which was also fixed.

When this brief tour was concluded I suggested that my
audience should climb aloft and have a look for themselves.
"And don't be crawling through the lubber hole," I said with a
swagger. I was pleased to see Holcomb's eyebrows rise and his
dark eyes express both surprise and approval. Between the forecourse yard and the lower tops'l yard there was now a small
platform welded to the mast. It was called the foretop and in

olden times used not only for handling sail aloft, but as a perch for riflemen in battle. There was a hole cut through the decking of this platform on both sides of the mast through which were passed the yard halyards, buntlines, clew lines, and sheets. It was also barely large enough for a man to squeeze through, if climbing to heights turned his blood to milk. The alternative was to use the futtock shrouds, which angled outward from the main shrouds to the perimeter of the foretop, and thus obliged the sailor to climb about 45 degrees past the vertical. There was really nothing to it.

To neophytes it just looked awful. I could not remember how far back in my lifetime I had read that anyone who crawled through a lubber hole was a farmer.

I took my hearties aloft, and they were impressed with my movements because they did not know how many hours I had been playing monkey in this very jungle, or of a peculiar quirk in my nature which allowed me to be quite at ease at heights up to 100 feet. Perversely, anything above that altitude, such as the view from a high building, made my blood congeal. Sailing boats of the more modern design have long abandoned ratlines as the means of climbing aloft to the upper rigging. In fact it is out of fashion for sailors to go aloft at all, and many boats would never be sold if the owner had to contemplate ever lifting his feet off the solid deck. With the great basic simplicity of modern sailing rigs, plus inherent material strengths, there is, in fact, little need for going aloft. The majority of repairs and mainte-nance can be done in some quiet harbour or shipyard, and whoever does the work is hoisted to his tasks in a bos'n's chair.

This is all very fine until something parts or snarls at sea, and then the fun begins. Every poor sailor who must then ride a chair aloft may do his own calculations as to the amount of "whip" created by a 60-foot stick swinging through an arc of 60 degrees while he clings to the end of it. At night it is unadul-terated hell for those on deck trying to ease the strain on their comrade aloft, who is nearly helpless to accomplish anything but the most simple tasks. And for all concerned the whole operation can be exceedingly dangerous.

I have always been more comfortable in a vessel offering some permanent means of going aloft. Particularly for cruising, the added windage of shrouds and ratlines is cancelled out by an added dividend in navigation. There is nothing quite so reassuring as a quick trip up the ratlines to spy an island or reef which from the deck would be invisible over the horizon, or to pick up a distant buoy, or navigate a difficult channel. The area visible to a sailor whose viewpoint is 10 feet above the water is a mere 3 1/2 miles! Radar has improved the situation for those who can afford it, but radar cannot show the navigator a shoal or a rock awash.

There was certainly no lack of ratlines on the *Albatros*. The shrouds of both masts were wormed, parcelled, and served, and they were all used frequently at sea.

Climbing the lower foreshrouds was like walking up a giant staircase. The rigging was set up bar taut and the ratlines themselves were of solid oak, so that even the most doubtful of our new crew felt secure. But once they had reached the foretop they found a change. To continue upward they must depend on "Lord Nelsons," which are simply hemp rope seized in ladder formation to the wire shrouds. Being of tender foot padding I had always detested Lord Nelsons, claiming they were for baboons; yet both Dickerhoff and Holcomb had said the *Albatros* would appear too heavy aloft if we used oak battens all the way, and they were right.

I was at least well qualified to demonstrate the proper way to climb any rigging regardless of its make-up, with the feet lightly on the ratlines and a firm handgrip on the shrouds themselves. "Then some wild night when you are up here and a ratline breaks – you'll still be here."

I also knew how to demonstrate how easy it is to go out on a yard and work – easy, that is, once you know how. I was aware that a new hand's first encounter with a yard is soured by a tremendous psychological block, rooted in a natural human reluctance to leave the security of a tree's trunk for the end of a branch extending outward a considerable distance over nothing. It is also a fact that the footropes on a square yard are totally deceiving, it being inconceivable to the uninitiated that they could provide solid support.

I knew there was no use trying to tell them so – so just go!

The same people who would soon be swinging from mast to ratline as easily as stepping out their front doors now crept inch by inch toward their destination. There were a great many "after you's," and nervous laughter, and much time and effort lost fiddling with the arm beckets, which eventually became such a nuisance we cut them away.

The footrope of a yard is far more than a wobbly string hanging beneath a spar. To accommodate the average sailor it must be hung at 3 feet 6 inches below the yard; if lower, the sailor's weight is thrown out of balance, the footrope has excessive swing fore and aft, and about all anyone can do is hang on to the yard and curse; if too short, the sailor cannot adjust his body to the yard and maintain his fore-and-aft position unless he is a midget. The strange thing about footropes is that the right length looks much too short and feels so until you learn to trust your precious body in a rather ludicrous position.

It may be stated with some certainty that during a sailor's first trip out on a yard-arm 99 percent of his energy is consumed in hanging on and the remaining 1 percent in looking about and wondering, What the hell am I doing up here? Yet in a surprisingly short time he stops trying to squeeze juice out of everything his hands, toes, and teeth can reach – he calms down and may soon become something other than decorative. He may even begin to enjoy his perch. Using his belly as a pad against the yard itself, he will venture ever larger rotations about its axis, so that when he leans far forward to reach down for a fistful of sail his feet swing up behind him on the footrope, then swing back again as he straightens and heaves up with both hands.

Good shipmates working together along a yard develop a rhythm so that their gyrations are synchronized, but we were a long way from such class, and the mere task of letting go a few gaskets caused so much commotion along the yard the shouting sounded like a protest march. By the time we had reached the t'gallant yard and gone through the business of setting, clewing up, and securing all four square sails, most of the confusion had evaporated. Everyone agreed it was great for the waistline. I saw no reason to douse their enthusiasm with remarks about our ship's present position in flat, calm water, and still moored firmly to the dock.

In the early afternoon we cast off and proceeded toward San Francisco Bay under the impetus of the supposedly resurrected African Queen. Enroute down the estuary we set the mainsail and rather smartly too, I thought, considering that the majority of the hands were new to the ship. While still in the protected waters we made for the yards and with only a minimum of delay cast off the gaskets on all four square sails.

By the time we returned to the deck we were feeling the first surge of the Bay and I thought darkly that on this little shakedown voyage we could do with a bit less wind. But I looked at Holcomb perched like an owl on the taffrail and saw no hint of warning in his deep black eyes. Rather, knowing him so well, I thought there was approval in the smile which compressed his lips. He bent into the shelter of his pea-coat collar to roll a cigarette and suddenly I felt very alone; which I later realized was exactly how he wanted me to feel. Murmuring a review of Lever's historic instructions, I ordered the helmsman (who was a girl) to fall off before the wind. We would begin by setting the forecourse.

It took ages. And by the time we had the lower and upper tops'ls set, and the t'gallant, and were heaving up the fore-top-m'st-stays'l and then the inner jib, and finally the outer jib, I saw to my astonishment that we had almost run out of Bay. And if I had entertained any doubts about the speed of the *Albatros* under such conditions I could now forget them. The afternoon breeze had piped up to at least 20 knots and we were skating along at very close to 10.

We braced the yards around as hard as we could and then "feathered" them slightly, that is with the forecourse set hard against the shrouds and each yard above it spoked a trifle more into the wind. Thus the chance of being taken aback was greatly reduced, since the helmsman had only to watch the t'gallant and hold a barely perceptible shiver in its leech. We were pointing as close to the wind as we could possibly go, and if the shiver increased it was only necessary to fall off a half-point or so.

So far all was well and Holcomb had not said a word. Nor had he moved from his perch, which was on the lee taffrail. I wondered if accident or tradition had caused him to settle there, since by historic custom the windward side of any quarterdeck was held the private domain of the Captain – phony or not.

Still panting from my exertions, I went to my mentor and said with as much pride as if I had designed and built the *Albatros*, "She goes right along doesn't she?"

"She do."

Then I saw that Holcomb was not entirely with me. He was looking ahead to the horizon and his eyes remained fixed there as if directing mine toward the same target. And suddenly I realized that he was not only looking ahead, but thinking ahead, which in my excitement and preoccupation in this shakedown I had neglected to do.

Although we had managed to skirt the western shoals of the Bay and still hold the wind, I now saw how the distance between the *Albatros* and the long Richmond bridge was diminishing with alarming rapidity.

We did not have a speed log aboard, so I hailed the fast power cruiser which had been watching the show from just off our port quarter.

"How fast are we going?"

Her skipper removed the cigar from his mouth and glanced at the array of instruments before him.

"Twelve knots!" he shouted.

I obviously had very little time to comply with Mr. Lever's solemn dictum and have "everything being ready before."

Moving closer to Holcomb for comfort, I said, "We'll have to come about in a few minutes."

"True. Unless you are awful mad at that bridge."

I had never seen a square-rigger coming about, hence I had been dreading this moment for months. It is one thing to read of

a manoeuvre and have it all fixed in your own mind and quite
something else to have all the right bodies in the right place
doing the right thing at the right time. A fore-and-aft-rigged
vessel missing stays or caught in irons during the labour of
passing from one tack to another can be embarrassing enough,
but somehow I had whelped the notion that a square-rigger
badly handled might result in an actual calamity. At least I knew
more than the crew. I had read a book.

Our rate of closure with the bridge was now augmented by
the swift tide south of its approaches. If we should miss stays
and be caught aback it was very obvious the combination of
tide and wind would carry us right against the bridge before we
could fall away and get organized again. In my nervousness I
sent a man below to stand by the African Queen.

At last all was in readiness with the crew spotted about the
ship according to Holcomb's soft-spoken suggestions. Two
men were forward to cast off and then belay the headsail sheets.
They would also cast off the forecourse tacks and belay the
opposite one when we had passed through the eye of the wind.
There were four men in the waist, two on each side to cast off
the lee yard braces and heave in on their opposites. We had
deliberately refrained from setting the mid and main stays'l, for
which conservatism I was now very grateful.

There were no winches on the *Albatros* except for the ancient
contraption employed to raise her anchors. The mainsheet was
hauled on a threefold purchase, so that with wind of any
strength sheeting in the main became all two strong men could
manage. This afternoon, with only Holcomb and myself available for the task, my apprehension was such I fancied I could do
it alone. For here was the bridge, all concrete and steel and
hardly a cable's length away. Still Holcomb failed to send me
any signal that the time had come.

We sheeted in the main as taut as we were able, which caused
the girl on the helm to complain she was almost hard over and
running out of strength. I told her to swallow a silence pill and
she said something about the difference between sailors and
gentlemen. I didn't care. The bridge was right there on the end

of the *Albatros*'s jibboom, about to be speared just as the police boat had been in far off Maassluis, Holland.

I wanted to close my eyes.

When I was certain it was too late Holcomb said quietly, "Perhaps you might care to bring her to now."

"Helm down!" I yelled. The girl let the spokes fly and gradually the bow swung around toward the wind. The headsails began to thunder and I called for their sheets to run free. We slacked the mainsheet as the deck became level. All of this was easy – standard procedure for any fore-and-aft rig, but now under square rig we were about to take on some very special education.

The *Albatros* had lost nearly all her way and I feared we were surely in irons.

Then I saw that a marvellous thing was happening and from that moment became a confirmed devotee of the square rig. Instead of doddering around on the opposite tack like a schooner or ketch, gradually losing turning momentum until you sometimes wondered if the old bucket would get around at all, the turning speed of the *Albatros* was rapidly increasing. The square sails, all of them now aback, were shoving her bow around as if a powerful tug were at work beneath her weather bow.

Holcomb was watching the t'gallant, then his eyes followed the mast down to the course. "Whenever you're ready," Holcomb said to me and nodded toward the men in the waist. They had been standing like actors waiting for a cue, the yard braces in their hands with only a single turn around the pins.

"Midships!" I called to the helm.

Then cupping my hands, I yelled toward the waist, "Let go and haul!"

The ancient cry of the square–rigger manoeuvring.

I felt self-conscious using it, an altar boy presuming to say the mass. I wanted to reach for my cocked hat, peg leg, and spyglass, and I could not put down a sense of great pride, because there were the yards swinging around of themselves and the men in the waist speeding them and checking their progress with the

lee and weather braces, and one by one the square sails were
filling, the t'gallant first, then the upper tops'l with a glorious
boom, then the lower tops'l, and when the big course rose up
against the forestay until the tacks were boused down and it
became as curvaceous and full as the ass of a sultana; and when I
saw that all of the square sails were pulling with a power that
seemed to actually live, I wanted to cry out my exhilaration.
Instead I managed a casual air so that the legendary coolness of
square-rigger masters, whether truth or fiction, would not be
desecrated by me.

Rigged as a schooner with the typical European depth of hull
forward, the *Albatros* had been a slob to bring about and had
sometimes barely made it. Now she was a new creature, vigor-
ous and alive. I looked aft and could barely believe the apparent
area consumed in our manoeuvre. We had come about in very
little more than our own length this first time and I wondered at
the feats we might accomplish once we had some continuous
practice. And I realized suddenly that we were shamefully over-
manned. British coasters of similar size and rig had often been
sailed by two men and a boy.

During the next hour we remained within the upper reaches
of the Bay and came about half a dozen times with varying
degrees of finesse. There were other manoeuvres I wanted to try,
particularly heaving-to, but the evening fog was already oozing
through the Golden Gate and my crew of assorted businessmen, students, and yachtsmen had to report back to their real
world of wives, study, and landlocked tribulations. Most of
them would never sail in a square-rigger again.

Our finale for the day was performed where we had begun,
just off the mouth of the estuary, and neatly cancelled out the
strutting conceit with which we had been infected. The time
had come to douse our square sails, and we discovered almost at
once how desperately we needed actual experience. I blessed
Holcomb for recommending we keep ample searoom, for
without it our general bungling might have brought about any
one or several of the serious misfortunes which had long
haunted me. As it was, the process of dousing and furling only

four square sails, none of which was large enough for a Cape Horner to blow his snoot in, took us one hour and a half. From a distance the exhibition must have caused old sailors to weep in mortification and it was a miracle someone was not hurt or gear damaged. With the evening had come a hard, no-nonsense wind sweeping between the city wharves and Treasure Island, and those on the yards found life vastly different than they had expected. The booming, recalcitrant sails were only partly to blame for our mass ineptness and confusion as we discovered one of the inherent disadvantages of the true square rig. The ulcer of exasperation quickly spread over the entire area of the foremast because it originated at the fife rail where all the sheets, buntlines, downhauls, clew lines, and tacks terminated. All of the lines were new, and well soaked with spray taken aboard during the afternoon. Now they were stiff, swollen, and ran through even the best fair-leads with a reluctance that was maddening. Although we had been at considerable pains to make up each line carefully and place it on the pin marked with its name, somehow there had been a mix-up and when we heaved on a downhaul we would find we were hanging on a buntline, or when we wanted to free a sheet and let it run, a buntline aloft would let go instead and the resulting explosion of sail would nearly shake the men off the yard. The more we sought to unravel the situation the worse we seemed to make it. It was as if all the crew had become apprentices to a nautical sorcerer, and I certainly became Captain Confusion. The t'gallant yard would only come halfway down, the port lower tops'l sheet was jammed taut somewhere in the maze aloft and, defying any gravitational possibility, the starboard clew garnet on the course had somehow wrapped itself around the end of the yard.

In his grandest manner Holcomb left the despair to me and I in turn passed it on to a certain McDowall, whose nature was such that he could deal with such matters without losing aplomb. It was he who eventually made order out of the spilled spaghetti of lines which dribbled about the foredeck.

McDowall was a marvellously complex man and we had

been fishmates for a season in the bone-racking *Mike*. He was very tall and very strong, blond, blue-eyed, and soft of voice. He often affected the manner of a simpleton, even occasionally allowing his jaw to fall slack while he pondered a problem. "Humph!" he would say as if the simplest matter was past his comprehension. Yet only hasty strangers fell for McDowall's private amusement. While he hemmed and hawed and scratched his head and confessed his utter bewilderment with whatever challenge was at hand, those who knew McDowall were not deceived. We knew he was an expert carpenter, a wizard plumber, a born mechanic, and among other things a first-class baker. It was fascinating to watch McDowall in the *Mike*'s galley, his great arms writhing like a pair of boa constrictors as he kneaded dough, or his powerful hands employed more tenderly when he plucked a straw from the deck broom and tested a cake.

When at last we made the calm of Oakland's estuary and all was once more shipshape and Bristol fashion about the ship, I called McDowall aft. Knowing he must be unwary and fatigued from his labours, I struck him between the eyes with an invitation I hoped he could not resist.

I asked him if he would care to serve as First Mate on a voyage to the South Seas.

He kicked a few invisible pebbles across the deck, scratched his head thoughtfully, and claimed he didn't rightly know just where the South Seas might be. So to please him, I solemnly explained where they were.

"Humph," he said when I had done gesturing toward the western horizon. "A body just might have a hankerin' to try it."

from *Song of the Sirens*,
Simon and Schuster, New York, 1968.

My Boat

Raymond Carver

My boat is being made to order. Right now it's about to leave
the hands of its builders. I've reserved a special place
for it down at the marina. It's going to have plenty of room
on it for all my friends: Richard, Bill, Chuck, Toby, Jim, Hayden,
Gary, George, Harold, Don, Dick, Scott, Geoffrey, Jack,
Paul, Jay, Morris, and Alfredo. All my friends! They know
    who they are.
Tess, of course, I wouldn't go anyplace without her.
And Kristina, Merry, Catherine, Diane, Sally, Annick, Pat,
    Judith, Susie, Lynne, Cindy, Jean, Mona.
Doug and Amy! They're family, but they're also my friends,
and they like a good time. There's room on my boat
for just about everyone. I'm serious about this!
There'll be a place on board for everyone's stories.
My own, but also the ones belonging to my friends.
Short stories, and the ones that go on and on. The true
and the made-up. The ones already finished, and the ones still
    being written.
Poems, too! Lyric poems, and the longer, darker narratives.
For my painter friends, paints and canvases will be on board
    my boat.
We'll have fried chicken, lunch meats, cheeses, rolls,
French bread. Every good thing that my friends and I like.
And a big basket of fruit, in case anyone wants fruit.
In case anyone wants to say he or she ate an apple,
or some grapes, on my boat. Whatever my friends want,
name it, and it'll be there. Soda pop of all kinds.
Beer and wine, sure. No one will be denied anything, on
    my boat.
We'll go out into the sunny harbour and have fun, that's the
    idea.

Just have a good time all around. Not thinking
about this or that or getting ahead or falling behind.
Fishing poles if anyone wants to fish. The fish are out there!
We may even go a little way down the coast, on my boat.
But nothing dangerous, nothing too serious.
The idea is simply to enjoy ourselves and not get scared.
We'll eat and drink and laugh a lot, on my boat.
I've always wanted to take at least one trip like this,
with my friends, on my boat. If we want to
we'll listen to Schumann on the CBC.
But if that doesn't work out, okay,
we'll switch to KRAB, The Who, and the Rolling Stones.
Whatever makes my friends happy! Maybe everyone
will have their own radio, on my boat. In any case,
we're going to have a big time. People are going to have fun,
and do what they want to do, on my boat.

from *Where Water Comes Together with Other Water*,
Random House, New York, 1984.

MUTINY ON *LA BOAT*

ARTHUR HOPPE

Mutiny! Now there's a subject that has stirred emotions and sold books, ever since the first author went down to the sea in ships. Look at *Mutiny on the Bounty*, say, or *The Caine Mutiny*. Titles like that spell b-e-s-t-s-e-l-l-e-r. But when you get right down to it, who loves Captain Bligh or Captain Queeg?

No one. Mention the word "mutiny" nowadays and everybody's on his feet ready to root for the mutineers. This is destroying our respect for authority.

For a change, then, let's take a captain who is a thoroughly decent sort, stern perhaps, but fair. Take a captain who is eminently considerate, one who, if he erred at all, erred on the side of overpampering his crew.

Take me.

Having become a sea captain by purchasing a yacht by mail, I learned almost immediately that while rank has its privileges, the burdens of command create inner tensions that try men's souls.

The week that followed my commissioning was an incredibly busy one, and I'll confess I was unable to give Meriwether even the minimum ration of attention required to keep any democratic marriage healthy. As a brand new sea captain I faced a score of fitting-out chores which had to be completed by the following Monday, embarkation date for our sun-filled, fun-filled two-week cruise. But, if I do say so myself, I faced them with the air of one born to lead. I stepped the towering mast ("Jesus Christ!"); I installed Meriwether's head ("Goddam!"); and I hung over the stern to apply the vessel's name on her transom in golden decal letters ("It's on upside down").

The name had been a problem anyway. Meriwether was for "One Basket," because, as she explained, ha, ha, "that's where we've sunk all our eggs."

"Put all our eggs," I said.

"Haven't we, though."

But I wanted a name that would breathe romance, and particularly a name which would retain the lovely Gallic flavour of *Fleur Bleue*. The French language, I feel, has class. Devlin had helpfully offered a number of suggestions, such as *Au Secours* and *Sauvez Vous*, but in the end I hit on one that was a natural. It was simple, to the point, and Gallic, yet, at Meriwether's insistence, easily pronounceable by the Coast Guard Rescue Coordination Center:

La Boat

I didn't really emblazon the name on the transom upside down. Not the whole name. Just the "t." Meriwether had been quick to catch the error, so that I was able to rectify it before it dried.

"It gives me a sinking sensation," she said, surveying the legend, *La Boaʇ*.

And that was about all she said during that week. For while I adapted readily to my new role as a sea captain, she appeared to find converting herself into a captain's wife most difficult. As a sea captain, my first duty, of course, lay with my ship. It would seem obvious to anyone that wife, children, and such chores as lopping back the ivy growing down the chimney must come second. It wasn't obvious to Meriwether.

"We're all going to go up in flames," was what she said.

"Don't you worry about it," I said, and I would have consoled her longer, but I had to get over to the boat to wire in the running lights which were absolutely essential to the safety of the vessel and her complement.

It will be recalled that the *Bounty*, according to legend, was launched in blood when a workman's foot was caught in the ways and he was flattened by the descending ship. A grim omen. It might be said of *La Boat*, on the other hand, that she was launched in tears. I'm not sure this wasn't grimmer.

But in analyzing the events leading up to the mutiny which sullied her name, I must concede that in certain particulars I might have charted a wiser course. One particular particular was the selection of a crew. My choice for first mate was, as the boating magazines archly put it, my first mate. And if Meriwether found it difficult to transform herself from a democratic marriage partner into a sea captain's wife, she found it nigh impossible to metamorphose again into a first mate. As a first mate she had certain inherent liabilities: in addition to her fear of water she was handicapped by an overweening maternalism toward the crew, in this case Dazey and Argee. And my only defence for the choices I made is that I had no choice.

It is not true, however, as Meriwether likes to tell the Boards of Inquiry she summons at cocktail parties, that I knew nothing about sailing when we embarked on that first and memorable voyage aboard *La Boat*. During the months I had awaited her arrival from Japan I had read many excellent books on the subject. And on that windy, overcast Monday morning, as I loaded the last of the stores aboard, I paused for a moment to glance at the bound volumes of *Learning to Sail*, *Sailing Made Easy*, and *Anyone Can Sail!* in their rack over the starboard bunk. Their presence filled me with a sense of well-being and quiet confidence. It was not shared.

Being the cautious and conservative-type sea captain, I recall wishing as we motored out of the Sausalito harbour into the white-capped reaches of San Francisco Bay that we had found time during the past week to put *La Boat* through at least one shakedown voyage to get the bugs out of her. Such as the bug of our newly purchased outboard motor which, when mounted on the transom, wasn't long enough to reach the water. The only hurried solution was for me to back edgily out over the stern and take a firm seat on the motor itself, thus submerging the propeller.

I feel the boating magazines would have been proud of the fine familial picture we made as we first put out to sea. Dazey, who immediately developed a mental block at differentiating between port and starboard, was at the helm as bosun. The ordinary seaman, Argee, was peeping fearfully out of the companionway and the first mate was crouched in a corner of the cockpit, checking the fastenings on her life-jacket while trying to keep a close count on the chickens she had hatched. I brought up the rear – or, more accurately, brought it down – vibrating cheerfully.

Without getting into technical details too complex for the lay reader, it is difficult to explain how I got the sails up. But I got them up. Eventually. I could tell because *La Boat* promptly lay over on her side like a mortally wounded elephant – like a mortally wounded elephant, that is, lying on its side going sixty miles an hour. The little bosun maintained a death grip on the tiller; the first mate managed to stick to her corner of the cockpit, the shur-grip soles of her boating shoes waving irritably over her head; and in the cabin the small fo'c'sle hand rattled around like a bean in a maraca. The outboard motor, not being designed to operate in a horizontal position, thoughtfully shut itself off. I now set our course.

To get to the Delta from Sausalito one must sail north across San Pablo Bay. This is too bad. San Pablo Bay is approximately ten miles long, ten miles wide, and, in most spots, one foot deep. It is ringed by mud flats leading uninvitingly up to low, brown, treeless hills dotted with grim oil refineries, a setting not immediately conducive to euphoria. Due to topographical phenomena, all the wind that hits the Pacific coast between Vancouver and Acapulco is funnelled across its shallow waters. This creates a wave action of interest primarily to masochists.

Soon after we entered this bay the first mate herded the bosun below. Several waves later she herded herself below and took what was to become her traditional place in the companionway, an apprehensive eye on my face, which she came to regard as a barometer of our fortunes. Should I look up at our bending mast with a thoughtful expression she was quick to ask if she might do something helpful. Like abandoning ship. It was thus I learned an axiom of command not in the Book: keep smiling.

The wind increased. The bay seemed a sheet of white foam. I kept smiling. Wanly. This was where the first stress developed in the chain of command. The mate gave a direct order to the captain: "Do something!"

I felt, perhaps wrongly, that this was no time to insist on

maintaining the proper channels of authority. Besides, the order was not without merit. Fortunately, chapter eight of the Book, entitled "Luffing the Main," flashed through my mind entire, much like a drowning man's autobiography. "Luffing the Main" entails inching out on a rope attached to the mainsail so that the sail becomes more and more parallel to the wind and commences to flutter or "luff." This takes the force out of the wind. The more the wind increased, the more I inched out on the rope, and eventually after a good many inches of rope, I had the whole sail fluttering away noisily.

This, it turns out, is very hard on the battens, thin strips of wood inserted in horizontal pockets along the after edge of the sail to stiffen it. Battens don't flutter – they snap. Ours did not snap; they exploded. Seeing pieces of one's new vessel flying off through the air, even such nonessential pieces as battens, is disconcerting. My smile began to jell.

Meriwether began to cry. I suddenly felt an overwhelming love for her, a love as sweet as that of the first days of our courtship and far more poignant. It surprised me. It was, I saw clearly, an emotion generated by our situation. Here we were, the four of us, with our food, our clothing, and our shelter, a self-contained family unit, independent of the world, battling against nature for survival, the destinies of us all lying in my hand, the hand that held the tiller. Meriwether was weak and good and feminine. The fears I felt when the boat had first heeled over were gone. I was now in command of both boat and family. It was my duty to protect and cherish Meriwether. I was strong and masculine and capable. I felt I had to tell Meriwether; she had to know.

"Dearest," I began . . .

"Stop talking," said Meriwether, the tears rolling down over her lips. "And do something!"

Doing something, I felt, was the least I could do. By now, however, I had arrived at the end of the mainsheet, a situation aptly described by landlubbers as "coming to the end of one's rope." Having come to the end of mine, I let it go. The sail and heavy wooden boom swung forward and banged into the wire shrouds holding up the mast, causing the whole boat, including captain and crew, to shudder.

In order to regain the end of the mainsheet I had to stand up. This meant letting go of the tiller. That meant the boat spun around in a tight little circle with all sorts of banging and crashing. And, all together, it meant more shrieks and cries and accusatory glares. Busy as I was in the hubbub, I was conscious of the ebbing away of my feeling of hairy-chested masculinity. I was sorry to see it go. For that one precious moment . . .

"Do something!"

"We'll be out of the bay soon," I said, when things had returned to their panicky normal. I had intended the statement as one of confident leadership. It emerged as wishy-washy appeasement.

After many another adventure calculated to warm the cockles of a rigging manufacturer's heart, we reached the yacht marina in Antioch at the entrance to the Delta area about sunset. My helmsmanship proved superb at this first attempt to berth *La Boat* and I hit the dock right on the nose. This was fortunate, as otherwise I would have smashed into the restaurant instead.

During the next two golden weeks, we spent many a sun-filled, fun-filled hour exploring the narrow Delta sloughs amid gay cries of "Watch out for that snag!" "Here comes a water skier!" "Good God, it's a tug and barge!" and, inevitably, "Do something!"

But it was not all adventure. There were days when we lay peacefully at anchor along the tree-lined banks, diving from the boat. Among other things, I dove for an old tennis shoe, size one, a child's fishing pole with fish attached, a dishpan full of dishes, and a pair of eyebrow tweezers. Not many a sea captain would go over the side for the first mate's eyebrow tweezers.

I think this idyllic existence would have healed the bruised psyches of the crew had it not been for the one insurmountable handicap we faced together – togetherness. For this, *La Boat* was admirably designed. The trouble with the 'tweendecks, as C. S.

Forester refers to the accommodations, is that there was less than four feet 'tween them.

The nights were fine. Meriwether and I slept in the cockpit, puly kool, underneath an awning stretched over the boom. The children occupied the bunks below, each ample for a full-grown man – a full-grown Japanese man. There had been some debate over their sleeping attire, but at last Meriwether agreed they could remove their life-jackets on turning in, seeing that should they contemplate climbing up through the companionway to go adventuring in the dark the first thing they would step on would be her head, an adequate alarm system.

The days were different, primarily because nobody would lie still. I recall one cozy family scene when through some disastrous mishap in planning all four of us wound up in the cabin at the same time. Meriwether was leafing through one of those *Let's Go Boating!* pamphlets I had picked up several months earlier for recruiting purposes.

"Listen to this," she said, removing Argee's elbow from her eye and gently shoving Dazey off her foot. " 'Boating brings the family closer together.' That certainly does hit the nail on the bull's-eye, doesn't it?"

I laughed, hollowly. But, oddly enough, Meriwether was, on the whole, far cheerier during those two weeks of fun-filled privation than she had been during the months I had dreamed of the boat's arrival. It wasn't that boating was better than she expected; it was that it was worse. And the cheerier she got, the gloomier I got. It's not that I'm a poor loser of Points. Lord knows, I have had enough experience losing. It's just that when you get as far behind as I was getting, you tend to lose interest in the game.

I kept thinking there must be some other basis for marriage. And what I thought about, more and more often, were those few magic moments on San Pablo Bay when I had unquestionably been in command of myself and my family, if not my ship. All this required, I knew, was self-confidence. But the trouble with acquiring self-confidence is that it requires self-confidence.

I remember the night the rat tried to get aboard. We were lying alongside the bank in Steamboat Slough, with anchors out fore-and-aft and a web of mooring lines secured to shrubs and bushes along the shore. I awoke around midnight to find Meriwether fumbling under my pillow for the flashlight.

"I sense it," she said mysteriously. "I sense it."

She snapped on the beam and there, sure enough, was a large rat tight-roping along one of the mooring lines, its nose aimed boatward.

"Don't, Meriwether," I said. "Don't throw . . ."

"Oooo," said Meriwether, ignoring my command. And she hit the rat on the very first toss. This was fortunate, as we had only one flashlight aboard.

I got mad. When I get mad I rarely boil. I stew. So I stewed for a good half hour and then I woke Meriwether.

"Look," I said in the darkness. "I told you not to throw the flashlight overboard. You did it anyway. You've got to realize that a ship can have only one captain. Only one person can be in command."

"Oh?"

I lit a cigarette. The flare of the match showed Meriwether up on one elbow, eyeing me quizzically.

"And I've been thinking," I said, after the match went out. "Maybe marriage is the same way. Maybe just one person should make the decisions."

"You do," she said. "This whole boat was your decision."

What seems so simple when you debate it with yourself becomes vastly complex when you debate it with your opponent. "What I'm trying to say," I said, "is . . . well, look at Christiana and Devlin – I think someone ought to be in command of the marriage. It's . . ."

"You *think*?" said Meriwether with that ability women have to get intuitively to the heart of the matter.

"Never mind," I said. I snicked my cigarette over the side and rolled to present my back to her.

"There, now," she said contritely. "You can be in command if you want to." And that didn't help either. In the morning, things were back to normal.

"How did you sleep?" I asked automatically.

"Not very well," she said.

"Me neither."

"Did you see that tugboat go by? It must have been about 4 a.m. – I was awake."

"Well, no . . ."

"It was an awfully big one," she said.

"It must have been before four. I was awake then. Because it starts to get light about five. There was mist all over at dawn."

"My elbow still hurts," she said, "from where I banged it yesterday on that bunk."

I thought of mentioning my sore foot, but it did seem better. Anyway, I felt we had come out, as usual, about even. Moreover, as it was the last morning there was much to do. I was just thinking of what commands to give when Meriwether said, "Why don't you untangle all those ropes over to the shore while I get breakfast."

"That's just what I was going to suggest," I said, and moodily went to do what I was just going to suggest.

So we floated gently down the sloughs, with me thinking my Bligh-like thoughts. What I needed to say was, "Mr. Christian, come here!" Unfortunately, just as I was getting nerved to re-take command I was unnerved by several circumstances beyond my control.

The first circumstance came as we stuck our nose, or bow, out into the wide Sacramento River where a dandy breeze was blowing. What happened – and I can think of no nautical manner of expressing it – was that our jib fell down. It just fell down, all by itself. I took it as an indication that our mast might follow suit, so I prudently lowered the mainsail, and, suppressing a weary sigh, assumed my seat on the outbbbboard mmmmotor.

Wind and tide were against us, a condition which would explain to any reasonable first mate why we ran out of gas. Luckily, a road cut along the riverbank at this point and I was able to borrow a few gallons from a passing motorist who thought being flagged down by a sailboat out of gas was very funny.

Sunset found our little expedition in the middle of nowhere, or, more specifically if not more accurately, in the middle of Suisun Bay, some four miles from the entrance to the Carquinez Straits, a twisting ribbon of water leading into San Pablo Bay. The sky was grey, the waves were grey, and off ahead and to the right were row upon row of silent, grey, moth-balled ships left over from the last of our wars. They had all the cheer of an elephants' graveyard.

But the mishaps of the day had, in a way, resulted in what I had hoped to accomplish by sheer force of personality: Meriwether had subtly relinquished command to me. Well, that's putting it strongly. She didn't exactly think of me as being in command, but there was no question that she now thought of me as being responsible.

And, as the greyed-over sun sank behind the grey, windswept hills, she inquired, with all due politeness, just where I planned to drown her and her children during the night. With the calm assurance of a good master I brought out the chart and showed her the legend "Small Boat Harbour" at the entrance to Carquinez Straits up ahead. We would be there by dark, *La Boat* moored snugly in a berth, we downing cold martinis and hot steaks in some gala restaurant. Such talk, I say, does more to cure grumbling in the crew than a cat-o'-nine tails.

Sure enough, as I predicted, we reached the entrance to the straits in the last glimmerings of light. It was so dark that it was difficult for the mate to make out the huge freighters plying up and down the narrow channel – difficult but not too difficult. I spotted the entrance to the Small Boat Harbour, ducked coolly under the bow of a lumbering steamer, and zipped in. Halfway in.

Small Boat Harbour, take it from this veteran sea captain, does not necessarily mean Small Harbour for Boats – it can also mean Harbour for Small Boats. This harbour was for very small boats, with very shallow keels. Fortunately, the bottom of Carquinez Straits, like the bottom of the Delta, is composed of mud: thick, black, slimy mud. And fortunately, if there was one thing I had learned during our sun-filled, fun-filled two weeks exploring the Delta, it was how to get out of the mud. So I rotated the outboard motor sideways, gave her the gun, and *La Boat* spun slowly around and with a gigantic slurp scooted back into deep water once more.

Back to the old chart. Happily, the chart showed a whole string of Small Boat Harbours down the strait. The law of averages would indicate that at least one was a Small Harbour for Boats and not the other kind. Due to technical difficulties it took several hours to disprove the law of averages. The chief technical difficulty was that it was now dark. The Book is very clear (Chapter Twelve) about "Piloting at Night": one simply follows the navigational lights which are posted along every shipping channel in such a simple manner that any reader of the Book can find his way. I scanned our limited horizon and, sure enough, there was a plethora of lights – red ones, green ones, white ones; sign lights, headlights; neon, fluorescent, incandescent; flashing, occulting, winking, and blinking. To pilot one's way through this complexity of luminescence required seamanship of the highest order, and strict care to stay within the glow of the street lights. Like any conscientious mariner I even managed to get a fix on our position: a highway sign which said thirty-two miles to San Francisco. The first mate eyed it wistfully.

It was along about the second Harbour for Very Small Boats that the children tired of the fun and cried themselves to sleep. It was after the third, or perhaps the fourth, that we ran out of street lights, the road inconsiderately curving up the hill at this point and away from the shore. The first mate cocked an eyebrow and aimed a loaded glare at the captain. I merely studied the chart as though I knew where the hell we were. This gives the crew confidence. The mate demonstrated her confidence by turning the boat around and around in circles. It seemed as good a course as any.

"Look out," cried the mate, her voice breaking a little. "Here comes a ferryboat."

Ferryboat! There's more than one way to skin a cat. The

ferryboat's track was marked on the chart and near its terminus on the other side of the strait was still another Small Boat Harbour.

"Follow that ferryboat!" I commanded.

"You mean out there . . . across the middle of that . . . with all those big ships. . . ." Meriwether suddenly lapsed into silence, perhaps overwhelmed by all the points she was accumulating. We tailed the 10:47 ferry to the far shore, executed a left turn, made out the harbour, and zipped in. Three-quarters of the way in.

This time, after considerable noisy gunning of the motor, I was forced to announce that disaster had struck at last: we were stuck thoroughly in the mud.

"Good," said Meriwether.

I took advantage of this expression of confidence by tossing our anchor over the side. Then I rigged the awning over the cockpit and we both slid into our sleeping bags, where I found myself facing the first mate's back. The wind gustily flapped the awning and the fog rolled in, washing out the few lights along the shore. This divorcement from the outside world elated rather than saddened me, and for a moment I felt another twinge of that love and protectiveness. I noticed Meriwether was shivering.

"Cold?" I said.

"Mad," she said.

I put a strong, masculine, protective arm around her. Tentatively. When this was ignored, I put my other strong, masculine, protective arm around her. After some hesitation, she rolled over. And everything was all right. In fact, everything was wonderful.

For about an hour. Then the tide came in and floated us free, unfortunately. This opened up several new chapters in the Book, such as: "What to Do when the Anchor Drags," "How to Moor a Boat to a Piling You Have Drifted Into," and "What to Say after the Mooring Lines Part for the Third Time."

The dawn was grey and grim; Meriwether likewise. It's amazing how quickly ladies forget these shipboard romances.

The noise I made chopping through the tangle of mooring lines holding us to the pilings was enough to arouse the children from their sound night's sleep. They poked up out of the companionway, frowzy-haired and still wearing their bulging orange life-jackets, looking like a nestful of newly hatched birds from the pages of the *National Geographic*. They requested their breakfast in appropriate tones. We motored off down the strait with the wind humming briskly in the rigging and the spray breaking aboard, whetting appetites. Due to the mood of the crew I refrained from calling their attention to points of interest, such as the rock jetty they had missed the night before. Narrowly.

"When's breakfast, Daddy?" said Dazey.

"Breakfast," said Argee, nodding to indicate he felt this was the proper course of action.

"I am going to take everybody out for breakfast as a celebration," I said grandly, and it was strange that nobody asked me as a celebration of what. "See? Right down there a couple of miles at the end of the strait is a Small Boat Harbour."

"It's the last one before you-know-what," said Meriwether, who had been studying the chart herself.

"I know," I said, "but I was talking to a fellow up at Steamboat Slough and he says everybody stops there on the way to the Delta. It's got a restaurant with fine steaming-hot food. So it must be a Big Small Boat Harbour. A Very Big Small Boat Harbour."

And sure enough, as we approached it we could make out attractive signs reading STEAKS-CHOPS-HAM & EGGS. There were rows and rows of fishing boats, power cruisers, and skiffs. It was, indeed, a Big Small Boat Harbour. It was so obviously a Big Small Boat Harbour that the mood of the crew changed perceptibly.

"Come on children," said Meriwether, "comb your hair. Dazey, put on that clean yellow shirt. And Argee, you . . ."

La Boat squinched to a shuddering halt. One-quarter of the way in.

It seemed incredible. We had run up against what must be a rarity: a Great Big Harbour for Small Boats. After we had extricated ourselves, I could tell by the look on Meriwether's face that she felt she was doomed to bobbing around on the water for the rest of her days, and sitting in the mud for the rest of her nights. This wasn't likely, however, as we were running low on gas.

As we executed our standard operating procedure for crises, going around in circles, it occurred to me that the gentleman who had recommended this Great Big Harbour for Small Boats was a power-craft, or shallow-keeled, yachtsman. But no more than four miles away was the city of Vallejo and the Vallejo Yacht Club, a venerable institution frequented by sailing, or deep-keeled yachtsmen, our own salty breed who depend on conquering the forces of nature to get where they are going.

"Motor on," I said.

The Vallejo Yacht Club lies up a quiet, protected channel, but to get to the entrance to the channel it was necessary to leave the quiet, protected strait and cross a small corner of San Pablo Bay. I gave my orders and the mate took her deep-water position, below. This left nobody to steer, so I lashed the tiller amidships and took my post on the outboard motor, finding that I could steer very well by simply twisting my hips, a motion that was communicated to the motor, although sharp turns did make me feel a bit ridiculous. Thus, prepared for the worst, we forged ahead.

It was the worst. The waves were a good twelve feet high and six feet apart, and instead of running with them as we had been coming up, we were now plunging against them. A third of the way across the first mate gave up shouting, "Do something!", braced herself on a bunk, gathered her children in her arms, and began to cry.

There is always a silver lining if one will just look for it. The silver lining here was that I was only sitting on the outboard motor half the time. As the stern of the boat rose over each wave, I would rise even farther to soar for a moment in vibrationless freedom. Of course, when the stern plunged down, I would plunge down, too. Occasionally, motor and captain would meet out of phase. But every silver lining must have its cloud.

As the stern rose over each wave, the bow, naturally, descended. "Descended" is not precisely the right word. It aimed for the bottom of San Pablo Bay like a sounding whale. Each time I bade farewell to the maternal grouping in the cabin. Each time, however, the bow would hit the bottom of the trough, shudder, and then slowly stagger up the oncoming wave, only to face another looming ahead.

On the descent I worried about the crew. On the ascent I worried about the mast, which was threatening to shake itself right out of the boat. And on the crest, as I soared free, I worried that when I came down, the boat would have gone on without me. Altogether there was more gratification than pain when motor and captain resumed contact.

So it was, with the first mate and crew crying hopelessly in the cabin, and the captain posting fearfully along behind, that *La Boat* rounded a jetty and slipped into the sheltered waters of the channel. There was one last wave, as big as the rest, one last whooshing descent, and then, as though a valve had been closed, nothing but flat, placid, barely rippled water. The crew raised their heads, surprise at being still afloat shutting off their tears.

My first emotion, too, was surprise. Next came relief; then, once again, love and protection. I had guided them all safely through dreaded San Pablo Bay, or at least a small corner of it; I, the master of our destinies, had conquered the awesome waters and had brought us all to safety. Home were the sailors, home from the sea. . . . Strong men, like me, should protect and cherish the weak and lovable, like Meriwether. We motored peacefully along the channel, into the yacht club, and expertly into a vacant berth. I shut off the motor, jumped ashore, and secured our mooring lines. We were safe.

As the liberty party prepared for going ashore, I felt the time had come for a rousing quarterdeck speech by the captain.

"We may be tired," I began . . .

"And cold and wet and hungry," Meriwether added help-fully.

"But now we're going to have a nice hot breakfast. And the most important part is that we've proved we can lick San Pablo Bay. It's certainly not going to be any worse out there than it was this morning. Sure, maybe we do have a longer stretch to go. But we've proved that our boat can take it. All we really had to fear was fear itself. And now that we've got confidence in our boat and in our captain, it won't be bad at all. That's what we need in life – confidence."

The first mate stepped silently off *La Boat*, followed by the bosun and fo'c'sle hand, both still wearing their bright-orange life-jackets. Single file they marched down the dock, through the yacht club, and up the street to the Greyhound Bus Depot, where the leader of the mutineers purchased three tickets to San Francisco. One-way.

It was then that I knew how the captains Bligh and Queeg must have felt. It wasn't so much what they did to you; it was the way they dreamed of doing it at all. And I think that in my identification with them I might have milked considerable enjoyment from my martyrdom had it not been for Dazey's parting words, meant, I suppose, consolingly:

"But you're not really a captain," she said, "you're really just a Daddy."

from *Dreamboat*,
Doubleday, New York, 1966, by permission of the author.

READING THE WEATHER

Wind Direction	Barometer Reduced to Sea Level	Character of Weather
SW to NW	30.10 to 30.20 and steady	Fair, with slight temperature changes for one or two days
SW to NW	30.10 to 30.20 and rising rapidly	Fair followed within two days by rain
SW to NW	30.20 and above and stationary	Continued fair with no decided temperature change
SW to NW	30.20 and above and falling slowly	Slowly rising temperature and fair for two days
S to SE	30.10 to 30.20 and falling slowly	Rain within 24 hours
S to SE	30.10 to 30.20 and falling rapidly	Increasing wind and rain within 12 hours
SE to NE	30.10 to 30.20 and falling slowly	Rain in 12 to 18 hours
SE to NE	30.10 to 30.20 and falling rapidly	Increasing wind and rain within 12 hours
E to NE	30.10 and above and falling slowly	In summer, with light winds, rain may not fall for several days In winter, rain in 24 hours

E to NE	30.10 and above and falling fast	In summer, rain probably in 12 hours In winter, rain or snow, with increasing winds, will often set in when barometer begins to fall and the wind sets in NE
SE to NE	30.00 or below and falling slowly	Rain will continue one or two days
SE to NE	30.00 or below and falling rapidly	Rain with high wind, followed within 36 hours by clearing, and, in winter, colder
S to SW	30.00 or below and rising slowly	Clearing in a few hours and fair for several days
S to E	29.80 or below and falling rapidly	Severe storm imminent, followed in 24 hours by clearing and, in winter, colder
E to N	29.80 or below and falling rapidly	Severe NE gale and heavy rain; in winter, heavy snow and cold wave
Going to W	29.80 or below and rising rapidly	Clearing and colder

GIRL STELLA'S GOING

FRANK MULVILLE

Being to the southward of our course had put the Azores almost in line between us and home. "Of course we'll go in," Patrick said, "it will be nice to get a run ashore in a brand new island." I was doubtful. "Would it be better to go straight on home?" Celia and Adrian agreed. "Let's go home," Adrian said. "We'll be late for school – and anyway I want to see the dog."

Dick, if anything, seemed to be in favour of seeing the Azores. "I must say I'd like to see the whaling boats," he said.

The argument kept us amused for days. "Look here, Daddy," Patrick said, "you can't go right past these lovely islands and not go in."

In the end I compromised. If we just went in to Flores, the most northerly of the islands, and stayed for a short time, two days at the outside, it wouldn't waste much time or take us far out of our way. We studied the Pilot book. Flores had a harbour of sorts, although it didn't say much about it. It was a whaling island – the last place in the world, I believe, where whales are still hunted with pulling boats using hand harpoons. If the whaling boats used the island there was no reason why we should not, and the port of Santa Cruz was on the lee side and should be well sheltered. "After all," Patrick said, "Sir Richard Grenville lay in Flores of the Azores, why shouldn't we?"

"All right – we'll go into Flores. But two days only," I decided. "We'll fill up with water," Celia said, "and get some fresh vegetables."

It was a bad decision. I knew it was a bad decision because a little voice inside me told me so – a decision dictated not by considerations of careful seamanship and what the Pilot book would call "a proper regard for the safety of the vessel," but by nothing more tangible than a passing fancy – a set of frail desires. It was trusting to luck instead of careful planning. Once

101

embarked on, it led inexorably on to other decisions, taken one by one and in themselves innocent enough, which built themselves up to produce a misfortune which, to our small world, was a disaster. The wind worked its way round to the southwest as we got closer to Flores and the glass went down slightly – nothing to worry about, but if it was going to blow a gale from the southwest it would be just as well to be safely tucked away in the lee of a high island. There is no radio beacon on Flores and, unlike any other of our major landfalls of the voyage, I would have to rely completely on my sextant. Flores is not a big island, perhaps half as long as the Isle of Wight, and there was no other island within a hundred and thirty miles of it except Corvo – a very small island immediately to the northeast.

I supplemented my sun observations with star sights in the morning and confidently pronounced an E.T.A. "You'll see it at half past two this afternoon, lying on the port bow, and there's ten shillings for the first boy to sight land." It was Tuesday, April 22nd, and we had covered 1,700 miles in thirteen days, an average speed of over five knots. At two o'clock Adrian sighted the island pushing its bulk out of low cloud fine on the port bow.

It took a long time to come up with the southern cape of Flores, and it was evening by the time we rounded it and came along the east side of the island towards Santa Cruz – close under great cliffs and mountains that dropped sheer into the Atlantic. White houses high up on the mountainside blinked their lights at us – we could see the gulls wheeling in tight spirals against the sheer rock face, and ahead of us the small town of Santa Cruz could just be seen before the sun went behind the mountain and everything was suddenly submerged in darkness. "What a pity. I thought we'd just get in before dark," I said to Celia. "We'll have to hang off till morning – how disappointing," she said.

We took the sails down off Santa Cruz, and just as we were making a neat stow of the mains'l two bright red leading lights suddenly showed up, one behind the other, showing the way

into the harbour. "Well, what do you think of that?" I said to
Dick. "Do you think they switched on the lights specially for
us?"

"Perhaps they did. Anyway it must be quite O.K. to go in at
night – otherwise the leading lights wouldn't be there."

I went below where Celia was. "They've switched on two
beautiful leading lights," I said. "I think we'll go in rather than
flog about here all night." "I think we ought to wait till we can
see where we're going," she said. I consulted Dick and we
overruled her. "Is everything squared up? Get the ropes and
fenders up and we'll go in," I said. I knew, deep inside myself,
that it was a silly thing to do. The little voice told me so again.
"You're a bloody idiot Mulville," it said. "Oh shut your blather
– I'm tired – I want a night's sleep."

When everything was ready to go alongside – the mooring
ropes ready, fenders out, side lights lit, boat-hooks handy,
anchor cleared away ready to let go if needed – I put the engine
slow ahead and went straight for the leading lights, and straight
for the black cliff which was all we could see behind them. Soon
we could hear the surf pounding against the rocks. "I don't like
it, Frank," Celia said, "I'm going below." "It's not too late to
turn back," the voice said. "Don't be such a bloody fool."

"Can you see anything, Dick?" I shouted to the foredeck.

"Yes – there's a gap right ahead – starboard a little."

"Starboard she is."

"Steady as you go."

"Steady." Suddenly we were between rocks – close on either
side. There was no turning now. A swell took us and swept us
forward. "Hard to starboard," Dick shouted. I spun the wheel,
my mouth dry as the bottom of a bird cage. "There it is – right
ahead – put her astern," Dick shouted.

There was a small stone quay right beside us – a dozen men
on it, all shouting at us in Portuguese. The swell was terrific.
G.S. was rearing up and down alarmingly. Dick threw a rope, it
was made fast and G.S. was pulled in toward the quay. "We
can't lie here," I shouted to Dick. "We'll have to get out again."
Just then G.S. grounded on a hard stone bottom. She only

touched once, not hard, and I put the engine astern and brought her a few feet along the quay – but it was enough to be unpleasant. "Anyone speak English?" I shouted. A big man came forward.

"I pilot," he shouted. "This harbour no good for you – tide go down – no enough water." He and two of his friends jumped on board. "Full astern," he said.

I put the engine astern and opened the throttle. The pilot took the wheel from me. "Neutral – slow ahead," he said. We seemed to be surrounded by rocks on all sides and the swell was playing round them, leaping into the air, and crashing down a noise like a steam train pulling out of a station. The pilot manoeuvred us back and forth – turning G.S. round with great skill as if he had known her ways all his life. "I don't know how you get in here," he said, "no one come in here at night." "Then what in Christ's name are the leading lights for?" "Fishermen," he said.

It was like the middle of Hampton Court Maze, but somehow the pilot got us out, backing and filling and turning until G.S. was clear in the open sea again. The saliva slowly came back to my mouth. "Give me a drink of water," I asked Celia whose white face was looking anxiously out of the hatch. "We take you Porto Piqueran. One mile up coast," the pilot said. "You O.K. there." We motored for a quarter of an hour to the north and then the pilot put G.S.'s head straight for the rocks. "Don't let him do it," a voice said. "Shut up for Christ's sake. I can't tell him his job."

There were no leading lights here at all – only the black face of the rock. "No worry," the pilot said, sensing my apprehension. "You O.K. here. Quite safe – no swell – I know way."

"Ça va bien," one of the other men said, thinking for some reason that I was French and wishing to air his grasp of that language. "Le Monsier Pilot – il le connait bien ici." The pilot was as good as his reputation. He took us straight toward a tower of rock, looming sullenly in the weak light of the stars, then hard to port for a few yards, then to starboard and to port again until suddenly we were in a small cove – a cleft in the rocks no more than sixty feet across but calm and still. "Let go anchor. Now we tie you up."

The pilot and his helpers climbed into our dinghy and ran out ropes to the rocks. They jumped nimbly ashore and fastened every long rope we had in the ship – three on each side. "Best ropes forward," the pilot said, "bad ropes aft. Wind come from west," he said, pointing to the sky where the clouds were racing towards England. "Always strong wind from west here."

I thought for a moment while they were working on the ropes. "Pilot," I said, "suppose we have to go out quickly. Would it not be better to turn her round, so she's facing the sea?" "No," he said, "strong wind from west – always face strong wind – best ropes forward." The little person inside me said "Make him turn her round, you weak idiot – this may be a trap." "Stop your bloody nagging."

They tied us up thoroughly, made sure that everything was fast and strong, and then they came down to the cabin and we gave them a drink. "By God, you lucky get out Santa Cruz," the pilot laughed. "No ship ever come there at night before. You fine here – you sleep sound." We put them ashore in the dinghy to a stone quay with a flight of steps hewn out of the rock face and they went off home. "See you in the morning. You sleep O.K."

We did sleep sound. G.S. lay as quiet as if she were in Bradwell Creek. The glass was dropping again and it was already blowing a gale from the southwest, but Porto Piqueran was quite detached from the gale – the only evidence of wind was the racing clouds far up above and an occasional down-draught which would sometimes break way from the body of the gale and find its way like some spent outrider round the mountain and down toward Porto Piqueran, where it would hurl the last of its dissipated energy at the top of G.S.'s mast, stirring the burgee forty feet up, making a faint moaning sound, and then dissolving into the night. Dick laughed, "This is a hurricane hole all right – there isn't enough wind in here to lift a tart's skirt."

"Don't laugh too soon," the little voice said to me as I went to sleep.

> The next morning Mulville was accompanied by customs officials into Santa Cruz and argued at length with the police, who wanted to retain their passports. He convinced the officials that if the wind changed they would need to have their passports with them in order to leave quickly.
>   Before their second night in Porto Piqueran they checked the warps carefully before they went to bed and found everything in order.

The two strongest warps we had were out over the bow, each made fast to a rock. On the starboard side there was a rope from aft to a ring bolt set into the rock by the steps, and another to a stone bollard at the corner of the quay. On the port side the longest rope led from aft to a big rock on the south side of the cove, and yet another from amidships. It was something of a work of art. "If you got out your crochet needles you could make us a balaclava out of this lot," I had remarked to Celia. In addition to her ropes the anchor was down, although I doubted whether it was doing any good as the bottom was hard and it had not been let go far enough out to be effective. Dick had been round in the day checking that the ropes were not chafing against the rocks and had served a couple of them with rope-yarns. "I reckon she'll do," I said to Dick, and we went to bed.

A boat is always there – you never stop worrying about her whether you are aboard or ashore. She is always a presence in the mind and you're conscious of her at all times. She may be laid up in some safe berth for the winter or hauled out of the water in a yard, but wherever you may be – at home in your virtuous bed or roistering in some gay spot, a chorus girl on each knee and the air thick with flying champagne corks – a part of your consciousness is always reserved. When the winds round the eaves of the house it has a special significance, and you check off in your mind, one by one, the possible sources of danger. Men lie awake worrying about their bank balances, their waistlines, their wives, their mistresses actual or potential; but sailors worry about boats.

A boat is something more than an ingenious arrangement of wood and copper and iron – it has a soul, a personality, eccentricities of behaviour that are endearing. It becomes part of a person, colouring his whole life with a romance that is unknown to those who do not understand a way of life connected with boats. The older a boat becomes, the stronger the power. It gains in stature with each new experience – people look at boats with wonder and say "She's been to the South Seas," or "She's just back from the North Cape," and the boat takes on a reputation in excess of that of its owner. *Girl Stella* had become a very real part of our lives – we each of us loved her with a deep respect.

I slept badly, frequently waking and listening. At two a.m. it began to rain, softly at first and then more heavily so that I could hear the drips coursing off the furled mains'l and drumming on the cabin top. At four a.m. I heard a slight bump and wondered what it was – then I heard it again and I knew what it was. It was the dinghy bumping against the stern. I froze in a cold sweat. If the dingy was bumping against the stern, the wind must have changed.

I got up, put oilskins on over my pyjamas, and went on deck. It was cold – the temperature had dropped three or four degrees – it was pelting with rain, and a light breeze was blowing from east by north – straight into the cove of Porto Piqueran.

I undid the dinghy, took the painter round the side deck, and fastened it off the bow where it streamed out clear. I went back to the cabin, got dressed, and called Dick. I tapped the glass and it gave a small convulsion – downwards. "Dick – wind's changed. We'll have to get out of here quick. The glass is dropping. We can't stay here in an easterly wind." Dick got up and put his head out of the hatch. The rain was pouring down and it was as black as a cow's inside. I believe he thought I was over-nervous, exaggerating. "We can't do much in this," he said, "if we did manage to get her untied and turned round we'd never get her out through that channel in this blackness. All we can do is wait till morning and then have another look at it." He went back to bed and was soon snoring peacefully.

The little voice said "Get him up – start work now." "Shut up – he's right – you can't see your hand in front of you – how the hell can we go to sea in this?" I walked round the deck. There was more swell now, and *G.S.* was beginning to buck up and down – snatching at her ropes so that sometimes the after ones came right out of the water. The forward ropes – the strong nylon warps – were quite slack.

I went down to the cabin, sat at the table, and tried to read. I made myself a cup of coffee and sat with the mug warming my hands and the steam wreathing round my face.

Then I went on deck again. The wind was beginning to increase, a heavy swell was now running, and small white waves were beginning to overlay it. The rain had increased and was now slanting with the wind and driving into the cove. *Girl Stella* was beginning to pitch and jerk at the two stern ropes with alarming force. Very slowly and reluctantly it was beginning to get light. I went below and shook Dick. "Come on – not a minute to waste – it's beginning to get light." I tapped the glass again, and again it dropped.

It seemed an age before Dick was dressed in his oilskins and on deck. "First we'll get the anchor up. It's doing no good there and it will only hamper us. Then we'll let go the head lines – leave them in the water – they'll drift to leeward and we'll come back for them later. Then we'll go astern on the engine and let her swing round on one of the stern lines."

We set to work. It was a relief to have ended the dreadful inactivity of the last two hours. As the anchor began to come up, Celia woke and put her head out through the hatch. "What's happening?" "We're going to get out of here – look at the weather – we're turning her round. Better get the boys up." In minutes the boys were up on deck in their oilskins and Celia was dressed.

The anchor came home easily and I started the engine. We cast off the head lines and prepared another line which would take the strain after we had turned, passing it round the bow so that we could fasten it to the stern line to starboard, which would then become the headline to port. Now the wind was howling with real ferocity – increasing every minute. The swell had become dangerous and was slapping against G.S.'s blunt stern and sending little columns of spray into the mizzen shrouds. I moved the dinghy painter from the bow to the stern and the boat lay alongside, leaping up and down and banging against the top sides.

We were almost ready when there was a twang like someone plucking a violin string. I looked up and saw that the stern line on which we were relying had received one jerk too many. It had snapped in the middle and the inboard end was flying back towards the boat like a piece of elastic. G.S. immediately began to move towards the rocks on her port side.

I jumped into the cockpit, slammed the engine into reverse, gave her full throttle, and put the rudder hard to starboard. She began to pick up. "Let go the port stern line," I yelled to Dick. He began to throw the rope off the cleat. "Throw it well clear – she'll come." The engine vibrated and thundered – the spray over the stern drove in our faces – the wind battered our senses but she was coming astern. "Good old girl," I muttered, "we'll get you out."

Then the engine stopped – suddenly and irrevocably – the bare end of the broken line wound a dozen times round the propeller. "Now you're in trouble," the little voice said.

G.S. began to drift inexorably towards the rocks – there was nothing to stop her – no ropes on the starboard side and no engine. "Fenders, over here, quick," I shouted to the boys and Celia. "Fend her off as best you can. I'll go over with another rope," I shouted to Dick. There was one more rope long enough to reach shore, still in the fo'c'sle locker. The top of the locker was covered with toys and books belonging to the boys and with Patrick's accordion. I threw them off in a pile on the floor and brought the bare end up through the fo'c'sle hatch. "Celia," I shouted, "pay it out to me as I go in the dinghy." As I got over the side into the *Starling* I felt G.S. strike the rocks – surprisingly

gently, I thought. Perhaps it was a smooth ledge and they would
be able to cushion her with fenders until we got another rope
out. I rowed desperately toward the shore, the end of the rope
wound round the after thwart of the dinghy. The swell was
washing violently against the stone steps. I could see the ring-
bolt but I couldn't reach it – as soon as the dinghy got in close it
would surge up on a swell, strike the slippery surface of the
steps, and plunge back. I took my trousers and my shirt off,
plunged into the sea with the end of the rope, upsetting the
dinghy as I jumped out of it, and tried to clamber up the steps.
But there was nothing to grasp and three times the weight of the
rope pulled me back. With a last effort I managed to roll myself
over onto the steps, reach up and keep my balance until I was
able to grasp the ring. "All fast," I shouted to Celia. I swam back
on board and clambered up over the bobstay. It was bitterly
cold.

Dick and I took the rope to the winch and began to heave.
The strain came on the rope and her head began to come round
clear of the rocks, but she had moved ahead slightly and the
rocks under her stern had shifted their position to right aft,
under the turn of the bilge, and had begun to do real damage.
They were too far below the water-line for the fenders to be of
any use. Then she stopped coming. The rope was tight but
something was preventing her from moving forward. Dick
went aft to look. "She's all tied up aft," he reported, "every
bloody rope in the place is tied up round the propeller and
they're all bar tight." I looked over the stern. It was daylight
now and I could see a tangle of ropes bunched up round the
propeller. "I'll cut them free."

Dick gave me his razor-sharp knife and I jumped over the
side again. I dived and saw that at least two ropes had somehow
got themselves into the tangle – I managed to cut one and came
up for breath. G.S.'s stern was just above me, the swells lifting it
and allowing it to settle back on the rock with all the force of her
great weight. I could hear the rock cutting into her skin – the
unmistakable cracking sound of timbers shattering under blows
of irresistible force. I knew then that she was done for.

I dived and cut the other rope, swam round to the bobstay with difficulty in the heavy swell, and dragged myself on board. Dick and I wound furiously on the winch – she moved a little further, and then, as the swells came more on her beam, she lifted and crashed down with an awe-inspiring crunch. She would move no more. As I went aft Celia was working the hand pump and Patrick jumped into the engine-room and switched on the electric pump. Adrian came up out of the saloon and I heard him say to Celia in a quiet voice, "Mummy, I don't wish to alarm you but the cabin's full of water."

"It's all over," I said to Celia, "everybody get into life-jackets. We'll have to swim for it."

Celia and I went below. The water was knee-deep on the cabin floor and was rising as we watched. She was still bumping, and every time she hit the rock we could hear the heavy frames splitting, the timbers crumbling. I looked at Celia. Her face was grey, her hair hanging in rat tails, and she had an expression of unimpeded sadness. We stood for a moment among the ruin. The ingredients of our lives were swilling backwards and forwards across the cabin floor, soon to be swallowed by the sea. Books given to us by the Cubans, their pages open and eager, as if they would convert the ocean to revolution, Adrian's recorder, clothes, an orange, the cribbage board, the kettle, a pair of chart rulers, rolls of film, my hat, Celia's glasses-case – objects which had somehow jumped out of their context to give mocking offence. The ordered symmetry of our lives was torn apart and scattered – haphazard and suddenly meaningless.

I could see in Celia's face that she had reached the end of a long journey. *Girl Stella* was a precious thing to her – something that was being thrown away in front of her eyes. The years of struggle with the sea were coming to an end – the pinnacles of achievement, the harrowing crises, the lighthearted joys and the endless discomforts had slowly spiralled upwards as we had progressed from adventure to adventure. Now they had reached an explosive zenith and for her there could be no going on. I knew in that moment she would never come sailing with me

again. I had at last betrayed her trust – forfeited her confidence
in me. Before, we had always come through – snatched victory
out of disaster – but now she was facing a fundamental confron-
tation of truth. I put my hand in hers – pleading for a glance of
sympathy.

Celia passed the life-jackets up the hatch to Dick, and then
she gathered a plastic bag and put in it the log books – the ship's,
the children's, and her own – and a few oddments. I found
myself unable to think – I was almost insensible with cold. I
grabbed my wallet and a book of traveller's cheques, the last of
our money, and stuffed them into the bag. I took one last look –
the clock and the barometer shining on the bulkhead, the cabin
stove, its doors swung open and the water ebbing and flowing
through the grate, the lamp swinging unevenly with a stunted
motion, and floating lazily across the floor, G.S.'s document
box, "*Girl Stella* – Penzance" scrolled on the lid.

On deck the boys were calmly putting on their life-jackets. I
bent down to help Patrick with the lacings. "This is the end,
Daddy," he said quietly, "the end of *Girl Stella* – poor, poor
G.S." Now she had settled deep in the water and her motion
had suddenly become sickening. She had lost her liveliness and
when she rolled to the swell it was with a slow, tired lurch. Her
stability, the quick sense of recovery, the responsiveness that she
always had, was gone. "Quick. She may turn turtle – we must
get off. I'll go first, then boys, then you, Celia and Dick last.
Grab the rope and pull yourselves along it. I'll help you up the
steps."

I jumped into the sea, found the rope and shouted back,
"Come on Pad – jump." Patrick hesitated for a moment, then
his body came flying through the air and he bobbed up, gasping
with cold beside me – then Adrian, then Celia. We pulled ourselves hand over hand along the rope. Now the swell was much
heavier and there were vicious seas breaking in the cove. It was
much more difficult to get on to the steps. The ring-bolt was
high up out of the water and it was necessary to let go of the
rope and swim the last few yards to the steps. My puny strength
was of no consequence in the swell – like a piece of floating stick

I was swept back and forth across the rock face, the small aperture of the steps flashing past as I was carried first one way and then the other. Then, more by some quirk of the swell than by my own efforts, I was dumped heavily on the bottom step and was able to scramble to my feet. I grabbed Patrick by one arm and heaved him up, then Adrian came surging past and I was able to grasp the back of his life-jacket and pull him on the bottom step.

Celia was more difficult. She was all but paralysed by the cold – she was heavy and slippery and there seemed to be nothing of her that I could grip. Then she managed to get her body half onto the step, and with Patrick helping me we pulled and rolled and tugged until she finally got herself clear and struggled to her feet. "Up you go – quick before the sea snatches you back again."

Dick had not come. I looked up and saw that G.S. had moved ahead and was now lying athwart a towering rock pillar. I saw that he had been below and had brought up the two sextants and placed them on a narrow ledge of rock which he could reach. G.S. was now low in the water and sinking fast. "Dick," I shouted, "come out of it – now." If she sank before he came he would be denied the rope, and I doubted whether he would be able to swim through the broken water without its help. He took a last and reluctant look round and then he jumped and we watched him working along the rope, hand over hand, until I was able to grasp his arm and he scrambled up the steps.

We stood in a dejected, shivering group on the little stone quay and watched G.S. work out this last moment of her span of life. A thing of grace and beauty – agile, sure-footed, tender in her responses to our demands – at the same time she was a block of solid assurance. We had always felt safe in her – we always knew that she would do whatever was asked of her. She was our home – she gave us a dignity which we would otherwise have been without.

She had come to her end not by any misdeed of hers – not through any wilfulness or delinquency – but by misuse, a sheer disregard of the elements of seamanship. I felt the dead weight

of my responsibility settle heavily on my shoulders. It was a
score against me that could never be wiped clean – nothing that
I could ever do would relieve me of the knowledge that I had
destroyed a thing of beauty.

from *In Granma's Wake*,
Seafarer Books, Camden, 1970.

2

CATCHING THE WIND

The least puff of wind stealing round the corners of the dock buildings stirs these captives fettered to rigid shores. It is as if the soul of a ship were impatient of confinement. Those masted hulls, relieved of their cargo, become restless at the slightest hint of the wind's freedom.

Joseph Conrad
The Mirror of the Sea

I've never been much of a racing sailor. On the Sunfish I found that in a one-hour race around the buoys of our little mile-square pond, I got more nervous, more upset, than I did racing an automobile at one hundred and forty miles an hour.

The tension in being out there in the Sunfish and having some guy pass me very, very slowly . . . creeping up on me and creeping up fast with me not being able to do anything about it . . . adjusting the sail every which way I could think of . . . doing everything possible to gain a little speed, and not making it . . . then this guy would get a little puff and go by. Well, I'd get back to the dock and I could hardly stand up, my knees were shaking so much. It's that kind of tension which led me to decide that I didn't need this much . . . this much fun.

Walter Cronkite

BLUENOSE

PHILIP AND BRIAN BACKMAN

Philip Backman led the fight in Lunenburg, Nova Scotia, to rebuild the great Canadian "ship on the dime." He published an early version of this article after Lunenburg had built a replica of the *Bounty*; the story raised interest and hopes, and the town's craftsmen soon set to work again. *Bluenose II* was launched from the town's docks in July 1963, with *Bluenose's* original skipper, Angus Walters, at the helm.

In 1920 the owner of the Halifax *Herald and Mail*, Senator William H. Dennis, offered a massive cup – the International Fishermen's Trophy – for competition among sailing vessels. They would have to be more than fast, for one stipulation provided that to qualify, a vessel must be a worker, and well able to earn her keep on fishing grounds amid Atlantic gales.

In the first race off Halifax in the same year, the trophy was carried off by a trim United States entry, the *Esperanto*, and the *Delawana* from Lunenburg was defeated. To local fishermen, the idea of a Yankee carrying away the silver cup was a humiliation to their fleet. The cup would have to be "brought home." An association of interested shipowners and others was formed, and a young Halifax marine architect who was already noted for his fast racing yachts was commissioned to create a vessel to be both a racer and a capable worker. It was not an easy problem to resolve, but William J. Roue eventually produced plans which were accepted by the committee.

Roue had no formal training whatever. He began building boats from shingles at the age of five, models of the vessels he had seen from his Halifax window. After leaving high school (curiously enough, over a disagreement with his teacher on pronunciation of a sea term), he was given a volume of what then comprised about all that was known about marine architecture. It was Dixon-Kemp's *Yacht Architecture*, and it was digested in detail by the young would-be designer.

When the committee commissioned him to design a fast schooner, Roue was not long puzzled. He had drawn the lines for a racing sloop, the *Zetes*, in 1910, which had sailed her way to the head of such sailing competitions of the time as the Wenonah Cup, the Prince of Wales Cup, and the Royal Engineers' Yacht Club Cup. She later went ashore at Greenbank, N.S., in a gale, and there she rotted. But *Zetes* had a greater destiny than being a fast racer, for she was to be the mother of the *Bluenose*.

Roue developed and expanded the basic design of the little sloop in the plans which the committee accepted for their challenger. After a winter of work, the 143-foot schooner *Bluenose* was launched from the shipyard of R.W. Smith and G.A. Rhuland. Those present on the morning of her launching on March 26, 1921, as well as those who had seen hull number two hundred rise from her keel block, were impressed by her long, plunging lines. She was built almost entirely of Nova Scotia wood, by Nova Scotia craftsmen, and few of them doubted that this product of their skills would do them proud.

Angus Walters would skipper her. Small, quick-tongued, but a commanding figure on the deck of his pitching schooner, he was affectionately noted for his love of hoisting full sail and giving his charge her head. He had made his first fishing trip in 1895 at thirteen years of age aboard his father's schooner. He had served a hard apprenticeship in the fishing and West Indies trade, learning to steer during off-watch hours under his father's tutelage, racing his dory against others for the bait wharf, and developing a will "to be at least as good a sailor as any other man." Sailing the *Gilbert B. Walters* in the first elimination race, he might well have won, had he not lost his topmast in the final leg of the contest.

Bluenose did not disappoint her guardians. In the ensuing races she "trimmed them all." The list of the vanquished forms an epitaph to the vessel they could not conquer: *Elsie, Henry*

Ford, Columbia, Gertrude L. Thebaud. These were the American challengers, three of them designed specifically by the best of marine architects to trim the wiry little skipper. Rival Nova Scotia schooners had tried too – ten of them – but they also were doomed to second place or worse.

The *Bluenose* had made herself undisputed champion of the North Atlantic fishing fleet, and that honour was never to be taken from her.

But the *Bluenose* was more than a racer. Those who knew her testify that within her lithe sheer was a soul embodied, a kind of indefatigable spirit. She was a fine fisherman, for she still holds the record for the largest single catch of fish ever landed in Lunenburg. But it was as if she knew that after the fish had been unloaded from her holds she would be groomed and dressed with her topmasts for another race. When the gun sounded, it was as if she suddenly came alive and anxiously awaited the command that would let her leave the arrogant challenger in her wake.

Gertrude L. Thebaud, a lithe and lovely schooner, was the only challenger ever to defeat *Bluenose*. A heavy sail-carrier, fishermen knew her by her high-peaked main gaff. She bore herself with the air of a Boston debutante – strictly Back Bay Boston – and well she might; she was that city's presentation piece in the high-seas court of international sailing rivalry. She took the series for the Lipton Trophy off Gloucester in 1930, but in the last two series for the International Fishermen's Trophy, she too bowed to the superior sailing qualities of the Canadian champion.

If there was any one of the American challengers to *Bluenose* which gained the grudging, even unreserved, admiration of the Canadian schoonermen, that boat was *Columbia*. And small wonder! She was about as pretty a thing as anyone could want to behold.

She came from the board of W. Starling Burgess, acknowledged as probably the greatest American designer of his day, a man imbued with a burning desire to achieve what no one else so far even had come close to: the humbling of *Bluenose*. This time there would be no question of the boat being a true schooner; he came up with a design that left no doubt of her ability to operate as a saltbanker. Just for good measure, he had drawn her smart enough to fill the role of a fresh fisherman as well.

She came down the ways with the sweet sort of look to her lines which, even before rigging, was enough to worry the Canadians. Her lean, sleek bow rode high, just like *Bluenose*, and she looked like something designed for no other reason but to personify the very essence of speed itself.

The American Committee had already picked her to challenge. She put in a season on the Banks, then spruced up and entered an elimination contest. Meeting the *Ford* and the old *Howard* in a race sailed in extremely light wind, she showed them both a clean pair of heels. Though the contest was not finished by any of the three boats within the time limit, she was far ahead of the Ford by the time the race was called. Soon after, she set out for Halifax for her bout with the Canadian Champion. She found *Bluenose* waiting and eager to do battle.

American authorities had contacted Angus Walters to discover whether he would object to Gloucester shipowner Ben Pine skippering their challenger. The race rules stipulated that the master of a challenger, like the vessel herself, had to be a working fisherman. It seemed that Pine, who was a chief investor in the Gloucester fleet, did not sail with any of his vessels to the fishing grounds.

Angus had known Ben for years. "He'll do fine," he said.

Race number one was scheduled for Monday, October 29, 1926. A breeze of about seventeen knots was blowing. *Columbia*, whose appearance claimed much favourable comment in the Nova Scotia capital, was understood to go like a startled deer in this sort of weather. But *Bluenose* too was anything but unhappy. Trimmed somewhat lighter in ballast than in previous contests, she handled as sprightly as her rival in a moderate wind. The lead of thirty seconds that Angus wrung out of the start was dissipated when he overstood the second mark, allowing *Columbia*'s master, Ben Pine, to race him neck-and-neck all the way to the Third Buoy. They reached it in a dead heat.

There followed what probably became the most talked of duel in the annals of the International Series – an out-and-out fight for the weather berth. Bow to bow, Pine pressed his advantage of position to force Angus to green water inside the mark. With all his cunning, the scrappy little Lunenburg skipper sought to shake off his tormentor, but Ben Pine hung on like a leech. By now, *Bluenose* was within spittin' distance of the "Three Sisters" ledge, ominous both in fact and prospect. A roar from the pilot to helmsman on *Bluenose* to bear away or strike the shoal brought an instant reply; the alternative was to ram *Columbia*! Squarely between the devil and the deep, Angus gambled on collision. *Bluenose* bore away from the ledge. Pine held to his course.

Immediately, Angus doused his staysail and swung his foresail to make her "wing and wing." A few seconds later his main boom struck the mainshrouds of *Columbia*, travelled forward to sweep the Yankee's forestays, and finally snarled in his jib, impudently towing the challenger for almost a full minute.

But that was it! *Bluenose* cleared suddenly and took off for home like all the hounds of hell were baying in her wake, crossing the line with a time of 1.43.42 to *Columbia*'s 1.45.02. Scant margin, but a clean win.

The night that followed bred arguments fast and furious. Ben Pine hadn't fought fair when he angled Angus toward the rocks – Angus was subject to protest by Pine because of the unofficial minute's "tow." It was a point for the rules, no denying – if anyone wanted to attempt applying them; but nothing could be further from the mind of either skipper, both of whom seemed to be in equal jeopardy. Both masters ignored the point. They looked to the next race to provide a more definite settlement on which was the better contender.

Columbia, reballasted and lighter than ever, was well out in front at the moment of the call–off, but with the stronger breeze *Bluenose* quickly put such nonsense to rout. At race's end, she was already tied up snug and proper at the dock when *Columbia* reached hers.

No one ever really knew for sure just exactly what made the *Bluenose* so fast. There is a wealth of theories, upon any one of which a fisherman will readily expound. Some say that it was from some "unfathomed quirk" in her construction; others say the credit is due to the designer, or to the sailing abilities of Angus Walters. Or it might have been the sheer of her hull, which, curiously, never left any dead water; perhaps to a last-minute change in her bow, ordered while she was abuilding when Walters decided that the forecastle would be too low. This turned out to be the most prominent distinguishing mark of the vessel – a defined angle which lifted her bowsprit higher, almost to the sky, when she rode a heavy swell.

The days when schooners raced from the Newfoundland Banks to their home ports with fresh-caught fish were fraught with danger. There was ever the threat of trouble and disaster among fishermen on the high seas, and the families that raised children without fathers or brothers were all too many. The disappearance of a schooner with all hands was not uncommon. In any case, many of the ships themselves fell victim to the toll of the sea. But it was neglect, rather than the sea, which spelled the end of the *Bluenose*. Many times in her career she proved her ability to withstand the worst that wind and wave had to offer.

During *Bluenose*'s maiden voyage as a fisherman, Angus Walters watched a full-rigged ship bear down until his vessel seemed certain to be rammed amidships. The bell was rung, the foghorn sounded, but no action was seen aboard the strange vessel. Walters and his crew finally took to their dories, rowing alongside the stranger, spoke to her, shouting for her to "keep off." It seemed certain the *Bluenose* would be cut in two, yet she escaped. Why, or how, is a question that remains unanswered to this day, for the full-rigger did not alter course, and missed the Lunenburg racer by "inches."

The *Bluenose* nearly came to grief again off Sable Island in 1926. Anchored off a lee shore of the Atlantic Graveyard, she was struck by what Angus Walters has described as a "grandfather sea." Her skipper and crew of twenty fought to bring her head up into the gale, but the schooner was swept forward, her cable snapped, fourteen stanchions smashed out, and part of the rail and bulwarks carried away. But even Sable Island could not add *Bluenose* to its list of victims.

"She kept heading up, biting her way into the gale," says Captain Walters, who had taken over the helm for the whole of the six-hour battle. "Don't know as any other vessel could have done it!"

In 1930 she grounded on the rocks of Placentia Bay, New-foundland. For four days she withstood the battering storms that snarled her rigging and swept her lifeboats overboard, and lived to sail again.

Five years later, *Bluenose* logged a King's admiration, and by the Atlantic's reckoning, her hardest – and perhaps her greatest – triumph. Britain was celebrating the Silver Jubilee of King George V and Queen Mary, and *Bluenose* was appointed an official Canadian representative at the event. She made a swift seventeen-day passage from Lunenburg to Plymouth. The port from which Drake once sailed to meet the Spanish Armada greeted the Nova Scotia fishing schooner with warmth and enthusiasm, memorable testament to the acclaim her exploits had earned for her from the island race of seafarers. No less a welcome awaited her from yachtsmen at Cowes on the Isle of Wight, and she was present at Spithead when King George reviewed his fleet for the last time.

The presence of the Lunenburg saltbanker among his battle-ships did not go unnoticed by the King. Shortly after the review, Angus Walters was summoned to the royal yacht, *Victoria and Albert*. He was received by the King and three of his sons – the Prince of Wales, the Duke of York, and the Duke of Kent.

"He was a very nice, ordinary sort of fella," Angus recalled later of the monarch, "though if I may say so, I thought he looked a little frail. Well, we chewed the rag for a while. He had heard some about the *Bluenose*, and he was very interested in knowing about herring fishing. Then the Prince of Wales, Edward, leaned over and explained to him about cod fishing and told him that we didn't fish for herring. Then he told me to come stand by him while they took our picture. He said it was a shame I couldn't come to London and see it on the screen. After we'd chewed off a little more fat, I went back to the *Bluenose*."

The King later sent word that he would come aboard to inspect the schooner, but before the hour of his visit arrived, Angus was told that the King unexpectedly had been called back to London and wished his regrets conveyed to the Lunenburg master.

"I was kind of sorry about that," Angus said. "I didn't carry any liquor aboard the ship that trip, but bein' as how he said he was coming aboard and all, I took him at his word and decided I should offer him a drink. I took him so damned common that I figured he'd be partial to it. So I sent ashore for a bottle of King George whisky."

Her highly successful mission at an end, *Bluenose* shook off her lines at Falmouth and cleared for home. By nightfall of the first day, a gale was blowing. It held with fierce wind and seas for the next four days. Laying to under jumbo and stormsail, the ship was leaking thirty strokes to the hour. Angus shortened sail until finally, with his vessel foundering heavily aft, he hove to under bare pole. As *Bluenose* rolled and pitched 150 miles out of Falmouth, one of her ten passengers managed to get the gramophone working. If the passenger meant the song to provide diversion, the weather witches heard it as a summons; for as the strains of "Anything Goes" filtered up from below decks, the biggest sea Angus Walters had ever seen, a giant, iron-fisted comber barrelled out of the dark and delivered the fourteen-year-old saltbanker a murderous broadside.

For the first time in her life *Bluenose* keeled over on her beam ends – her below decks flooded with tons of water. In one blow the ocean had smashed both boats, the deck-house engine box, the foreboom, and the main boom jaws; the galley was uprooted and in shambles, and her port bulwarks had vanished. During the minutes she stayed under, Angus gave up hope she could ever survive. But the mangled champion painfully and slowly righted herself. By now the pounding had opened her seams aft. Angus mustered crew and men passengers and raised flooring planks to shift pig iron ballast forward.

Bluenose's passengers marvelled that even during the height of the hurricane, their masterful captain took time at intervals to come below in high spirits and joke them out of preoccupation with their predicament. Finally the winds abated. Angus brought his wounded charge about and ran for the Channel. He dropped his hook in Plymouth Sound a week after sailing from Falmouth. Except for four hours of the voyage, his mainsail had remained furled. One of his passengers, a veteran of seventeen years' Naval Service, recalled the storm as the most terrifying sea he had ever encountered, and gratefully credited his life to the seamanship of Angus Walters and the incredible qualities of his magnificent saltbanker. Said Angus himself: "I was never prouder of her."

Lunenburgers still remember a sunny morning one September during the Fishermen's Exhibition, at the height of the saltbanker's career, when spectators had packed the wharves for the water sports. Beyond the lighthouse at the harbour entrance were four young schooners, racing on the final leg of a scheduled contest. All at once a fifth schooner hove into view beyond the headlands. It was only an instant before somebody recognized the familiar silhouette and shouted *"Bluenose!"* and the crowd turned to watch. She was late for the exhibition festivities, returning with her holds full from the Banks. Her topmasts were off, and she lay low in the water. Walters promptly hoisted all possible sail and joined the race to harbour.

Here your Sunday-morning fisherman will say little more, as drawing on his pipe, he'll look again past the now empty harbour, perhaps remembering the way the crowd shouted and cheered that day when the *Bluenose*, heavy-laden, still crossed the finish line minutes ahead of the nearest rival.

In mid-summer of 1933, *Bluenose* stowed her fishing gear and sailed for Lake Michigan as Canada's representative at Chicago's Century of Progress Exposition. For the rest of the season the steps of thousands of admiring visitors sounded homage on the deck of the nautical celebrity. A newspaper story from 1938, following another *Bluenose* victory, tells its own story of the sentiment that was building up around her: "Seafaring folk of Lunenburg will greet 'Queen of the Seas' when she arrives at her home port," the account reads. "A half-holiday will be declared for school children, while a parade of bands and decorated automobiles, to take Captain Angus and his proud crew through the streets, is being arranged."

But then Canada and the United States became busy with war, and there could be no interest left for the thrills of schooner racing. The submarine battle was at its peak, fishing prospects in the Atlantic were doubtful, and the diesel engine was replacing sail.

Angus Walters had long since opened a dairy business in the town, and the *Bluenose* was less than herself under a substitute master. Besides, she was beginning to slip into debt, for money was still owing on the heavy powerhouse installed within her three years previously. *Bluenose* was owned privately by a group of shareholders in the *Bluenose* Schooner Company, and her losses were taken personally. Sentiment and interest were hidden by a nation's preoccupation with war. There was but one solution. The *Bluenose* would have to be put up for auction. Then one hour before the Queen of the Fleet was to go on the block, Angus Walters handed over $7,000 from his own pocket to the sheriff.

"I still have faith in the *Bluenose*," he said then, "and I think it is a disgrace that the people of Lunenburg and Nova Scotia would have let her be put on the auction block. I still will protect the *Bluenose* with all I have, for she served me too faithfully to be let down."

But her days were already numbered, and she waited them out, tied to a dock until 1942. The West Indies Trading Company needed fast, light sailors to haul freight between the islands of the Caribbean, and so they made a bid for the vessel.

Little choice was left Walters, who now held the controlling shares. His almost frantic efforts to raise a fund to keep her had been unsuccessful, even among his fellow townsmen, who had lost interest in their famous ship's fate. The *Bluenose* would suffer a final indignity. Bereft of her sails, she would die a freighter.

To the historian it was the last chapter in the age of sail; but to most, the death of the *Bluenose* was like the passing of a revered and beloved statesman. She had returned time and again to her Lunenburg, Nova Scotia, port, carrying pride and honour to a nation resting between the storms of two world wars. The aftermath of the second of these wars had seen her forgotten. Now she had met her end. Her back was broken on a coral reef, and, abandoned, she was left to rot away in waters foreign to her graceful hull.

Angus remembers the day she left as a painful one.

"I cast off her lines one overcast day in May. If I may say so, there was a lump in my throat. Somehow, I knew it was good-bye. We'd seen a lot together in fair weather and foul, and the *Bluenose* was like a part of me."

The trim Americans who challenged her, for the most part, had gone too, or else were not to be long in following her. None survived to make the final voyage to the scrapper's wharf. *Mayflower* was burdened with a third mast shortly before she was lost; *Esperanto* was caught by the claws of Sable Island; *Columbia* met her end there too, and she took her crew with her; *Henry Ford* sank off Martin Point, Newfoundland; the sea claimed *Elsie* off St. Pierre.

The Gloucesterman *Gertrude L. Thebaud* had been the champion's greatest rival. Ironically, she foundered not far from the spot which marks the final resting place of the *Bluenose*.

The belief of Lunenburgers in a schooner with a soul was spontaneous, not merely one designed to illuminate a growing legend. In dozens of interviews, I had heard the sailing qualities of the old champion attributed in turn to her designer, her builders, her crew, a freak run of luck, an early frost setting her beams, and of course, to the Captain himself.

Hundreds of tourists yearly detour to chat with the 83-year-old Angus Walters. He can be found in a large white house, around the corner from his dairy, where he lives alone with his little dog. He has mellowed since the days he stood on the deck of his schooner and scowled and snapped at newsmen whenever he heard the Americans were building yet another challenger:

"I don't care for their Mae Wests, Annie Oakleys, or Greta Garbos," he had said, "or if they want, their Clark Gables. I'll stick to my fisherman's rig."

We talked in his living room, furnished with pictures and other mementoes of the *Bluenose*.

"Any changes I made in the original, you know, were all above water, and had no effect on her sailing. I think a lot of people thought that change in her fo'c'sle made her faster."

"Angus – what *did* make the *Bluenose* the ship she was?"

Aware my question was more than common, I'd expected a ready reply. Instead, the aging mariner sat musing in silence for several moments. When finally he spoke again, it was to deny himself credit in favour of the hand of nature.

"I think I know what it was. I think it was the way her spars was stepped. If the rest of her is good, a vessel's spars will pretty well tell what she'll do. Somehow, the *Bluenose*'s spars was stepped mathematically perfect, in a way that no man could do. I think that was it. I don't feel as there was a vessel that ever came out of Lunenburg that had her sticks stepped that perfect."

I said goodbye to the Captain and strolled along the wharves. The harbour was bare and empty. Only two steel draggers were tied to their docks, and a small fishing smack was splitting the silence that ruled over the bay. It was getting dark. The sun was beginning to fall behind the golf course across the water, and the little lighthouse at harbour's entrance was only barely discernible. I realized that I too had become caught up in Lunenburg's almost tearful memory of a ship.

Angus Walter's final words stuck with me: "If they build another, I think I'd like to see how she goes."

from *Bluenose*,
McClelland and Stewart, Toronto, 1965.

LIPTON'S LAST CHALLENGE

ALEC WAUGH

Sir Thomas Lipton, the Irish grocery clerk who built a world-wide tea company, tried five times to win the America's Cup. *Shamrock I, II,* and *III* were swept in straight races; *Shamrock IV* won the first two races in 1920, but couldn't seal the victory with a third win. In 1930 Lipton sailed to Newport to make his final attempt.

On the fourteenth of April, 1930, *Shamrock V* was launched by Lady Shaftesbury. Never had Lipton appeared more confident. He spent his eightieth birthday on the *Erin* watching *Shamrock V* at work. "I am out to do it," he said. "I mean to do it."

There was the old vigour in his voice. He had issued his first challenge lightheartedly enough, but the caprice had become a passion now. He had cracked his jokes. He had said that he got better publicity when he lost than when he won. There was nothing people liked better, he said, than a good loser. But he was no more sincere when he said that than is the novelist who, when he has at last written the novel of his life, will not allow himself to be congratulated on his reviews but pretends that what really pleases him is the sum that he has snared from Hollywood. Whatever he may have thought in 1899, there can be no doubt now that he wanted desperately to win. He was an old man of fourscore years. If he could pull it off at last, it would be indeed a chance that would redeem all disappointment, that would settle every score, cancel every grievance.

During the early summer of 1930 tributes as warm as any he had been ever paid were profusely proffered. On July 8 in the Fishmongers' Hall he was lunched by the Honourable Company of Master Mariners. Both the Prince of Wales and Ambassador Dawes were present.

The Prince expressed the belief that even in the United States a victory for *Shamrock* would be popular. The Ambassador said, "Britain has shown us that she possesses the fastest airplane and the fastest car. If she produces the fastest yacht, American disappointment will be assuaged by her appreciation of the fine sportsmanship of this veteran now making his fifth attempt." Rudyard Kipling, who was wearing a soft collar that the representative of the *New York Times* described as being both American and of ample dimensions, nodded his head approvingly. As Lipton rose to speak, the cheering could be heard right across the thousand-year-old Billingsgate Fish Market that lay below the windows of the dining hall. He stood for a moment straight and tall, looking down at the crowded tables.

How often in the past over the last thirty years had he not risen at this and the other table to reply to this same toast, his health. Already across the Atlantic committees were discussing details, secretaries were preparing invitation lists of banquets in his honour. The familiar scene would be re-enacted, the familiar speeches made. There was nothing all that special, for Lipton, about this particular occasion. Was he, though, as he stood there for a moment silent, warned by some premonitory voice that this was the last time he would stand in London at such a table? Did he guess that this luncheon in his honour was in fact London's good-bye to him? "Your Royal Highness, Your Excellencies, my lords, and gentlemen." For a sentence or two his voice boomed with its rich brogue through the familiar opening, then gradually it began to falter; he hesitated, checked, began a sentence, then stopped altogether. He intended to speak extempore, but he could not manage it. He picked up the manuscript of his speech, put on his spectacles. He looked very old as he stood there, peering through his glasses, reading out the same expressions of goodwill that he had been making for thirty years, the familiar peroration about there being no sportsmen like Americans, that whenever he was dealing with Americans, in business as in sport, he could be certain that he would get fair play.

He had looked old on that July afternoon in London, but he had fully recovered his vitality ten weeks later when the

Leviathan sailed up from quarantine on a foggy September morning. Never had he had such a welcome. New York was in the mood to honour him. Last autumn the stock market collapse had broken many minor bank balances. But the buoyant optimism of the city refused to believe that anything serious had happened. It was just a settling of the ground. The summer had been long and warm. There was a keen bite in the September air. It was impossible to feel depressed upon such days.

New York was in the mood to put on a show. And Jimmy Walker and Grover Whalen were the men to do it. The fog did not help them any, and the heavy wind interfered with the nationwide broadcast they had prepared, but thousands lined the Battery, excursion boats paddled alongside to cheer. A special tug with a police escort came bustling out. "Even when I came here as an emigrant I was never received by the police," he said. "I'm certainly getting to be the devil of a fellow."

He had his sallies ready. To Mary Curley, daughter of the mayor of Boston, he wisecracked that he had always known that Boston had the most intelligent citizens in the country, since they had thrown the tea overboard when they had discovered it was not Lipton's. It was a triumphal progress, with the ferries saluting him and fireworks being shot up through the fog, with the police escort leading him to the Biltmore and a man shouting from the sidewalk. "You've got to win the cup – I've put so much money on you that I'll be in the workhouse if you don't." "Reserve a bed for me too," Lipton shouted back. Even at the turn of the century it had not been better.

This time it had been decided to hold the races at Newport instead of Sandy Hook. The weather was likely to be better. The crowd would be easier to control. Never had the fashionable resort known more excitement. Special cars were running from Chicago, the harbour was filled with yachts, the narrow streets were blocked with automobiles, blimps purred noisily in the sky above, Ocean Drive was made a one-way street, the Saunderstown and Jamestown ferries were put back on summer schedule, the hotels were crowded; everything was set for the biggest match in the history of yachting.

And then –

But it is difficult to explain, difficult to record dramatically what happened then. A yacht race is very difficult to describe. It is too technical; it is too long-drawn. There is all that tacking, that manoeuvring for position. Only the expert can tell what is being attempted and what is being threatened. You can describe the setting, Newport with its long stretch of sand, its low line of dunes, its naval base, its old town section along the waterfront. You can describe the fleet of three hundred craft following the race. You can describe the city of Lowell furnishing an orchestral concert. You can describe how back in England, in Gosport, the shipyard was lit with electric signs and the streets were thronged with crowds impatiently waiting for the bulletin. You can describe what happened on the *Erin*, but the race itself, the drama of the actual race, that eludes description. A yachtsman could describe it for other yachtsmen in terms of technicalities, but to the layman it would be incomprehensible. The recorder of that week at Newport can only report the facts.

The first race was won by *Enterprise*. It was a straight there-and-back race. Owing to a shift of wind, there was no windward leg, and in the opinion of that sound judge, Herbert L. Stone, there was no reason why good sailing should not have won the race for *Shamrock*. It was a race that in point of fact told little. Harold Vanderbilt said afterward that it was a good race and the *Shamrock* was a fast yacht. Lipton's comment was, "If I were not disappointed I would be in a mental home. I'd be more optimistic of getting first prize if the last boat over the finish were the victor." Even so, it was an open issue still.

It was the second race that was decisive. It was a foggy day, with the yellow lightship off the reef standing out in contrast against a grey-blue background. The racers faded away like dream ships in the mist, and the guests on the *Erin* had to listen to the race by wireless. Probably very few of them realized what was happening out there in the fog. The first leg of the race was the first trial to windward, and the superiority of the *Enterprise* at every point showed that the outcome of the series was not in any doubt. As Stone says, "The crew of the *Enterprise* knew it and the crew of the *Shamrock* must have sensed it."

Lipton must have known it too, but he did not allow his knowledge to interfere with his duties as a host. He was resolved that the atmosphere of the party should not be overcast. He did not discourage Miss Evelyn Law, the showgirl, when she offered to dance a hornpipe if the *Shamrock* won. When the result came through he turned laughingly toward his guests. "There'll be a big change after tonight; I'm going to put the ladies in full charge," he said. He then turned to one of the prettiest of his party. "How would you like to be captain?" The answer came back pat: "I'd like to be your captain any time, Sir Thomas." But when the party dispersed "a gloom thick as the fog that had blotted out the end of the race pervaded the *Erin*." "It's a great disappointment," Lipton told the press. "Something apparently is wrong."

He knew that he was beaten, as surely as the skipper of the *Enterprise* knew that he won. "I make no comment on the race," said Vanderbilt.

In England the press was trying to provide an alibi by explaining the *Enterprise*'s victory in terms of the Duralumin mast and the new drum winches, the general tone of their reports being that "gadgets had beaten manpower." Which was, of course, to a certain extent true; *Enterprise*, owing to the mast designed by W. Starling Burgess, whose father had beaten the British challengers of the eighties, needed less ballast than *Shamrock* did, while an innovation in the boom enabled the mainsail to slide from one side to another and take in more breeze. Captain Nicholson described the Burgess mast as the greatest engineering feat in the development of racing yachts. Stephens was less enthusiastic. He was a conservative and remarked that a boat like *Enterprise* didn't need yachtsmen but hurdy-gurdy grinders from the Bronx. It was just an affair of turning handles. "How much," he wrote, "mechanical contrivances contributed to *Enterprise*'s snappy work with the sheets and halyards it is hard to say. Certainly the trimming was accelerated by the drum winches below. Also the backstays were better tended mechanically than by hand. The Duralumin mast contributed. It weighed fifteen hundred to two thousand pounds less than *Shamrock*'s."

There were many technical explanations of the *Enterprise*'s better showing, but it must at the same time be pointed out that all these gadgets were available for Captain Nicholson. And Lipton was too good a sportsman to put up that kind of alibi. He knew the answer. He was up against something stronger than he had met before. During the last ten years yachting in America had advanced far faster than it had in England. Possibly there were more rich men in America who could give their time and money to it. But that again is another alibi. The fact remains and is incontrovertible that yachting in America touched in 1930 a high peak, and that among many great yachtsmen Vanderbilt was first. He loved the sea; he knew the sea. He stood at his own helm and beat the best that a syndicate of millionaires could put against him. The victory of *Enterprise* was not the victory of gadgets but of personality. Her skipper was a great sportsman in a great day of sportsmen. And when memory lists the figures of that decade, as it recalls them in their youth and vigour, Lenglen and Borotra; Red Grange and Babe Ruth; Dempsey, Carpentier, and Tunney; Jack Hobbs and Bobby Jones, there in the forefront of that proud gallery must stand the picture of Harold Vanderbilt, tall, thin, determined, in white flannels and blue yachting coat, bent over his wheel under a slouch canvas hat.

Never in his long career was Lipton's sportsmanship put to sterner test than in the last two races. Always up to now, even though he had been beaten, he had put up a good fight, even in 1903. But this time it was only the generosity of the press that prevented the match from being written off as a walkover after the second race. Lipton displayed high courage. How tested his temper was can be shown by an incident on the day of the third race, when the British warship, the *Heliotrope*, sent over ten sailors as the *Erin*'s guests. The sailors were embarrassed and stood rigidly at attention when he greeted them. Their lack of response annoyed him. "What's the matter with you? Don't you speak English?" he snapped. A second later he was apologizing, was putting them at their ease, leading them over to the buffet, assuring himself that they were having a good time. It was a momentary flash of temper, but it showed the strain he was living under.

It was the only sign he was to show. To his guests aboard the *Erin* he remained a genial host. He had little hope that the third race could end any differently from the other two as he seated himself on the main deck of the *Erin* in an easy cane-backed chair. Only a miracle could win the race. For a moment it half looked as though that miracle might have happened. *Shamrock* outmanoeuvred *Enterprise* at the start. If she could hold her own to the windward mark there was just a chance that she might win on the run home. He watched her eagerly through his glasses. A quarter of an hour passed. Half an hour. *Shamrock* still held her own. Was there, after all, a chance? Was fate to play into his hands at last? His excitement mounted. His natural optimism was reasserted. And then suddenly, in a second, it was all over. Another accident. The mast had snapped. Lipton jumped to his feet and ran over to the rail. The bright and buoyant creature, agleam of green and white that a moment earlier had been battling foot by foot and yard by yard in the desperate struggle of the windward thrash, was now a helpless wreck, wallowing in a shroud of canvas.

The last race was sailed two days later. By now public interest had begun to wane. The result was beyond question. Nevertheless, there was a large crowd upon the *Erin*. It was a long, slow-passing day for Lipton. He breakfasted late and without hurry, not joining his guests till the yachts were jockeying for a start. At the start there was some excitement when *Shamrock* shot into the weather berth at the line, but soon she fell off to leeward, and when it was realized that she could not point with *Enterprise* on the crucial windward leg, hope failed. With the race a third over, *Enterprise* was a mile and a quarter ahead, with *Shamrock* following "on wearying wings." Most of the morning until lunch Lipton spent upon the bridge. He was alone and glad to be. This was the end, not of a race, not of a series, but of something more, of all that had symbolized for him during thirty years the romance and glow of living. Never again would he watch a small green cutter spread its immense wings of sail on this side of the Atlantic. It was the end and his heart knew it. It was over, his life's grand passion – the challenge, renewed and re-renewed, and all that went with it. Never again. He was acquainted in that hour with the common lot. He was old who had once been young, and the tale was told now.

On the windward leg *Enterprise* eased up a little to guard against any unforeseen weather freak or breaking-point pull. But toward the end she was canvas-covered and driven out again, with every thread of hemp and wire holding, to break the record for the course by three minutes and five seconds. As she approached the finishing line Lipton left his guests to chatter on the sun deck and gathered the reporters round him at the after rail. "It's no good," he said. "I can't win, I can't win." He shook hands with them one by one. They remarked that he had lost his buoyancy of manner. He looked tired and worn, with the twinkle gone from his eye. He moved dispiritedly among his guests, seemingly glad to be able to throw off at last the mask of gaiety with which he had covered his defeats. At the same time he was loath to have his friends depart. He wanted to prolong to the last moment this "last time."

Next day, the *New York Times* in its leader said, "If sentiment could have gained the victory, the America's Cup would be in the hands of Sir Thomas Lipton," and its tribute to Harold Vanderbilt was commiserative. "It was not an easy, it was almost a thankless task to defend the America's Cup when thousands of his fellow countrymen were almost clamouring for failure." Through the country there was a general feeling of anticlimax, of disappointment, of everybody wishing that it could have turned out differently; an unsatisfactory feeling and by no means a generous one to Vanderbilt, who had put up one of the finest performances in the record of the New York Yacht Club; a feeling, however, that was fortunately to be dissipated within a few hours of *Enterprise*'s victory by a letter that appeared on the front page of the *New York Times* over the signature of Will Rogers.

"What do you say to this?" the letter ran. "Let everyone send a dollar apiece for a fund to buy a loving cup for Sir Thomas Lipton bigger than the one he would have got if he had won, contributed to by everybody that really admires a fine sports-man. Send it to, I would suggest, a Lipton Cup Fund in care of Mayor Walker in New York. Let Jimmy buy it and present it on behalf of everybody with an inscription along this line: 'To possibly the world's worst yacht builder but absolutely the world's most cheerful loser.' You have been a benefit to man-kind. Sir Thomas, you have made losing worthwhile."

The idea caught on at once. Jimmy Walker welcomed it. "There might be some doubt about his ability to win the cup, but no doubt about his ability to capture our hearts." Letters approving the scheme flowed in. Edward E. Spafford wrote: "Mr. Lipton has come to this country on several occasions for the purpose of lifting the cup. He has lifted the hearts of the people of the country, who are anxious for him to lift a cup filled with the admiration of the people," while Patrick Quinlan of the Associated Silk Manufacturers suggested a peerage because of his efforts in cementing international goodwill – "Earl Lip-ton of Tyrone." Within ten days sixteen thousand dollars had come in, and Lipton himself had so recovered his good spirits and good humour that by the time he sailed on the twenty-seventh of September he was promising to make yet another challenge for the cup.

from *The Lipton Story*,
Brandt and Brandt, London, 1950.

THE YACHTS

WILLIAM CARLOS WILLIAMS

THE YACHTS

contend in a sea which the land partly encloses
shielding them from the too-heavy blows
of an ungoverned ocean which when it chooses

tortures the biggest hulls, the best man knows
to pit against its beatings, and sinks them pitilessly.
Mothlike in mists, scintillant in the minute

brilliance of cloudless days, with broad bellying sails
they glide to the wind tossing green water
from their sharp prows while over them the crew crawls

ant-like, solicitously grooming them, releasing,
making fast as they turn, lean far over and having
caught the wind again, side by side, head for the mark.

In a well guarded arena of open water surrounded by
lesser and greater craft which, sycophant, lumbering
and flittering follow them, they appear youthful, rare

as the light of a happy eye, live with the grace
of all that in the mind is feckless, free and
naturally to be desired. Now the sea which holds them

is moody, lapping their glossy sides, as if feeling
for some slightest flaw but fails completely.
Today no race. Then the wind comes again. The yachts

move, jockeying for a start, the signal is set and they
are off. Now the waves strike at them but they are too
well made, they slip through, though they take in canvas.

Arms with hands grasping seek to clutch at the prows.
Bodies thrown recklessly in the way are cut aside.
It is a sea of faces about them in agony, in despair

until the horror of the race dawns staggering the mind,
the whole sea become an entanglement of watery bodies
lost to the world bearing what they cannot hold. Broken,

beaten, desolate, reaching from the dead to be taken up
they cry out, failing, failing! their cries rising
in waves still as the skillful yachts pass over.

from *The Collected Poems of Williams Carlos Williams, 1909-1939, vol. 1,*
New Directions Publishing Corporation, New York, 1938.

THE RACING EDGE
TED TURNER AND GARY JOBSON

Satellite broadcasting pioneer Ted Turner first captured the world stage when he defended the America's Cup in 1977 and discovered that he enjoyed the attention. He won the Cup on *Courageous*, with master tactician Gary Jobson at his side.

Jobson: I hear you talking to reporters a lot about why we compete in sailing and other sports. What do you think is the value of competition, particularly in sailing?

Turner: I would say that we have a need to compete. It's as natural as sleeping or eating. We have a need to excel. And sailing is very good at bringing it out.

J: What challenges you to win? Of all the people I've ever sailed with, I've never seen anybody as strong-willed to win on the race-course. What is that?

T: I've got a larger dose of motivation than most people have. Some people are born fleet of foot, make great runners. When basic characteristics were doled out, I got more than my share of competitiveness. That's probably all. In fact, it may not be all that healthy.

J: Some people say that competition can bring out the worst in people, and others that competition can bring out the best.

T: I would say there are a lot of people who get more enjoyment and camaraderie and friendship out of sailing competitively than in sailing just for relaxation. But the competition ought to be kept in perspective. Sailing is sport – at least, it's supposed to be. It ought to be fun. That doesn't mean you can't give it everything you have; but when poor sportsmanship and skinning the edges of the rules and so forth fall into it, as they have in certain areas, that's not good. Sailboat racing ought to be fun.

J: Do you think the key to success in sailing is persistence – just plugging away at it? Some people sail for forty years and never get in the top half of the fleet.

T: I'd say that's one of the abilities you have to have to win in anything. You have to be persistent and you have to be dedicated. You have to be hardworking. I've never run into the guy who could win at the top level in anything today and didn't have the right attitude, didn't give it everything he had, at least while he was doing it; wasn't prepared and didn't have the whole program worked out. On the other hand, you have to have the ability and you've got to have good sense. And that's true in every aspect of life. Sailing is a brains game to a large degree, as well as physical. And you've got to be able to figure out what's going wrong and correct it. To get to the top, you have to have the ability and the attitude, I'd say.

J: What are the great offshore races in the world? Which would you rank as, say, the top five or six?

T: I prefer courses that keep the fleet fairly close together, so that fluky weather conditions are minimized. A point-to-point race over a wide expanse of ocean – the Bermuda or Honolulu race, for example – can be a challenge, but it is not as true a test of sailing ability as the St. Petersburg-Fort Lauderdale race, say, or even the Miami-Nassau race, in which you have two marks that you have to turn. That keeps the fleet pretty much on the same course. I would say that the Fastnet Race is probably the most competitive one in the world.

J: How about the Mackinacs?

T: They're great too. All the big-name races are great, because they attract top-level competition. I like the Hobart Race, too, because the coasts of Australia and Tasmania keep the fleet fairly close together.

This may be a good time to say that I enjoy fleet racing

actually more than match racing. It's always really interesting when the boats are closely matched and crews and skippers are evenly matched in ability. But match racing just isn't as challenging, on the average, as racing against a twenty- or thirty-boat fleet. If you're a little faster than the other guy, it's no contest. In a fleet race, a guy that's a little bit slower, for whatever reason, does have an outside chance. In a match race, he really doesn't, since he's always being covered.

J: What was the roughest race you've been on?

T: Obviously, the Chicago-Mackinac, which you just mentioned, would be a candidate. It can be nasty and cold on the lakes, even in summer. The Sydney-Hobart race, with those southerly busters coming up from the South Pole, that's really rough, and the Trans-Atlantic race, with the westerly gales, can be pretty bad, even though the wind is primarily behind you. The Lauderdale race is another one, if a norther comes through in the winter – or any SORC [Southern Ocean Racing Conference] race when a real bad cold front comes through, which is fairly often.

J: I haven't been with you when it's really rough – blowing sixty – but I've been with you at the point where safety becomes a factor. You want to hold the chute as long as you can, but then it starts blowing just too hard for the chute, so you take it down a little early. Where do you draw the line?

T: Fortunately, I always have pretty strong boats. I have not allowed myself to get caught up in the craze for light boats and equipment. When the wind starts to really come on, it's better to be prepared than to have to go right to the edge. In other words, once you've gotten down to your storm canvas, you may not be going very fast, but there's not much that can go wrong. You're not likely to lose your rig if you've got a good stick in the boat. Incidentally, we discovered in the Sydney-Hobart race on the *Pied Piper* that a great storm rig, fast as the devil for downwind running in extremely heavy air and heavy seas, is a mainsail – a number two genoa – winged out to windward and a reacher out to leeward. That's a heck of a good rig if you have a double-grooved headstay, as most boats do now. The boat was much more controllable than it was with the spinnaker, and we were going, I think, just as fast, maybe faster, because we weren't yawing or rolling as much.

The most frightening time for me, and I think when you get into the most trouble, is when you have a spinnaker up going downwind in marginal conditions. The wind is strong, and the seas are running rough. You never know when you're going to wipe out. Upwind it's not that bad, because no matter how hard it blows all you have to do is put on smaller sails. It's uncomfortable changing them, but once you are down to the right canvas, the reaching is not a problem – up to fifty or sixty knots, I think.

J: When you're going downwind in that kind of breeze, do you ever sail by-the-lee?

T: By-the-lee in heavy wind is pretty dangerous. And in the kind of winds we're talking about, you can't fly a blooper because the bloopers are basically light and they'll blow out. Your blooper usually blows out just about the time you really need it.

Let's face it, though: only two or three percent of sailboat racing is done in winds over thirty to thirty-five knots. You're not going to win much by being a great sailor in winds over thirty knots.

J: When was the first time you aspired to win the America's Cup? Is it something you always wanted to do?

T: I think the first time was when I was in college at Brown. I had the good fortune to watch the first twelve-metre defense, in 1958, and I remember the boats: *Columbia* and *Sceptre*. I was out there watching the first race. We were on a sailboat about thirty feet long, owned by the family of a friend of mine. We were near Castle Hill, and they towed the boats by – both white, if I remember. The crews were all big, muscular men, with their matching shirts on. I'm sure that at the time I didn't just decide I was going to go out and win the Cup, but I was pretty impressed. At the time I had never sailed on anything bigger than a Y Flyer or a Lightning.

I remember when I thought Lightnings were like J-boats. I was ten years old and I was sailing a Penguin. I thought, Boy, if I ever get a Lightning, that would really be out of sight! And then when I did, I really enjoyed it. Lightnings are a lot of fun.

In fact, I enjoyed every boat I ever sailed. It doesn't really matter what size boat you're sailing. The sport is the same, whether it's Penguin or an Interclub dinghy or a Laser or a twelve-metre or a Class A offshore racer. Same wind, same waves, same principles; just a lot less agony and grief in a smaller boat.

J: Some people think that the best big-boat sailors are the ones who have gone through the fire in small boats first.

T: Absolutely. I say that a good small-boat background is essential, starting with dinghies and then on to a little sloop, with spinnaker and so forth. I mean, to go straight into big boats without sailing small boats at least a number of years would be like trying to go to college without having gone to high school.

J: Do you think it's good to stay in touch with small boats when sailing big ones?

T: It's good if you have the time to do it. If you ask me, sailing is so much fun that it's best to do it in all sizes of boats. The average weekend sailor might be able to make a couple of big-boat races a year or something like that. The rest of the time he's sailing in his own club on small boats. Of course, most people sail small boats and don't really get a chance to race offshore, because of the time and money involved.

A couple of years ago, before I bought the baseball team, I got a Y Flyer again, and I had as much fun sailing that as I do the bigger boats. The only reason I'm not sailing every weekend in small boats right now is simply because I don't have the time. But they're just as much fun as the big boats, maybe more.

The main thing is to buy a boat you can afford to campaign in a first-class manner. There's nothing sadder than to see a guy with a boat for which he can't afford first-class equipment because the boat's too large. It's like buying a bigger house than you can afford to maintain. If you want a big boat, the thing to do is check out a used one, particularly in one-design. Normally all it will need is sails and maybe a few more fittings and so forth. You just have to be sure it's not too heavy.

One thing, though. Whatever size boat, it's important to race a high-performance boat if you want to raise your level of racing. Low-performance boats teach tactics, since they are relatively close in speed; high-performance boats teach good boat handling techniques, and that is how to improve most quickly. If you want to be really good, you need to be in a high-performance or Olympic-class boat.

I have tended to sail the highest-performance type of boat I could, and I think it's been a major factor in my success as a sailor. I started in a Penguin, which was good experience because it requires good balance or you capsize. After several years I got into the Y Flyer, another relatively high-performance boat. And I really started making progress when I got into the Flying Dutchman, which in the sixties was probably the hottest boat around. My keelboat sailing began in a 5.5-metre, which was definitely the most sophisticated small keelboat ever built.

These days 470s are excellent. So are Lasers and Finns. And there are a number of other boats in the high-performance class: the Thistle, 505, and Scows.

J: Ted, there really isn't that much match racing going on in this country, or in fact the world. Is this what makes the America's Cup so interesting?

T: Well, the biggest challenge of the America's Cup is to get into the America's Cup – figuring out how to get a berth. But of course the fact that the boats are so large and expensive is the reason it gets the publicity. And it does attract the best sailors.

You know, the level of racing in the America's Cup has

improved. So much time and money is devoted to it that you can reach a level of performance, with the practice and continual working on the sails, that is pretty impressive. You have sail-makers sailing on the boats and working on the sails daily.

Still, I would say that going to the Olympics and winning a gold medal is a far greater challenge than defending the America's Cup, because, first of all, there's a lot more people you're competing against. There was a total of, I think, only seven boats in the entire America's Cup, whereas in the Finn class at the Olympics there are probably five to six hundred sailors who try for a slot, and those are the finest sailors. Then too, the Olympic sailor is a much younger fellow, because of the physical demands of boats like 470s, for example. It's just not a boat that somebody in his forties would be sailing. On the other hand, you're going to have a basically older group in the America's Cup anyway, because of the complexity and the money and experience required.

J: The average age on *Courageous* was thirty-three, and that was young compared with a lot of the twelve-metre campaigns of the past.

T: I think we had the youngest afterguard in history.

J: How do you put your crews together? What do you look for; what are the qualities for a successful crew?

T: Of course, the nature of the crew depends on the size of the boat. As the boat gets bigger, you have more of a division of labour. An FD crewman, for example, has to be as skilful a sailor as there is. He's got to be the spinnaker man, the jib man, the hiking man, the tactician, the navigator. The helmsman just hangs on and tries to keep the boat going fast through the waves.

Of course, on a Laser or Finn, you are the crew. When I sailed a Finn and wasn't doing well, everybody used to say I cussed my crew. I'd talk to myself: "You stupid son-of-a-gun, you. You can hike out harder." You know – when they're going by on both sides. I found I really enjoyed sailing on two- and three-man boats more, because I like the camaraderie of having somebody along.

Now, when you get on a bigger boat, the crew becomes more of an organizational deal. On a twelve-metre, you have one guy who is the tactician, one guy who is bowman, and so on down the line, with eight guys leaning over the side and a guy trimming the jib. In a way, it becomes simpler. On a twelve you can take somebody who really doesn't know that much about tactics but is a good, strong, willing worker, and he can be a very important addition to the crew just by grinding. On a big boat you also need to consider getting a group of guys who will get along with one another, especially if you're going to stay together for more than one series. Your greatest premium, though, is on organization and recruiting, just like it is in basketball and baseball. Having the experience to know what kind of equipment to get and who to put your money on.

Another thing on that. From the skipper's standpoint, and even from every crew member's, you have to be extremely tolerant when you are on an offshore boat, because people are going to make mistakes, and the more people the more mistakes. The chance for mistakes is about equal to the number of the crew squared, so every additional crew member increases that percentage quite a bit. I personally enjoy the camaraderie and the challenge of the larger group, but there are a lot of people who don't want to bother with that. I know some tremendous sailors who are not really good on large boats – not because they don't have the ability to sail them, but just because they find it difficult getting along with all those people. They can't put up with the hollering when somebody makes a mistake; they simply like to do things independently. This is one of the great things about sailing: there's room for all kinds of people.

J: About three hundred people have asked me, "How do you get on a twelve-metre crew?"

T: One way is to buy your way on. But you've got to be good then. I'd say to sail on a twelve-metre you need to be a good small-boat sailor – not necessarily a skipper, but you need to have both small-boat experience, and a lot of it, and the big-boat experience too. Most basic of all, it's good to find out who has twelve-metre aspirations, from both a syndicate and a skippering standpoint, and to get to know those people, since they pick the crew.

After getting the boat [*Courageous*] I did the best I could at putting together the most mature and experienced crew I possibly could. Since the other two boats were already under way and they had already begun to select their crews before I even had a boat, they had the first- and second-round drafts and we drafted third. But there were still quite a few good guys available in the third draft. We had a couple of rookies, but also plenty of experience.

When we got to Newport, if I remember, we had some sickness, and we brought in a couple of tremendous substitutes. You've got to have a good bench to win in anything. But other than that, I don't think we changed the crew from the first day of the summer until the last day, though of course we had tryouts for a couple of positions up in Marblehead before coming down.

I'd say we put in eight or nine hours a day every day in practice, and we were deadly serious about what we were doing, but what with the length of the campaign, I tried to keep it as light as possible, so we didn't burn ourselves out. We had plenty of energy left – emotional energy as well as physical – for a good push at the end.

I remember once in the middle of everything just taking a sail and having lunch at Block Island. That day *Independence* broke down. Ordinarily, I don't find it beneficial just to go out and sail by yourself. It's like playing tennis by yourself; you can knock a ball up against the wall and get a little exercise doing it, but it's a pretty low-key workout. But we'd been working extremely hard, so at that point we just cruised over to Block Island. We did some tacking and jibing drills on the way over. I think we changed sails at the time just to practise, but we went the straight line. A lot of guys had never been to Block Island, and we went ashore, had lunch for an hour, then sailed back.

J: What about your own frame of mind, as skipper? How would you assess your emotions at the time of the America's Cup, aside from just being up for the competition?

T: I was ready. With all the big-boat experience that I had had in messing around with *American Eagle* and doing a lot of sailing on larger boats, one-tonners and larger, I learned plenty. You know – sailing *American Eagle* ten thousand miles and then the disastrous *Mariner* campaign, when we learned how to eat humble pie. But that in itself is something you need to learn, because in twelve-metre racing you need to have a lot of humility. You're not sailing your own boat; you're working for a committee, the New York Yacht Club selection committee, and you're working for your syndicate. So you have to be a little bit of a politician, in the better sense of the word. You have to be a gentleman, and you have to do what is expected of you on the water as well as off. I mean, going around and writing "turkey" with a grease pencil on another guy's boat, like they do in the Finn class, doesn't make sense in a twelve. If they found out who did it, you'd be taking a walk down the dock the next day. You ought to be a gentleman and make the yacht club and your competitors happy to have known you. Good sportsmanship and reasonable standards of conduct are important.

J: What did defending the Cup mean to you in the end, after it was all over?

T: Like any international-championship regatta, particularly the first time, it's a tremendous experience. I remember when I first went to the Lightning Internationals up in Buffalo. I was so impressed just to be there and meet all the real big cheeses in it. So there was excitement and elation and satisfaction at having accomplished what we set out to do, and reaching what is certainly one of the great pinnacles in yacht racing.

And there was a sense of relief, too, that it was over. I spent all year getting ready for those Cup races. When we went to New-port and when we were up there sailing, I wiped almost every-thing out of my mind, just about every waking moment, except for maybe a couple of hours in the evening when I'd relax and watch a ball game.

J: It kept building up day after day.

T: The pressure was intense for the summer. Everyone was trying so hard to do a perfect job, so there was a sense of relief when it was over and we could all go home to our regular careers, which seemed like they would almost be vacations. I know that every man in the crew, including myself, felt the strain. Those races last so long. When you're behind, you keep trying to tack to get away, for hours and hours, and it's so hard to do that it feels like somebody has taken a whip and beaten you on the back.

And there was a lot of work even when we weren't racing or practising. We'd watch Ted Hood when he was sailing against *Enterprise* – we watched both Hood and North to see how they were reacting when they raced against each other. We checked their sails and how they were tacking, looking for the good things they were doing and for the chinks in their armour.

J: I think knowing your competition is a very important thing.

T: It's certainly important in the America's Cup, or any match race. A lot of it is psychological. I think our good start in June gave us a leg up and gave our crew a sense of elation and optimism, whereas a sense of gloom and defeatism crept into the other two boats. It was important that we maintained this edge, though we came close to losing it in July.

Somebody said to me after it was over, "You guys were so good. Did you ever make mistakes?" So I told him about the first time against *Independence* when we were up there with all of our people green and went into the tacking duel. Those kids cleaned our clocks. Losing track of where the trim tab was was kind of fun.

J: That was my fault. I locked the rudder one way and trim tab the other.

T: We just stopped – had to take two tacks right at the mark.

J: Would you say our ability to change jibs quickly was one of our major keys to success on *Courageous*?

T: Absolutely. We had the right jibs and we had the right system and the right personnel to change them. You have to have all three. And then we had spent the time to know which ones to use under which circumstances. The right sails, the right people, the right system, and the experience to know which one should be up when. I think that particularly helped us against *Enterprise*, because I think *Independence* certainly had the right sails and knew which ones to have up. They didn't change as often as we did, but they had the system. I think maybe they didn't have as much confidence in their personnel as we did to make the changes in critical situations. And if you'll remember, Robbie Doyle, God bless his soul, didn't have as much confidence in our ability to do it as we did. But we never had a major foul-up, to my knowledge, changing a jib. We changed them a lot. We practised it a lot, too. We practised it because there's no room for error changing jibs on a seventy-foot boat while tacking.

J: As far as practising, you had everybody following the same routine, a set routine, even on non-race days.

T: It's just like in baseball: you're so much better off with a set lineup than you are changing things around, because you just can't get too proficient in what you're doing – particularly on a large boat, but even on a small one. And the more people involved, the more you have to integrate. Any one person failing to do his job in a tack or a jibe causes the jibe or tack to miscarry. Had a sail change been wrong, we could have ended up with a sail in the water, and it would have cost us the race. Just the slightest little fitting going – remember when we lost the backstay? That's the end of the race. Your crew has to have every single possible manoeuvre or circumstance, fore and aft, down to where you don't even think about what it is when it occurs, because usually when something busts or breaks or miscarries, you don't have time. You've got to have it all planned out. And you practise so that after a while nobody even has to say anything.

J: I remember you saying that you believe a lot of people would rather race by rating. There are a lot of people who like to race by rating, I'm sure, because the sting of defeat is not so great.

T: You always have oodles of excuses, you know: small boat, not my weather, and so on. I would say that handicap offshore racing is a relatively low level of competition, compared with one-design.

J: Do you think the boat builders are setting up a market for one-design?

T: Absolutely. Having been in the boat business, I know the best thing in the world a boat builder can do is establish a proprietary product like the Laser. That way, all he has to do is maintain the same standards for all boats. And he can charge whatever he wants, because no one's competing with him in the same marketplace. They make money on that sort of thing, whereas in building Lightnings or Flying Dutchmans or a class that anyone can build, there's no money in it at all, and there's no promotional budget available, no marketing, no advertising – not even any dealers usually, since there's no room for a dealer markup. This makes it very, very difficult to buy a new custom ocean racer. You have to go to a designer and you have to get a builder, and you don't know what it's going to cost and you don't know whether it's going to be good or not, because you're building a new design. If you buy a J-24, you know what you get; or a Laser, Windsurfer, Sunfish, or Hobie Cat.

J: So offshore racing is dominated by the proprietary products. They're also easier to buy and sell. Let's talk a little about mental preparation. How do you psych yourself?

T: I stay psyched up all the time. My two sports teams play every day, and I take the role of underdog, so for me it's nothing to be psyched. At least when we're racing it's only once every two weeks or once a weekend.

J: What about the question of how much time to devote to sailing? Some people seem to get hooked on the sport and lose a sense of proportion. They allow it to rule their lives.

T: It can be a problem. I would have to say that your business comes first. If you want to give your full time to sailing, you can sail twelve hours a day, three hundred sixty-five days a year, and you can compete in a regatta somewhere every weekend. It's a great field to be in, even though I would caution young people who are thinking about it. It's not as much fun when you do it for a living as when you do it for a hobby. I think if you asked anyone over forty who has spent his career in it – particularly in the racing area (I'm not talking about yacht brokerage) – you'll find a lot of heartaches.

So if it's not going to be your vocation, then you shouldn't give it more importance than it really has. One of the unhealthy things today, I think, is that many people spend more time playing than working. I've spent a lot of time sailing, but I've spent a lot more time working, and had I not been successful in business, I could never have achieved success in sailing. It took money, and that came from my business. Your career provides for your sailing, so your career should come first.

J: I find that sailing is great, but a big part is getting around and meeting people and seeing different places. I'd never been to Mackinac Island, for example, before we raced there last summer.

T: You have the best of all worlds. You're really more like a teacher – a teacher and coach – particularly since so many of your goals have already been achieved. I think that's great. You don't have to prove anything; you can go out and really enjoy it. Share your knowledge with others.

That kind of life is a lot more interesting than that of a sailmaker, who is dealing with all the customers who'd like to blame the fact that they're not winning on their sailmaker. You can get out and race, and somebody's going to be last; you can't blame that on the sails.

J: What are the important factors a sailor should weigh in looking toward the next year's campaign or the next two years'?

T: It depends on the sailor's budget, the amount of time he can devote to his racing, how important it is to him in the overall scheme of things. If he is a beginner, he could be shooting to be in the top half of his local fleet the next year, and if he has been down at the bottom, that's a very worthwhile and interesting goal. I don't think you ought to set unrealistically high goals for yourself. It's disappointing if you don't make them.

J: So you should set a goal.

T: You don't really have to, but I think it's always more fun to have something in mind that you want to accomplish. If you don't have a goal, it's harder to achieve something.

J: And your goals – how do you go about planning them each year?

T: I sit down and think about a year in advance as to what events we're going to attend. After the America's Cup, though, it was a pretty easy year. You build up to it, and then it's best, I think, to take a little time off to yourself. Relax a bit.

J: Do you get nervous before you go out racing?

T: I used to get tremendously nervous; not as much anymore. Let's face it: I'm fidgety and high-strung. Years ago I used to have a bad case of nerves, and a lot of times I would clutch up. I can remember sailing in a boat one time and my foot started shaking uncontrollably, so I almost fell out of the hiking straps. It was a Sears semifinals, and I had to pass a boat to win. I didn't.

I guess I was so intense in sailing that I clutched there more than in any other area. It's one of the worst habits you can have, because if you're going to clutch in a tight sailing situation, then you will in other situations too – in an automobile, for example, when another car is coming at you. There are a lot of guys who have that problem.

J: How can you overcome that?

T: You have to work hard on it, the same way you work on quitting smoking or biting your fingernails. It doesn't hurt either to tell yourself that this race is not that important, that you're going to have a good time. But the real solution is confidence, and that comes with experience and hard work. Then, once you overcome the problem in sailing, it will be a lot easier to overcome it in other areas as well.

from *The Racing Edge*,
Simon and Schuster, New York, 1977.

PREPARING TO WIN

DENNIS CONNER AND PETER ISLER

Dennis Conner has compiled one of sailing's greatest racing
records; like Conner, interviewer Peter Isler has won Olympic
medals and the America's Cup.

Isler: What is the most common error you see out on the race
course?

Conner: In local racing I always see people come out of the
harbour with 15 minutes to go, thinking they have a chance.
That's ludicrous. They have no time to choose the sails to put
up, to make sure the mast is tuned, to have the cunningham and
outhaul adjusted. They don't even have an idea which way the
wind is going to shift; they may not even know the course. Lack
of preparation is the biggest problem, and it separates club and
amateur sailors from those who are really world class.

I: As helmsman, what do you concentrate on before a race?

C: Preparation. That may seem mundane, but it's failure to
know the little things – like what the weather is going to do, the
state of the tide, details in the sailing instructions and the late
notices on the bulletin board – that can result in poor performance or even disqualification. Before you leave the dock you
make sure all your equipment is there, that no one has borrowed
life-jackets and that all your gear is working. Go through a
check list before you leave.

I: What about the weather?

C: Having an idea of what the weather, wind, and tide are going
to do can make or break the race. It is important to know what
to expect before you leave the dock so you can make the proper

sail selection, make sure you have the right spinnaker sheets on, and check that your boat is set up properly. But you should also keep in mind what you will need if you are wrong. For instance, even if light air is predicted it's not a bad idea to have that 3/4-ounce ready as well as the 1/2-ounce and the #2 ready to go up as well.

I: And once you leave the dock?

C: Get your head into the game right away. Start thinking about the wind direction and velocity and writing data down every 20 minutes so you can spot backing or veering patterns. A piece of tape on the deck with everything written on it puts all you need to know right in front of you.

I: Do you get head-to-head readings on a boat that has no fancy electronic instruments?

C: That's the best way, even if you do have an electronic read-out. Then you can check compasses and check telltales and masthead fly against the electronic readout to figure out if there is any wind shear – a difference in wind directions between deck and masthead level.

It's important to get an idea of what the wind is aloft and on the water, because the upper wind is a good indicator of where it might shift later on in the day. It's also a good idea to get your headings on each tack and derive the true wind from that and compare it to your head-to-wind readings, which will also help you determine where it will shift later.

I: I've noticed that you are very tuned in to a wind shear, especially sailing in San Diego. What other information do you look for?

C: I think a wind shear is one of many indicators you must be constantly aware of in your environment – clues to what the wind might do – like smoke on the horizon or boats sailing at different angles, different coloured patches on the water. Those are all data for your mental computer.

I: What should the crew be doing at this time?

C: Double-checking spinnaker packing, getting the magnetic courses from mark to mark, checking for shallow water on the race course. If you have a new boat, it doesn't hurt to calibrate the speedometer. For instance, if you know a One-Tonner should go 6.7 knots upwind from the polar curve, you can check your own One-Tonner's speedo. If it's a 50-footer and you know from experience you should be going 7.4 knots, calibrate the speedo before the start, otherwise it will take five critical minutes during the race to realize that your calibration is off.

I: How much do you rely on the numbers and how much on feel?

C: I've found that the best way to sail is to rely on what your instincts tell you. If you need to check those instincts, look at similar boats around you, compare how you are doing with them to see if you're pointing or footing, gaining bearing or losing bearing; then look back at the numbers.

I: What are other good gauges you might use instead of electronics?

C: Before the start, I like to find a boat that's being sailed just a little faster and sail alongside. Then I check her leads, sail trim, all the speed-producing elements. I compare our pointing angles and then change what I have on my boat to match and check again.

I: So you would recommend gauging yourself against the best boat?

C: Not necessarily. It doesn't help your morale or your capability if you are already off on boat speed. It's better to choose a boat that is close to you in speed – that way you can see what improvements you need and make ones that will count.

I: You mentioned the other day, at the start of the Manzanillo

Race, the benefit of taking a flight over the race course to see the wind. Just how much do you rely on local knowledge and is it a real advantage?

C: Local knowledge is important, of course. One thing that is dangerous about it, however, is that it can give you a preconceived, but wrong, idea of the conditions in a familiar racing area. Sometimes, for example in big races or regattas, the course the committee sets is a mile or two away from the one the local fleet normally uses and the conditions can be completely different. It is a mistake to apply preconceived ideas based on the topography of one place to a slightly different location.

I: Do you have any favourite starting approaches?

C: Starts depend on the competition. If you are sailing against Peter Gilmour for the America's Cup and you have a boat that doesn't turn too wide, you might choose to use more of a traditional time start and take away his advantage of manoeuvrability.

In a fleet race where the pin is favoured, most top level, aggressive sailors sail on port and then tack onto starboard into the pin. But if you have good boatspeed you don't have to get the best start to win the race – you just have to avoid the mistakes that could ultimately prove fatal.

I: I've noticed when you start a big boat with an unfamiliar crew, you tend to steer more to speed up or slow down rather than let the crew do it by trimming or luffing the sails. Why?

C: Communication is important when you are sailing with a new group of people. You can never communicate enough and it's optimistic to think that an unfamiliar crew is going to perform optimally. In any manoeuvre before the start – accelerating or decelerating, or changing sails – it's asking for high risk and low reward to count on the unfamiliar crew to bail you out.

I: So you should try to make it as easy on them as possible?

C: Yes. And try to communicate exactly what your wishes are and try not to change the game plan. But, if you must change plans, do so when there is adequate time, and recommunicate your desires.

I: You have sailed with the best. If you disagree with your tactician, who has the final say and how do you avoid controversy?

C: Generally, a pecking order has to be established. A helmsman who is not confident will delegate authority to a tactician. It's a decision the person in charge has to make. The best sailors want a lot of input from their tacticians, but the buck stops with the guy who is steering the boat.

I: When you watch kids sailing Lasers, for example, you see them turning the rudder a lot. What is your theory on steering?

C: The smaller the boat, the more you can get away with steering a lot. I'd say quick motions on the tiller can help, but there's a fine point between that and sculling. Yes, it's fast and effective but the legality of it is another story. On a bigger boat, if you oversteer you are just interrupting flow and slowing down.

I: Is there any best training ground?

C: My advice would be to sail daily where there are steady winds because you need to sail regularly in steady winds to develop boatspeed. I think southern California is the best training ground in the States; it's not like Long Island Sound, where local knowledge is a big help and you can regularly take advantage of wind shifts and currents. Major world championships are usually held in areas that require boatspeed, not in places where shifts or local knowledge can skew the results.

Besides, look at the record – the best sailors for the past 35 years come from southern California (myself excluded).

I: Finally, what are five tips you would give an up-and-coming skipper?

C: One, establish your priorities so that sailing is as important to you as possible. Two, sail as much as you can – there is no substitute for time in the boat. Three, work hard on your equipment because the better equipment you have, the faster you go – and you won't break down. Four, sail with the best sailors; learn from their experience. Five, work hard to enjoy your sailing.

from *Yachting*, May 1988,
with thanks to Charles Barthold.

A SEA DOG PRIMES HIS GUNS

CRAIG NEFF

Dennis Conner isn't like other folks. He isn't even like other sailors. People who race sailboats and people who write about people who race sailboats have been trying to figure him out for years. Why did Dennis say this? Why did Dennis do that? What is Dennis up to now? More often than not the answer is a verbal shrug. "That's Dennis," they say.

Conner, the skipper of *Stars & Stripes* and the most perplexing personality on the America's Cup scene in Australia, is a wily and fierce competitor whose mind is on sailing 100 percent of his waking hours. His racing companions say they form tag teams so that late at night Conner always has someone to talk to about sailing. While lesser skippers race for the sport of trying to win, Conner races in order to win. He has defined his sport in his own terms, and his opponents have been forced to accept his definition, like it or not. At the same time, Conner's definition means he can neither court the sometimes useful role of the underdog, nor can he expect to be granted its dispensations even when, as in this year's America's Cup competition, he might well deserve them. He is feared and respected by many, admired by some, and loved by very few. After three decades at the top in the tight, gossipy little world of sailboat racing, he remains an enigma, of whom a yachting journalist said, "He's done it all. He's the best there is. His only flaw is that he's Dennis. He's his own Achilles' heel."

This week, in the semifinals of the Louis Vuitton Cup, the 3 1/2-month-long series of races to determine the challenger for the America's Cup, Conner has arrived at his moment of truth. He must beat Tom Blackaller and his double-ruddered *USA* in a best-of-seven series or be eliminated from Cup competition altogether. In Sunday's Race 1 he got off to a stunning start, taking a thriller from Blackaller by just 10 seconds. And on

162

Monday Conner won again, by three minutes and two seconds, leaving Blackaller a formidable catch-up task. (The winner of that all-American series will meet the winner of the *New Zealand – French Kiss* series in the challenger finals, starting Jan. 13.)

The stakes would be high at this point in an America's Cup "summer" no matter who was involved, but when Conner and Blackaller, longtime California rivals with many old scores to settle, are slugging it out in what Conner likes to call "a game of life," the battle, for the moment, overshadows the war. It is a perverse but genuine tribute to Conner and to his reputation as a competitor to say that his losing would be bigger news than Blackaller's winning.

Until 1983, when Conner and his red-hulled *Liberty* lost the America's Cup, the urge to explain Dennis sprang from his success, a competitive record unequalled in his generation of racers. In small one-design boats, medium-sized ocean racing boats, and massive 12-metre campaigns, he has won everything that matters most to people who devote their lives and their fortunes – or someone else's – to the sport of racing sailboats. He has won the Star class world championship twice, the Southern Ocean Racing Conference circuit four times, and he has helmed two America's Cup winners: *Courageous* in 1974, when he was picked out of the chorus line, so to speak, to share the wheel with Ted Hood; and *Freedom* in 1980, when, to his eternal credit, or shame, depending on who's talking, he reinvented America's Cup campaigning.

The $200 million America's Cup exercise in extravagance that is going on in Western Australia right now was set in motion by Conner and his unprecedented two-year, two-boat *Freedom* and *Enterprise* campaign leading up to the 1980 Cup. Until then the typical America's Cup program was five months long, cost around $1.5 million, and bore a striking resemblance to sport. Conner's businesslike approach changed all that. With exhaustive attention to detail, thousands of man-hours devoted to crew work and sail testing, and the spending of previously inconceivable amounts of money, Conner laid waste the defender trials that summer. *Freedom* won 45 out of a possible 48 races, while

Courageous, sailed by Ted Turner, and *Clipper*, steered part of the time by Blackaller, had only four wins between them.

Turner, the last of the true 12-metre amateurs, was so disgusted with the turn the game had taken that he quit 12-metring for good. Blackaller, a San Francisco sailmaker, who, like Conner, has twice won the Star class worlds but who, unlike Conner, would prefer to be racing Formula One cars, has twice tried to beat Dennis at his own game: in 1983, with *Defender*, a boat and a program that came nowhere near measuring up to Conner's, and this year with *USA*, a gamble on a revolutionary design.

Twelve-metre skippers like Conner and Blackaller are the rock stars of sailing. Typically, they are dashing figures in a glamorous sport who look and feel their best at the wheels of their boats, preferably wind-whipped and wave-lashed. Conner, whose weight goes up and down, mostly up, and whose face has a boyish softness that belies 30-odd years of sun and salt, does not fit the mould. He is a star, nonetheless, because in one sort of boat or another he has beaten them all.

An America's Cup syndicate is a small corporation. Its product is a sleek, 65-foot, 55,000-pound racing machine that is as fast and strong as the corporation's resources of time, talent, and money can make her. Most 12-metre skippers view the business side of racing as a necessary evil, a tedious means to a possibly glorious end. They attend to the endless details of preparing their boats because they have been doing it since childhood, and they know that preparation wins races. They scrounge for funds because they have to. However, they would gladly sail a dinghy through an icy gale on the North Atlantic with a broken collarbone if it meant they wouldn't have to put on a blazer and show up for a sponsor's cocktail party.

Conner, by contrast, loves it all. "I come from fairly modest beginnings," he says. "To me it's kind of a rush to get to go and meet people like Edsel Ford or Mike Dingman at the Henley Group, to walk in and see them and be on a first-name basis. I never would have had that opportunity if I hadn't been there asking them for help. I find that fun. I called on Donald Trump and asked him for $3 million. I told him we'd name the boat *Trump Card*. He gave it a lot of thought. The point is, I enjoy that. I'm a businessman. Sailing is my hobby. It's fun to be a small businessman and to go see how the heavies operate, and see what life is like at the top in another game, if you will, the game of making money."

Conner is a businessman. He owns a carpet and drapery manufacturing business in San Diego, where he has lived all his life. He also dabbles in real estate. But his real business is the 12-metre business, and though he sometimes tweaks his American rivals – professional sailors like Blackaller, John Kolius, Rod Davis, and Buddy Melges – with his technical status as an amateur, he admits he spends as much time at the game as they do. More, some say.

Fund-raising is fun for Conner because he has found a way to make it a contest. Though it would probably have surprised the Aga Khan, the principal backer of the now eliminated *Azzurra* syndicate, to learn that he was in direct, personal competition with a San Diego draper, he was – at least in Conner's mind. Earlier in the trials Conner said, "I have had a chance to compete here against the Aga Khan, against Michael Fay [the banker who heads the *New Zealand* syndicate] and the whole country of New Zealand, against the French nation, against the New York Yacht Club with all the effort and muscle they can bring to bear. I like the challenge."

Rumour has it that Conner sometimes makes 100 phone calls a day. Blackaller groans at that. "There are a hundred phone calls I can make a day to help my program," he says. "I can only force myself to make about 10. I just can't do it. I don't have that kind of discipline. That's one thing Dennis has, a remarkable amount of discipline. He must."

Blackaller is the most vocal of Conner's detractors. Part of Blackaller's Conner-baiting is gamesmanship born of a rivalry that dates back to 1967, when they first met in the Star Western Hemisphere championships. The other part is genuine antipathy. As Blackaller sees it, Conner has taken the fun out of the sport. "I don't like his style and I don't like him personally," says

Blackaller, who is as candid in public as Conner is guarded. "And I'd like to get him the hell out of sailing. I think he hurts it. I keep trying to get him in my own way, but it's hard. He's tough. And he knows I think he's tough. You've never heard me say that Dennis isn't a top sailor and a tough competitor. You've got to crawl over his dead body to win a race. That's always been true. But God, the way he does it is just awful."

No one, least of all Conner, can match Blackaller at dealing with the press. Blackaller's wit is quick and his *joie de vivre* is contagious. Conner is mistrustful of the press, and his responses to questions often seem devious. Experience has taught Conner that silence is his best defence against Blackaller.

"When Tom started criticizing Dennis [in Newport in 1983], Dennis probably didn't know how to react," says Malin Burnham, president of the *Stars & Stripes* syndicate. "As it kept coming and coming he finally decided and is now convinced that when Blackaller criticizes the most is when Blackaller is having trouble winning races. So Dennis just doesn't go back at him. What I'm saying is that Dennis has, with maturity, learned that many times it's better to keep his mouth shut, and I think he's respected for that." On occasion, however, and most unpredictably, Conner's frustration overcomes his caution, and he lashes out at an opponent he suspects of cheating or a reporter who asks a needling question. "If you're such an expert," he said to a New Zealand reporter who pressed him too hard one day, "why are you sitting out in the audience instead of sitting up here sailing a boat?"

For better or worse, the way Conner does a 12-metre campaign is the way it is done. This year, with the exception of *French Kiss*, every syndicate with a prayer of winning the Cup built at least two boats, some three, spent gruesome amounts of money, and devoted at least two years to the effort. The one-boat Cup campaign is now an anachronism.

"Sailors are quick to copy and improve," says Conner. "That's why you have to keep moving. They're following in your footsteps in the snow. If you stop for just a minute they'll be by."

That's what Conner learned in 1983. It wasn't that he didn't try, or work as hard and long as he ever had, or spend as much money, or sail as well. He did all those things. But in the area of research and design his organization was weak where the Australians were strong, and Conner was beaten. No one who watched his last press conference in Newport's dingy Armory on September 26, 1983, is likely to forget the sight: Conner alone and exposed under blinding TV lights, tears running down his tanned cheeks, an incongruously jaunty straw hat jammed squarely on his large head. At that point it was painfully clear that the burden Conner had carried through the long, bitter summer was too much for any one person, even Conner. The old joke – if the America's Cup were ever lost it would be replaced on its pedestal in the New York Yacht Club by the head of the skipper who lost it – wasn't so funny, after all.

"It's kind of ironic," says Conner now. "One year you do a fantastic job and win and you get 50 job-well-done letters. Then you lose and you get stacks of letters about what a nice job you did. I actually got more credit for losing than I did for winning. Now everybody writes, 'Dennis Conner, world's best sailor, world's foremost 12-metre helmsman.'"

Until now Conner's Cup campaigns have been dictatorships. He held all the strings, and he kept them short. After winning the Cup in 1980 he demanded and got a no-cut contract, a guarantee from the syndicate backers that he could not be dumped in mid-campaign should things go badly. Conner's debut at the helm of a 12-metre rose out of just such a situation. Bob Bavier, skipper of *Courageous* in 1974, was abruptly and rather cruelly replaced during the August trials by the veteran Hood and the relatively little-known Conner, who handled the starting manoeuvres.

This time around Conner has stepped back a bit. After *Australia II* copped the Cup with a winged keel that was a leap forward in 12-metre design, skippers such as Conner who were contemplating grabbing it back had to face the fact that high technology, very high, had hit the 12-metre game. Technologists, scientists, and aerospace experts were the key to the 1987 Cup, and the syndicates needed someone who could speak their language. Conner chose John Marshall.

Marshall, 44, had served as Conner's mainsail trimmer on *Liberty* in 1983. A biochemist by training, with a degree from Harvard, he did a stint as a research fellow at the Rockefeller Institute in New York and has a background in sailing and sailmaking. He is also president of Hinckley Yachts, of Southwest Harbor, Maine. For the *Stars & Stripes* syndicate Marshall's assignment was to coordinate the work of the scientists and naval architects.

"It goes against Dennis's nature to lose any element of direct control," Marshall said last month at the syndicate headquarters in Fremantle. "He's uncomfortable, particularly with technology and having technologists determine his fate. In this game technologists do make mistakes. There have been Olympic gold medallists out there [Marshall waves an arm in the general direction of the Indian Ocean] struggling to stay out of last place because their boats were hopeless. Dennis lived through that in '83, having a piece of equipment that was inferior and then being asked by the world to do a superhuman job. The last thing he wanted was to be back in that position, yet he had to decide to put himself in that position because there's no hope of winning if you don't have very, very strong technology."

Conner has to know people a long time before he trusts them, which is why there are many familiar faces from earlier campaigns around the *Stars & Stripes* compound. Closest to Conner is Tom Whidden, his tactician. Whidden, 39, has been sailing with Conner since 1979. A tactician is said to be the eyes and ears of the helmsman. He relays information about what is going on on the race course and what he thinks the helmsman should do about it. Ideally, the relationship between helmsman and tactician is based on total trust. The tactician says, "Tack," and the helmsman tacks. "In the old days," says Whidden, "I'd say 'Tack,' and Dennis would say, 'Well, why?' But that doesn't happen anymore. He used to pride himself that he was both tactician and skipper and that the tactician was just back there to pull the running backstay. He realizes that's not in the program's best interest anymore. That's part of the maturing of Dennis Conner on the race course. He's more disciplined. In Newport he would do things sometimes that weren't right just out of being impulsive."

Whidden can kid Conner where others can't, or don't. The day after the Cup was lost in 1983, the *Liberty* group was packing its belongings, in preparation for leaving Newport, when the phone rang. It was Ronald Reagan calling for Conner. Betsy Whidden, Tom's wife, who had answered the phone, relayed the message to Tom, who yelled out the window to Conner, "Hey, Dennis. The President's on the phone. He wants to tell you you screwed up."

"That was the best thing that came out of all that," says Whidden. "Dennis didn't laugh as hard as we all did, but he laughed. He thought it was funny. I think Dennis likes to be the centre of attention, not the cause of it, or however you say that. He likes to be on the front end of the joke, not the other end."

Conner is much better known in Australia than he is in the U.S., having been the engineer of Australia's Cup defeat in 1980 and an agent of the perceived perfidy of the New York Yacht Club in the winged keel controversy of 1983. He was also the star a year ago of a TV commercial on behalf of an Australian state lottery. While some Australians viewed the TV ad as inappropriate, most saw it as a generous and pleasantly self-effacing gesture. The ad began with Conner saying, "Remember me? I was the skipper who lost the America's Cup."

The Conner syndicate has worked hard on its image. Lesleigh Green, a Perth public relations woman who worked for Alan Bond in 1983, was hired to smooth its way with the press, and the citizens of Fremantle were invited to an open house at the syndicate headquarters before racing began. The effort was rewarded with goodwill, friendly headlines, and an editorial in a local paper that read, "From an enemy to be hated [Conner] has become already in just a few days someone to be admired."

Most effective of all, however, was an impulsive gesture of Conner's. On a September afternoon, soon after Conner's arrival in Fremantle, 12-year-old Tim Cook, who was hawking newspapers along the waterfront, spotted the *Stars & Stripes* skipper and asked for an autograph. Conner replied with an invitation for Cook to go sailing, written on the back of a paper beer coaster. A few days later Cook had his sail on *Stars & Stripes*, the syndicate had a headline to tack on its bulletin board (CONNER MAKES A DREAM COME TRUE FOR A NEWSBOY), and young Cook had this to say: "He's a generous bloke."

"Anything that's kid-oriented is Dennis's idea," says Judy, Conner's vivacious, red-haired wife. "It's something he does all the time. This is going to sound funny, but he does not like children. He doesn't play with them and things like that, but I think he wishes that somebody had taken more of an interest in him as a child and taken him sailing. So he offers those opportunities because that's where he thinks he missed out."

Conner grew up near the San Diego Yacht Club in a family that had neither interest in sailing nor the means to sail. Before Dennis was born, his father had a commercial fishing boat. "Albacore," Dennis said a few weeks ago. "A fairly small, 60-foot albacore boat. I think my grandfather owned part of it. It wasn't exactly meagre, but it wasn't a great living and I think, ultimately, my mother laid down the law and said, 'When are you going to get a regular job?' So he went to work for Convair during the war. He eventually worked up into an engineering-type position in estimating [production costs], even though he didn't have the background. Basically he worked there till he died. Actually today is his birthday. He died about three or four years ago. Maybe five years ago. Time flies."

Conner never wanted for food or clothes or a decent house or schooling, but he was alone a lot and he desperately needed to be good at something. Sailing became his vehicle. He learned it by hanging around the yacht club making a nuisance of himself.

"He was a pest, a pain in the ass," says Burnham, who was 15 years older, handsome, wealthy, and a very good sailor. "He was always searching out older people for advice – he was always underfoot, wanting information. Why do you do this, and why do you do that? On one of the San Diego-Acapulco races there were five of us aboard. Dennis was by far the youngest, and he was one of those kids who never wanted to cleat the sheet down. And this was overnight racing. He always wanted to change something. An inch here, half an inch there. For a long time we called him Sak, for Smart-Ass Kid."

Conner's heroes were San Diego's hotshot sailors, a world-class bunch that included Star champions Burnham and Lowell North. His mentor and father substitute, however, was Ashley Brown, whom Burnham describes as "a successful ocean racer . . . an old-time, seat-of-the-pants sailor who was always coming up with new ideas . . . a San Diego institution."

"Dennis was always going to Ash," says Burnham. "Every Monday after school he would end up at Ash's house waiting for him to come home from work so he could ask him about the weekend sailing, either Ash's races or Dennis's."

Although Conner became a junior member at the San Diego Yacht Club, he never had his own boat as most juniors did. An $800 Starlet was beyond his means. In fact Conner was 27 before he bought a half interest in his first boat, a 33-footer, for $1,700.

"I've always known how much I have in my checking account, if you know what I mean," Conner says. "For the first 35 years of my life I could have told you how much, within a couple of dollars, I had in my pocket. But I couldn't tell you now if I had $20 or $50."

Suddenly Conner stands up behind the desk of his cramped office in the *Stars & Stripes* Fremantle headquarters and begins emptying his pockets. Several bills and an American Express Gold Card tumble onto the desk. He counts the money, puts it back in his pocket and sits down again. "It seems to be about $200," he says. "Things have changed. For the better."

courtesy of *Sports Illustrated*
from the January 5, 1987, issue.
© 1987, Time Inc.

A Beauty's Second Launching

Duncan Brantley

"Ohmygod!" That's what people say when they see the boat for the first time. "I just sit there quietly, waiting for them," says the boat's owner. "Then, sure enough, they say it. Every single one of them."

The boat is *Endeavour*, one of 10 near legendary J boats built in the U.S. and Great Britain for the America's Cup in the 1930s. The owner is Elizabeth Meyer, a 37-year-old Baltimore heiress who spent five years and $10 million to restore *Endeavour* after finding her rusting away, a forgotten hulk, in the south of England.

The prime of *Endeavour*'s life was the America's Cup summer of 1934. Owned by Sir Thomas Sopwith, developer of the famous Sopwith Camel airplane of World War I, *Endeavour* was perhaps the most magnificent yacht ever sailed. Her midnight-blue hull measured 130 feet from tapered bow to tapered stern, her flat-topped "Park Avenue" boom – wide enough for two people to stroll arm in arm – was 65 feet long, and her towering mast rose nearly 17 storeys above the teak deck and supported 20,000 square feet of canvas. The deck was completely flush, with not even a lifeline to mar its silhouette or separate her 33-member racing crew from the drink. She also had that most elusive of qualities – speed.

In the summer of '34 everyone agreed that *Endeavour*, the English challenger, surely was faster than *Rainbow*, the U.S. defender of the Cup. Even Harold S. (Mike) Vanderbilt, *Rainbow*'s owner and skipper, said he had never seen anything like the way *Endeavour* could accelerate out of a tack. With just a bit of racing luck, *Endeavour* rather than *Australia II* might have been the first challenger to wrest the America's Cup from the grip of the New York Yacht Club. *Endeavour* easily won the first two races of the best-of-seven Cup series, but a tactical error cost her the third race. In the fourth race Sopwith, *Endeavour's* skipper, protested a dangerous manoeuvre that *Rainbow* had made while trying to pass. But because Sopwith failed to hoist his protest flag immediately after the incident, the race committee, adhering strictly to the rules, refused to hear *Endeavour's* protest. With a 2–2 tie in hand, *Rainbow* took advantage of a demoralized *Endeavour* crew to go on to win the series 4–2.

The sailing world's fascination with J boats began taking hold in the America's Cup trials of 1930 when the enormous yet graceful new sloops replaced the earlier schooners and cutters. Ten of the new boats were built quickly, six in the U.S. (*Rainbow*, *Ranger*, *Enterprise*, *Whirlwind*, *Yankee*, and *Weetamoe*) and four in Great Britain (*Endeavour*, *Endeavour II*, *Shamrock V* and *Velsheda*). Yet even in their heyday, the J's were as doomed as dinosaurs. Their cost, both in construction and upkeep, was ultimately prohibitive. The J's raced in the America's Cup only three times – in 1930, 1934, and 1937. Another Cup series was anticipated in 1940, but by then World War II was under way in Europe, and within another year all American J's had been scrapped for their bronze hull plating and lead keels. By 1958 only three J boats remained, all in varied states of disrepair – Sir Thomas Lipton's *Shamrock V*; *Velsheda*, which was named for the three daughters (Velma, Sheila, and Daphne) of British Woolworth's chairman, W.L. Stephenson; and *Endeavour*.

Impractical for either racing or cruising, *Endeavour* had passed from Sopwith to a series of owners, one of whom sold her for $22 to a man who rescued her from the muddy banks of the Medina River on England's Isle of Wight, only to leave her stranded until 1984 on a spit of land near Southampton.

By 1984 Elizabeth Meyer was known in sailing circles for being rich and eccentric. She had inherited from her family a healthy chunk of *The Washington Post*, and in the 1970s she made a fortune of her own, investing in waterfront land on Martha's Vineyard in Massachusetts. After graduating from Bennington College with a degree in English, Meyer, who had long been interested in sailing, began writing free-lance articles for nautical magazines. During that time she published a very funny one-shot parody of those magazines, titled *Yaahting*, which sold more than 40,000 copies. Perhaps most of all, she delighted in titillating the gossips in sailing enclaves such as Newport with her antics. For example, her friends once received Christmas cards bearing a photo of Meyer and her boyfriend at the time (Mr. Really Wrong she calls him now) naked on a hotel balcony in Costa Rica.

Those who know Meyer describe her variously as impatient, determined, witty, stubborn, wild, and fun. She has an opinion about everything, and her language, says America's Cup sailor Gary Jobson, is "as salty as anybody's I've ever sailed with."

In the early 1980s several events combined to change the course of Meyer's life. In 1981-82 her parents died of cancer within seven months; in 1984 she was found to have a benign brain tumour. Surgery was performed successfully that year and again last summer, but the operations left Meyer frustrated. "I can't remember numbers anymore now," she says with a grin. "I have to write them all down."

Numbers had suddenly become very important to Meyer, because in 1984 while she was in England researching an article on the history of the J class for *Nautical Quarterly*, she had seen what was left of *Endeavour*. By this time, mastless, keelless, and rusted, the boat sat in a wooden cradle next to an abandoned seaplane hangar on Calshot Spit, on England's south coast. "I grew up worshipping J's just like every other sailor did," Meyer says. "I felt sorry for her, and I felt somebody had to do something. At the same time, I got a sinking feeling because I knew it would be me."

Meyer bought *Endeavour* from the Englishman who had paid $22 for her, promising as part of the deal never to divulge the amount she gave him. Her next move was to find and talk to the original owner, Sopwith, who was 97 at the time and disinclined to listen to yet another dreamer talk about restoring *Endeavour*. Not until he had his banker check out her finances did he decide Meyer was worth an interview.

"You're a damn fool," Sopwith bellowed when the two finally faced each other at his home in Hampshire. "These boats were preposterous even in the '30s."

"Then you think I shouldn't do it?" said Meyer.

"I didn't say that," Sopwith said, and until his death in 1989, at 101, he contributed invaluable advice to the reconstruction project.

Returning to Calshot Spit, Meyer set up a makeshift boatyard, erecting a plastic shed over her broken-down prize and hiring six people to work on her full time. She herself oversaw the rebuilding of the steel hull and the new, 70-ton lead keel. But after a promising start, things went less smoothly. Because *Endeavour* was so big and, literally, one of a kind, most of her hardware had to be custom-made, which proved to be time-consuming as well as costly. The reconstruction fell far behind schedule, and the enormousness of Meyer's task began to dawn on her. "God knows why I'm doing this," she said at a particularly low point. "I'm so scared. Sometimes I wake up at 4 a.m., shaking."

Meyer's difficulties were compounded by British immigration officials who, she says, hassled her; by the local tax man, who dogged her footsteps; and by the county council, which, she says, tried to stick her with an exorbitant rent for her yard. In addition, an anonymous malefactor repeatedly cut the power to the yard. Even when, after 18 months of work, *Endeavour* was finally ready for relaunching, Meyer's old worries were replaced by new ones. "I kept thinking, The boat is going to go in the water and I'm going to sink to my knees with grief. She's going to be ugly and funny-looking and weird."

Then on August 10, 1986, before a crowd of 600 well-wishers, Meyer smashed a magnum of Louis Roederer champagne across *Endeavour*'s bow and the boat slipped gracefully into the English Channel. Meyer's relief was palpable. "O.K.," she said. "The boat looks great. Nobody's going to laugh at me for doing this. I realize the social insignificance of it, but I think in human terms it is significant. To me, it's like restoring the Statue of Liberty."

With *Endeavour* finally seaworthy but still an empty shell, Meyer had her towed to the Royal Huisman Shipyard in Vollenhove, Holland, reputedly the finest yacht yard in the world. In June 1987 *Endeavour* moved into Royal Huisman's biggest shed. There, joinery craftsmen slowly created, at a cost of approximately $3 million, an elegant Edwardian-style interior far different from that of the original.

Today *Endeavour* is as unconventional as her owner, an intriguing mix of historic preservation and modern maxi-boat technology. Below decks are five elegant staterooms and, in the main saloon, a marble fireplace surrounded by gleaming cherry cabinetry. On deck are the latest in coffee-grinder winches, as well as a 51-foot spinnaker pole made of carbon fibre. In another departure from tradition, Meyer rejected brass or bronze hardware, which requires constant polishing, in favour of nickel, platinum, and stainless steel.

"Elizabeth restored *Endeavour* in such a grand style that the boat is really a piece of art," says Jobson. "*Endeavour* is the finest yacht in the world today."

The reconstruction of *Endeavour* was completed in May 1989. What had taken five months and $165,000 to build in 1933 required five years and $10 million to rebuild 55 years later. Meyer blew a good part of her fortune, but she has no regrets. "I just wanted someone to restore a J, and the fact that it was me is less important than the fact that it's been done."

Meyer's reward came last summer when *Endeavour* made her Newport debut in a much heralded three-race series against *Shamrock V*. (The restoration of *Shamrock V*, which is now owned by Newport's Museum of Yachting, was aided by a $1 million gift from Meyer.) Twelve hundred boats turned out to watch the return of the J's. Ted Turner, the 1977 America's Cup winner, and Jobson were the skippers, and a spot in either crew was so highly coveted that not one of the 71 who were invited sent regrets. *Endeavour* won the series 3-0, but the magic of what Meyer and her money and her obsession had wrought went beyond winning a race and beyond even the gratification of seeing a beautiful object preserved.

"The only analogy I can make," said an *Endeavour* crewman, Jerry Kirby, "is if I was a baseball player and wanted to play in an All-Star Game, that I could bring back Babe Ruth and Satchel Paige and we could all get together and have a game. It's like that."

courtesy of *Sports Illustrated*
from the April 16, 1990, issue.
© 1990, The Time Inc. Magazine Company,
with thanks to Linda Verigan.

3

Coming About

When you keep getting headed, it's time to tack.
                                                First Rule of Sailing

When I left Europe to start my sail around the world, I had no generosity. I was a greedy bastard. All I could see in life was to have a boat, go to nice places and work as little as possible. During the voyage I began to change.
                                                Bernard Moitessier

I had no nation now but the imagination.
                                                Derek Walcott
                                                The Schooner Flight

Since tides, like the movements of sun, moon and stars, were phenomena that man could not influence, it was man's natural conclusion that they affected his life. Just as farmers regulated plowing and sowing by the phases of the moon, so sailors and fishermen believed that flood tide meant strength, and ebb tide, weakness. If an old salt lay at death's door, his family and friends watched the tide. If he survived an ebb he would improve with the flood, but he would always die on the ebb.
                                                Samuel Eliot Morison
                                                Spring Tides

COUSTEAU: THE POET

RICHARD MUNSON

Cousteau's silhouette is forceful and lean. His head has been compared to that of an ancient stone sculpture: half man, half bird, mythic and eternal.

Cousteau's face actually shelters two distinct personalities. The gaunt cheeks, hooked nose, and large-lidded eyes present a solemn, almost sad countenance. But when the Captain smiles, his cheeks crinkle, and his eyes roll upward in mischievous wonder.

Cousteau's ideas are equally diverse, spanning the gulf between the practical and the visionary. He invented the useful aqualung, but he writes surrealistic poetry. He is a successful executive, but he believes business is inconsequential compared with the life of a pelican or a dolphin. Over a meal his conversation ranges from French wine to whale communications to nuclear war to the phenomenon of the sun rising and setting each day.

Cousteau claims his desire to "have fun" has integrated his life's activities. "I was playing when I invented the aqualung," he declares. "I'm still playing. I think play is the most serious thing in the world. When I see someone who becomes serious and announces his work as a great discovery, I burst into laughter."

The Captain displays his playful intellect frequently, and each of his colleagues seems to have a favourite tale. Ghostwriter James Dugan remembered a particularly tense planning session for an early submarine device. After listening passively to the discussion for several minutes, the Captain announced: "Well, I think it will work and perhaps bring valuable information, but the important question is, 'Will it be fun?'"

Cousteau has tried to realize as many of his own impulses as possible. In his eyes the perfect life is for a man to be "pushed by

181

his instincts, needs, pleasures, drives, and to play without measuring the consequences."

In his more practical and self-centred moments, however, the Captain admits that this "ideal" life-style is not for everyone. He argues that if too many individuals practised such free-wheeling ways, the planet's beauty and ecological diversity would vanish. Yet he maintains that special and creative men – like him – shouldn't be restrained by governments or rules.

Much of the Captain's career, in fact, has been spent searching for freedom. Goggles delivered the young naval officer to the vast freshness of the undersea world. The aqualung liberated him from reliance upon surface assistants. And the diving saucer enabled him to descend to the farthest reaches of the ocean.

Diving also offered Cousteau a supernatural escape. "From birth," he explains, "man carries the weight of gravity on his shoulders. He is bolted to earth. But man has only to sink beneath the surface and he is free. Buoyed by water, he can fly in any direction – up, down, sideways. Underwater, man becomes an archangel."

To describe his quest for total freedom, Cousteau outlined what he feels are the world's three basic philosophies. First is the philosophy of the stones, which is based on stopping time. In this approach, which the Captain claimed never to have accepted for himself, you "build estates and acquire things in the hope that it will last and make you immortal."

The second philosophy, one which Cousteau abandoned in the early 1970s while he filmed the ABC television series, is of the lovely but short-lived rose. "You take full advantage of the instant," he said, "trying to make each instant beautiful and fruitful. You are ornamenting yourself to produce and to die, but the trouble with this approach is that it's also very vain."

The third and the Captain's ultimate state is of the wind. "You just blow wherever you want; it doesn't matter. You don't need ornamentation; you just need the current of air. You are organized nothingness. That's what we are, carefully organized nothingness."

Cousteau, however, does differentiate between positive and

negative nothingness. "I prefer to blow in palm trees or a field of flowers than in cement," he admitted. "I prefer to do things that give pleasure."

Cousteau ranks Bertrand Russell as his idol, someone he describes as a complete man who embodied the philosophy of the wind. "Russell's work for me," he says, "is the fantastic combination of a great scientist, a good writer, a human character who loved women, life, and who had the courage to go to prison for his ideas." The Nobel prize winner, who died in 1970, was jailed while campaigning for nuclear disarmament. He also lost teaching positions because of his outspoken agnosticism and his alleged advocacy and practice of sexual promiscuity.

Russell's religious arguments greatly influenced Cousteau. "The whole conception of God is a conception derived from the ancient Oriental despotisms," argued the philosopher. "It is a conception quite unworthy of free man." The Captain, in response to questions, expresses a similar distaste for religious worship, calling it debasing rather than ennobling.

Russell also taught Cousteau to avoid sentimentalizing history and to live for the moment. "A good world needs knowledge, kindliness, and courage," declared Russell. "It does not need a regretful hankering after the past or a fettering of the free intelligence by the words uttered long ago by ignorant men."

Most important, the British scholar, although primarily noted for his work in mathematical logic, convinced Cousteau that logic would not satisfy his thirst for truth, that the inspiration guiding poets brings them nearer to reality than anyone else. The Captain has declared:

When I reason, when people reason, they come most of the time to logical absurdities. I find poets closer to the truth than mathematicians or politicians. They have visions that are not only fantasy. They have visions that are, for some reason they cannot explain, an inspiration that guides them and brings them by the hand, or by the pen, closer to the truth than anybody else in life. It's the light. It's the star we should be guided by. Poetry, and poetry under all its forms. Poetry in anything you are doing. The only remedies to the logical absurdities are utopias.

Cousteau's pragmatic side, however, argues that these visions must be "reasonable utopias." He has spent much of his life proposing ways to adjust the human community so that men and women don't harm others or future generations. "I think the only usefulness of people today," he said in the mid-1980s, "is to make sure they are able to pass along to the future generations an inheritance that is as good as what we've got, and maybe better."

Critics scoff at some of Cousteau's specific proposals. At his seventy-fifth birthday party, for instance, the Captain declared that he "would devote all of his remaining efforts" to transferring 1 percent of the world's military budget to a vast exchange of children. "Imagine a world where all seventh-graders would have to spend a year on the other side of the fence," he demanded. "It would not only be a great opening for their minds, but it would be a formidable barrier against war." One sceptical politician chuckled and said no one would seriously consider such a plan.

Many of Cousteau's television fans would be startled by his private thoughts on subjects such as marriage, which he defines as an archaic device that "people use to avoid facing the fact that we are all solitary and perishable." And love, he maintains, is simply "a drug to blur the truth that a couple is not a couple but a juxtaposition of two alone individuals."

Fans also would not recognize the dark thoughts that frequently appear in Cousteau's personal log. "At times," he recently wrote, "I find myself flirting with the morbid idea of lassitude. The constant breakdowns, repairs, delays, empty me of resolve. And in the bilges of my mind, I deeply resent anybody and anything which interrupts our dream of action, of protecting the seas and water life. Even the necessity of dry-docking for repairs becomes adversity."

Even though Cousteau relishes his star status, he aggressively protects his privacy. His personal life, he declares firmly, "is no one's business but my own." When reporters press him for details, he grows testy: "I don't want you to know if I drink coffee or tea or have adventures with my secretary. . . . Out! This is my life. It's my privacy. Hands off!"

The Captain particularly avoids questions about his marriage. For almost four decades, he and Simone have spent little time together, largely because she's remained aboard *Calypso* while he travelled around the globe. On the road Cousteau is an acknowledged flirt who likes to chat up and charm young women, and they seem to be drawn to the glib celebrity. He's been known to arrive at a new location and immediately ask, "Are there beautiful women here?" Some society staffers suggest Cousteau maintains a typical Frenchman's appreciation of the opposite sex.

In an age when tabloids report the personal habits of celebrities, Cousteau's revealed idiosyncrasies are not that revealing. He is a connoisseur of wines, his favourite being the French Côtes du Rhone; he enjoys tea rather than coffee; he avoids dairy products and animal fats, especially in hamburgers; he occasionally smokes small, foul-smelling cigars; his breakfast usually consists of dry toast with orange marmalade; he claims never to read novels, finding fiction to be a writer's egotistical display; he gets his rest from ten-minute catnaps in taxis and on planes; he exercises each morning, often completing a hundred push-ups; he spends a lot of time flying but never feels safe in airplanes; he hates mountains, finding them "oppressive things"; his close friends call him "Pasha" (the Old Man).

What is clear is that millions idolize Cousteau, not merely because he is a charming celebrity but because he embodies that yearning we have to live by our impulses. The Captain projects a sense of eternal youth.

Friends who have known Cousteau for many years say he possesses a special "control" over nature. The weather clears on his command. Fish perform. The coral appears to part so *Calypso* can pass through.

Few associates attribute Cousteau's achievements to super-natural forces, and none deny the Captain's many setbacks when he films in the wild. Still, they maintain that Cousteau has more luck – or what they describe as magic – than any other person they know. Shooting nature scenes requires a tremen-dous amount of patience. The sea must be clear and calm. Enough light must be available to expose film adequately. The animals must accept the presence of divers and execute their required scenes. Even Cousteau admits that the process is an emotional roller-coaster of expectation and frustration: "We can spend three months waiting on *Calypso*, unable to do any work, and then suddenly the weather turns perfect, the animals are there, and the film can be picked up in 24 hours."

Still, Cousteau's presence often seems to minimize the frus-tration. According to Jan Cousteau, Philippe's widow, "He always brought good weather. It may have stormed for days, the boys were playing bridge, Monopoly, Scrabble, getting restless. Then the Captain came and the sun shone. When he left, the bad weather often returned."

Cousteau senses this magical quality, and he doesn't mind showing off to strangers. Sara Davidson, writing for *The New York Times Magazine* in 1972, recalled her first meeting with Cousteau when he invited her for a swim during a thunder-storm. "It is dark as night and I am shaking with cold," she remembered. The Captain looked up at the black sky and announced that the sun would shine soon. Davidson chuckled at the absurd prophecy. "There is no one in sight," she wrote, "no sound but the rain and the tinkling of metal on sailboats. A minute later, the water is lit up as if by a klieg light."

Luis Marden, a National Geographic correspondent who often accompanied *Calypso*'s early expeditions, also witnessed Cousteau's remarkable abilities. Near Assumption Island in the Indian Ocean, Marden had spent days underwater trying to photograph the blast from a miniature volcano, presumably caused by the spout of a hidden animal. He lay on his stomach for endless hours, his camera trained on an individual cone, only to have nearby volcanoes explode. Whichever one he selected remained dormant. Cousteau finally dived to see what was keeping the cameraman busy and frustrated. The Captain examined the scene for a moment, pointed his forefinger at a nearby sand cone, and flipped his thumb like a trigger. The pyramid erupted. Back on board, Cousteau credited his feat to "fantastic luck," but Marden claimed more profound powers were at work.

No doubt much of Cousteau's "control" over nature simply results from his having carefully observed the sea and its creatures for so many years. He has acquired a sense of the animals' habits, and like other experienced sailors, he has learned to "read" ocean waves and currents. Still, *Calypso*'s crew maintains that the Captain's talents are unique. Acknowledging his biased perspective, Philippe once noted, "I have known highly skilled seamen who make use of echo-sounding equipment as they would a precise and impersonal instrument, but I feel sure that, to my father, it is something much more than this. He had guided us precisely to the spot we were searching for, with as much sureness as if he were actually walking on the sea floor, with no hesitation whatever, using the ship and the elements themselves as a virtuoso might use his favourite instrument."

Cousteau's communion with the sea has evolved. He recalls that at the age of three or four "water fascinated me – first floating ships, then me floating and stones not floating. The touch of water fascinated me all the time, but the real interest in the ocean came when I was already in the navy. I turned to the navy as a career, in the beginning, because of my love for water and because of my desire to travel and see the world."

At age twenty-six, after suffering the automobile accident that almost paralyzed his arms, the young officer turned to swimming for recuperation. The physical exercise, however, became a spiritual journey when he placed his goggled eyes beneath the sea's surface. Underwater his body became weightless, free of earth's gravity. He could float with liberty throughout what he described as the "embracing medium."

"The spirituality of man cannot be completely separated from the physical," Cousteau wrote after one of his early dives. "But you have made a big step toward escape simply by lowering yourself under water."

Cousteau's mystical experience, of course, blended with the sheer adventure of opening up a new world – the undersea world – to man. He remained for many years on the cutting edge of that exploration, with the experiments and the revelations providing an intoxicating thrill. Much of Cousteau's early public appeal, in fact, resulted from his obviously joyous enthusiasm for the experience of discovery.

By the early 1960s Cousteau sought practical results from his otherworldly adventures. "Undersea exploration is not an end in itself," he declared. "The privilege of our era, to enter this great unknown medium, must produce greater knowledge of the oceans and lead to assessment and exploitation of their natural resources."

The leader of the Conshelf expeditions imagined man colonizing the ocean floor, tapping its resources to lengthen life and memory, to retard aging, and to cure illnesses. "Organic anaesthetics can be extracted from marine animals, eliminating the need to introduce synthetic chemicals into our bodies," he predicted. "Cephalotoxin is a poison found in the saliva of the octopus that hinders the coagulation of the blood. Elecosin is also found in the octopus's saliva; it may one day be used to control high blood pressure."

Some twenty years later Cousteau joined environmentalists in condemning the exploitative destruction of the seas. He still imagined raising fish for food, mining minerals from the sea floor, and extracting energy from the ocean's waves, but he no longer promoted permanent colonization. The Captain claimed that humans remain aliens underwater and the undersea environment "is not ours."

Cousteau's environmental perspective may have evolved over the years, but his dedication to self-promotion has remained

constant. Since the age of thirteen, he has placed himself in front
of his own cameras and recorded his actions and thoughts in
scores of books. Still, he exhibits a charming humility before
strangers. A young reporter once exclaimed that the Captain
had become a true international legend. Cousteau's response
was short and quick: "Bull!"

"If you begin to believe in yourself," Cousteau continued,
"you're sentenced to become a joke. We're nothing, none of us."

Even in reflective moments, Cousteau argues that introver-
sion and egomania result only in hollow pleasures. "We enrich
our own souls when we reach out to enrich the souls of others,
to gather and appreciate and absorb not the manufactured
wealth of society but the natural wealth of the universe," he
wrote in the society's newsletter. He submits that "self-
extension" is the only route to happiness and that it can be
achieved through creation (such as writing and filmmaking),
knowledge (such as science and expeditions), and love.

Cousteau is no isolated individualist; he relishes his relations
with colleagues and friends, and he operates the *Calypso* and the
expeditions as team efforts. Although he clearly directs activities and enjoys his own suite aboard the ship, he shares meals,
thoughts, and honours with his crew.

"The history of the *Calypso* is important to me for its scientific importance and its technological value," the Captain
declares, "but above all it is a story of human adventure. I can
more easily recall the person with whom I did something than
remember what I did."

Regardless of the gruelling work, the long hours, the lack of
family life, and the dangers, Cousteau has had no trouble attract-
ing divers, sailors, engineers, and scientists to the *Calypso*.
Many, as the Captain admits, were "sensitive men, men who
have not found happiness or peace in leading an ordinary life."
Some sought adventure and exploration; others pursued solitude and meditation.

The crew came from diverse backgrounds. Mechanical engineer Armand Davso was a street cleaner in Marseilles when he
first saw Cousteau's early films. Albert Falco, who has been at

Cousteau's side for thirty-five years, was a champion spear
fisherman, known for having killed fish with everything from
sewing needles to curtain rods. André Laban, an early diver, was
trained as an engineer and a chemist. Cameraman Louis Preze-
lin performed rescue dives for the French Air Force, while
sound engineer Guy Jouas served in the French merchant
marine.

Participants have been selected for their ability to fit in with
the rest of the crew. They must withstand pressures imposed by
nature, mechanical breakdowns, and, according to the Captain,
the "stress from too much to do, too far to go, too little time."
For three-month stretches, they often work seven days a week
and twelve to sixteen hours each day. "We lose about one person
a year," Cousteau says, "but people who are accepted and cher-
ished by their friends will stay, maybe 20 or 25 years. It's like a
transplant, an organ transplant. It is rejected or accepted. That's
the way we make our team."

Camaraderie dominates everyday life aboard *Calypso* and
Alcyone, and mischief seems to be its most obvious expression.
Guy Jouas, the sound and electronics engineer who has been
with Cousteau for more than two decades, is the team's most
noted prankster. He once tied all the crew members' belt loops
together; when he issued the call for all hands, his colleagues
jumped up from the dinner table together and abruptly fell into
a heap. During the Canadian expedition Jouas glued Jean-
Michel's cold-weather boots to the deck, enabling the crew to
enjoy a hearty laugh as the young Cousteau rose from his chair
and sprawled forward headfirst. For Jean-Michel's forty-ninth
birthday, Jouas produced a cake in the shape of a humpback
whale; the design included a tube, filled with confectioners'
sugar, that ran from the whale's blowhole to a foot pump on the
floor; when Jean-Michel leaned over to examine his present,
Jouas delivered a full charge of white powder into the birthday
boy's face.

The Captain has often shared credit willingly with his companions. He clearly conceptualized and developed *The Silent
World*, but according to Louis Malle, a successful filmmaker

today, "Cousteau was graceful enough to give me credit as co-producer of the film. I was only 23, and it gave me a wonderful start on my career. I have kept a passion for documentaries from my days with Cousteau and *Calypso*. I cannot forget that I was lucky enough to work with Cousteau. I learned a lot from him. Those years are really my golden years of filmmaking."

Armand Davso, the first engineer aboard *Calypso*, proudly remembers when a visitor asked Cousteau how he produced such beautiful films. "That's easy," replied the Captain, "it's because Armand made me the best cameras in the world."

Despite the apparent humility, Cousteau views himself as special, apart from the common man, and "chosen." He declares, "When one person, for whatever reason, has a chance to lead an exceptional life, he has no right to keep it to himself."

The Captain and his family, in fact, believe they have a unique mission to witness and report of the wonders within and the challenges to the planet's water system. At times the Cousteaus have assumed this task as if it were a noble burden. Philippe once wrote:

> We were akin to those knights-errant who travelled across the world and returned to tell the king the news of the Holy Land or of Mauritania. We were different in the sense that we would bring the story of our adventures not to a solitary king, but to millions of people. When one thinks of it, however, the task becomes enormous. We could imagine each of our future viewers, and knew he would be hoping that we brought back accounts of things that were beautiful, true, and intellectually rewarding. Each of them was investing some degree of confidence in us, and this implied a heavy responsibility. We could no more deceive this confidence, this patience, this need for information on the marvels of the deep than we could have abandoned a blind man we might have been guiding across a busy street.

Cousteau's perspective may be filled with vanity, but he says straightforwardly, "I'm not interested in achievements. I'm interested in having an interesting life myself and sharing it with the public on television."

Still, as the Captain approaches his eightieth birthday, he is being showered with awards for his lifetime contributions to science, television, and film. Both the United States and France delivered their highest honours to Cousteau during his seventy-fifth year. France awarded him la Grand Croix dans l'Ordre National du Merite (the Grand Cross of the National Order of Merit), and President Reagan bestowed the Presidential Medal of Freedom at a White House ceremony.

In November 1987 Cousteau was inducted into the Television Academy's Hall of Fame along with Johnny Carson, Jim Henson, Bob Hope, Eric Sevareid, and the late Ernie Kovacs; his citation reads, "With his underwater explorations, he unlocked the ocean's colourful treasures from the depths of obscurity to the eyes of the world above sea level." Later that same month he travelled to New York to receive the Founders Award from the International Council of the National Academy of Television Arts and Sciences; the prize recognized the Captain's presentation of television programs to more than 115 countries and at least 250 million homes worldwide. Shortly thereafter he was welcomed into the Television Movie Awards Hall of Fame.

In 1988 Cousteau joined a select group with Sir Edmund Hillary and Jane Goodall to receive the National Geographic Society's Centennial Awards for "special contributions to mankind throughout the years." His name also was placed on the United Nations Environment Programme's "Global 500 Roll of Honour for Environmental Achievement." And he was recently elected to L'Académie Française, the elite guardians of French culture and literature.

Like few others, Cousteau has maintained his celebrity status for decades. In 1953 *The Silent World* became an international best seller. In 1969, a year after *The Undersea World* series began, opinion surveys identified the Captain as one of television's most popular personalities. In 1985 a *Good Housekeeping* magazine poll found Jacques Cousteau to be one of the world's ten most admired men. In 1989 Cousteau claimed that each of his documentaries reaches half a billion people – one tenth of the planet's population.

Even *Calypso* has become an international symbol that evokes delight and enchantment. While cruising up the Mississippi River, it was greeted by thousands of well-wishers lining the riverbank, sometimes in the pouring rain. The admirers waved until the small ship passed out of sight, expressing thanks for the years Cousteau had transported them out of their living rooms into worlds they would never have seen or could barely have imagined.

Captain Cousteau is one of the rare Renaissance men of the twentieth century. In addition to his noted filming, writing, and engineering achievements, he plays the piano, paints, composes poetry, and comments on international affairs. He speaks English and German fluently, understands Spanish, and reads Russian.

Cousteau has met and entertained the world's political and cultural leaders. "I'm pretty good with presidents," he claims. He has also maintained lengthy correspondence on aesthetics with various artists. Pablo Picasso, for instance, accepted the Captain's gift of black coral, revered in many Middle Eastern cultures. "After his death I met his wife," Cousteau remembers, "who told me Picasso had the coral in his hand when he died. He liked to touch it, to feel its smoothness with his fingers. That was moving for me."

Both a pragmatist and a dreamer, Cousteau has been able to connect seemingly unrelated facts and to communicate his concepts clearly to a wide audience. "While the world looks at life through a microscope," observes Jean-Michel, "my father looks at it through a macroscope."

The Captain has consistently sought intellectual stimulation. He once described his explorations of the undersea world as "inspiriting." He didn't mean spiritual or religious, "but a life full of daily inspiration like that to which man has risen as a result of creative developments in his past – the Greek concept of ethos, the High Renaissance, the 18th-century revolutions."

Although best known for his films and television broadcasts, Cousteau gained significant stimulation from writing scores of books. Most publications reported on his adventures or offered information about various undersea animals. Several – including *The Silent World* and *The Living Sea* (1963) – enjoyed critical and popular acclaim. In recent years, society staff writers – primarily Mose Richards in New York and Yves Paccalet in Paris – have converted the Captain's shiplogs into manuscripts on his odysseys; Cousteau simply polishes the drafts, using his red pen to rewrite sentences.

On three occasions, the Captain has tried to present his comprehensive vision of the world. Not surprisingly, the multifaceted author developed complex amalgams of ideas and data.

In the late 1970s Cousteau convinced Doubleday & Company, a large U.S. publishing firm, to advance approximately two hundred thousand dollars for the development of *The Cousteau Almanac*, billed as "an inventory of life on our water planet." The Captain and Philippe jointly conceived the book as an extension of the Involvement Days at which they had arranged diverse displays on the environment. The book, according to original plans, "would be an almanac – lively and witty, but a solid reference as well. It would be a browsing book, filled with maps, lists, lore, cartoons. It would carry short articles and statistics about virtually every major environmental issue in the world." The book, in essence, was to convey the interconnectedness of all the planet's living systems.

After developing a detailed outline, the Captain turned the project's management over to Mose Richards, a talented editor who hired a team of twenty-five writers and researchers and solicited articles from approximately sixty independent authors. Cousteau visited the society's New York City office every few months to check on the book's progress and to offer his latest insights and suggestions (some of which, such as the proposed chapter on lovemaking, were ignored by the staff).

The staff team spent about eighteen months trying to reflect the breadth of Cousteau's interests.

The final document "is about the entire world," said Richards. "It is a planetary inventory of living, an attempt to help people find their place in the great global organism of which we are part, in its flows and circles, and in the sweeping developments that are changing it rapidly in our age." The 838-page book, completed after Philippe's death, included some of the features of a regular almanac, such as statistics on population, incomes, and per capita energy consumption. But it also presented short profiles of futuristic bicycles, disappearing species, and energy-efficient buildings. Moreover, it encouraged citizen action by profiling "wavemakers" and by suggesting tactics for organizing political campaigns.

"It's a monument of data on uncorrelated things," boasted the Captain. The heavy and complex book was popular in France, but it sold only forty thousand copies in the United States, far below Doubleday's original estimates.

In the mid-1980s Cousteau decided to create another massive compilation of thoughts, this one to be titled *The Peace Almanac*. "It will not be what people think," he explained. "It's going to discuss scientifically the importance and role of violence in evolution and the selection of species."

When the Captain proclaimed his idea for the book, "everybody just rolled their eyes," said Richard Murphy, the society's staff scientist. "Then he gave an outline to me, and here we are, doing it! The guy is an unbelievable mover."

Cousteau turned the project over to Elisabeth Barbier, an editor working out of the Fondation Cousteau offices in Paris. Progress was slow, largely because the Captain managed to speak with Barbier only three times over a two-year period. The Cousteaus also couldn't agree on a definition of peace. The Captain and the French-based editors wanted to focus on North-South issues, while Jean-Michel and the U.S. staff expressed more interest in East-West relations. While Cousteau continues to explore peace issues, his son cancelled the book project in summer 1988, claiming he could not locate a commercial outlet.

Cousteau's third writing project, being done in concert with Susan Schiefelbein, a former editor for *Saturday Review* and a longtime Cousteau ghostwriter, will be the Captain's "book of ideas." It's been in the works for almost a decade, and Cousteau still occasionally writes notes to Schiefelbein about the manuscript, but he isn't sure it will ever be finished.

The proposed treatise will present Cousteau's views on the future, illustrating the wandering insights of his creative and unorthodox mind. According to Schiefelbein, it will be "a conversation about life, an application of what he's seen to social issues."

Speaking about a future scenario that might be included in the publication, Cousteau said, "After all the dangers of the Bomb and starvation in the Third World have come to pass, finally, by gene manipulation, we achieve the eternal. People don't age. They die only by accident. Then what should they do? Recreate evolution from the beginning! They create a super zoo with every possible mutation as part of a favourable environment, and we get back to where we are now! Finally, they communicate with other civilizations that are developing, and they all end up eternal. Then they decide not to fight anymore – no more star wars. There's a big meeting, and it's like Olympus because they're gods – and you're back to the original Greek concept of the gods on Olympus ruling the world! So that's how I see the future of the universe."

from *Cousteau: The Captain and His World*,
William Morrow and Co., New York, 1989,
by permission of the author.

How to Prepare for an Ocean Voyage

Robert Gould

Preparation for an ocean voyage is a demanding science that requires careful thought and planning. The intention here is to offer a guide to such preparation, and to clarify the pitfalls and dangers that should be of concern. A long-distance ocean voyage is as different from coastal sailing as a trip to outer space is from a flight to a nearby city. It is more like scaling Mount Everest than taking a hike into town.

The ocean is unpredictable. It's possible to sail to Bermuda in light to moderate winds with clear blue skies and fluffy, fair-weather clouds. With a week of light weather conditions prior to sailing, the seas might well be down. There may be no distant storms to send endless reaches of twelve-foot rollers to mar the serenity of the voyage. My experience, however, and that of countless other sailors, is that the sea is often harsh and cold, weather conditions are changeable and can be frighteningly violent, and the longer you are at sea, the greater your chance of getting clobbered.

In considering the type of boat for an ocean trip one should look for stability. A shallow draft, beamy vessel with a high centre of gravity will, if turned turtle, stay there. It may be more stable in the upside-down position with its mast in the water than it is right-side-up. Don't go to sea in such a boat. You want solid, stiff construction. Whether a boat is of light, medium, or heavy displacement, quality of construction and stiffness of the hull and deck are of vital concern. Have the boat surveyed and describe your plans for her to the surveyor. He will be able to advise you on how to prepare her for sea so your risks are minimized.

What is your boat like in moderate conditions with winds

blowing twenty to thirty knots? Does she sail on her ear? You will be very uncomfortable spending a week or more at a forty-degree angle of heel. Much better to find a boat that is stiff enough in those conditions to sail at twenty degrees. What is her displacement? Light displacement boats will usually have faster passages, but will have an increased risk of hull damage in extreme conditions or upon colliding with a solid object at sea (barrel, container, log, boat, rock, or whale). The spars on a light displacement boat have a greater incidence of failure, as they are usually designed to cut windage and weight. A fast passage may mean five days at sea rather than eight, but a lot can happen in five days on the ocean.

Anything that can prevent the need to go on deck in a blow is of value. Roller-furling sails of all types should be considered for the main as well as the foresails. A running forestay can be kept at the shrouds when not in use and set on a quick release lever. This will allow you to set a working or storm jib without having to drop the big roller-furling genoa. Alternatively, a staysail stay can permit you to run up working or storm sails and may even be set on roller-furling.

A storm trysail of adequate size, perhaps twenty to twenty-five percent of the size of your mainsail, should be permanently set in a bag at the foot of the mast, with its slides in their own sail track to one side of the main track. This allows a quick hoist in rough conditions and will let you douse the main and tie down a wildly swinging boom while you sheet the storm try-sail to a heavy block on your stern.

This points up a little-known fact. Many boats do not heave to well under the traditional backed jib and trimmed, reefed mainsail. They will actually fall off the wind and lie beam on to the seas. These same boats will lie nicely, head up to the wind, with a storm trysail or triple-reefed main sheeted in tightly and the helm brought over hard to weather. The trysail isn't big enough to drive the bow through the eye of the wind but holds the head up to the gale nicely. If you think your boat won't heave to, try this little trick. Even with a boat that will heave to with a backed storm jib, just using the trysail is a safer and more reliable way of handling storm conditions and can be carried in worse weather. Backing your jib and sheeting in the main is okay in a smoke southwester in Buzzard's Bay when you want to stop for lunch, but not for a storm at sea.

Finally, you do not want a massive cockpit that can be easily swamped. This will drag the stern down and prevent her from lifting to the seas. The cockpit should be self-bailing and the drains should be large enough to drain her in two or three minutes. You must be able to secure cockpit lockers, and they should have adequate rubber gaskets to prevent the ingress of water at extreme angles of heel. A raised bridge deck to protect the cabin from a flooded cockpit, and sturdy companionway slides that can be fixed in place with a throughbolt, shock cord, or other such means, should be considered.

Personal safety equipment should include safety harnesses with extra-strong metal fasteners and webbing for each member of the crew. Have them aboard and please, please use them! Personal strobes and man-overboard poles and drills are all well and good, but are meant to correct a serious mistake. The best treatment is prevention. Such mistakes must never happen. It is extremely difficult to manoeuvre a vessel in rough conditions and pluck someone from the water. Jacklines should be strung from the rear stay to the mast and from the mast to the bow. All crew should clip on before they leave the safety of the cabin and should stay attached until they go below again. Having the jacklines in the centre of the boat allows crew to reach the line from the safety of the companionway ladder, and eliminates the need to unclip from one line and reattach to another simply to move from one side of the cockpit to the other.

The slight inconvenience of having to use a harness is far outweighed by the security of knowing that you or your crew will not disappear at sea. You may also want to consider double lifelines with stanchions through-bolted to the hull, and a safety net if there will be children aboard. Do not allow your crew to go to the rail except in absolutely calm conditions. Many a body has been recovered at sea with his fly undone. In bad weather and at night, when a trip to the head is not easily accomplished, have the crew use a plastic bottle with a secure cap. Have women use a plastic bedpan, obtainable from many pharmacies. Privacy can be assured with a modicum of consideration for your crew's feelings.

As for the boat's interior, one should strive to prevent the crew from being struck by flying objects, or themselves becoming airborne. To ensure this, each crew member should have his own lee cloth at least sixty inches wide attached to his bunk. Nylon netting is often more comfortable than stiffer cloth and may be cooler. When clipped to the cabin wall above the berth, a lee cloth will hold one in like a cocoon. All drawers should be positively secured, either with ties or latches, so that the contents don't fly about the boat in a knockdown. You'll want adequate handholds, and rounded corners on all furniture help prevent bruises or more serious injury. Radios, sextants, books, refrigerator tops, and kettles on the stove can all be potentially lethal, so find a secure place for everything and secure everything in its place.

Batteries should be in permanently positioned boxes with tops that are secured so they can't come out even if you turn turtle. Ventilators should have screw-on covers for the ultimate storm. Anchors *must* be tied down or they won't stay on your bowsprit. I would recommend that every seagoing boat invest in three types of pumps: one or preferably two manual high-output bilge pumps, an electric bilge pump with a strainer, and an emergency, engine-driven, very-high-output pump such as that produced by Jabsco for potential disasters. A bilge-water alarm and a gas detector are also useful. If you plan to go to high latitudes, consider a diesel furnace.

Other valuable items that you may want aboard can run the gamut: life raft, emergency supply canister, masthead tricolour light, radar reflector, and assorted communications equipment such as single side band or ham radio, VHF radio, emergency position-indicating radio beacon (EPIRB). Coast-Guard-required safety equipment includes life preservers, flares, horn, bell, and fire extinguishers. Various sizes of tapered wooden plugs, underwater epoxy, spare parts, and tools should also be carried.

Radar is a luxury, but in fog can become a necessity. It's either that or worry a lot. The newest units are modest in cost, within the reach of many sailors today. Radar is also a great boon to local piloting and navigation. Radomes (radar emitting beacons visible on the boat's radar) in the tide-ripped waters between the Isle of Wight and the Brittany coast of France kept us on course in heavy fog when little else would.

All ports and hatches should be inspected for strength and security before you put to sea. If you have any doubts, build storm shutters out of Lexan and use them. Make sure that you have access to the stuffing gland of your propeller shaft so that it can be tightened if it develops a leak. Put a hose clamp both on your propeller shaft and on the rudder post; if either decides to part company with the boat, the clamp won't allow them to fit out the through-hull and will prevent a disastrous flood.

At least three anchors should be carried. Five would not be too many. Two CQRs and a yachtsman or Herreshoff anchor are of the most value. One of your anchors should have 200 feet of chain and a windlass to work it. The other may be equipped with 12 feet of chain and 250 feet of line. The CQR holds well in sand and mud and has more holding power than the Danforth in borderline conditions. The yachtsman will hold on coral, rock, or kelp. I have designed a fitting for the bow pulpit that permits this anchor to be kept on deck ready for use at all times. The Bruce anchor holds well in mud and sand but does not dig in well in hard-packed sand or kelp. I do not recommend it, as it has no advantages over the CQR and does have several limitations.

Check all your seacocks for ease of use and lack of corrosion. Have double hose clamps on all hoses leading to the seacocks. Ground your mast to the keel with #0 – #2 cable as a protection against lightning damage. Get all the charts you will need for both the crossing and any ports you might need to visit on the way in case of an emergency.

For long-distance voyagers, a SatNav is a valuable, mod-
estly priced piece of equipment and has great accuracy. For the
long-distance voyager who leaves the safety net of coastal
Loran C chains, there is no better method of fixing your
position. Best of all, SatNav is there every day and night, often
several times a day, with an updated position in any kind of
weather. While you certainly should bring your sextant and
know how to use it, because any electrical device can break
down, don't scorn the benefits of today's technology. Too
many good navigators have been fooled by currents or have
been prevented by cloudy skies from taking celestial observations. The bones of their vessels litter the seas. The technology
is available. Take advantage of it.

Some form of self-steering is vital for the lightly crewed
yacht at sea. It is too cold in the North Atlantic to stand intermi-
nable watches in forty-degree weather, with cold rain and
twenty-five knots of wind slowly but inexorably freezing each
molecule in your feet and working up from there. Do that six
hours a day for three weeks and see how you feel about ocean
sailing! Either an autopilot or a windvane is valuable. Each has
its advantages and disadvantages. The windvane requires no
power to run and works well for the small vessel with limited
power and fuel capacity. It is useless, however, when you must
power your way through calms, canals, or fjords. It frequently
does not work well in light airs or on downwind reaches unless
half a gale is blowing. To my mind, if you have the fuel capacity
to run your engine to charge the batteries for three to four hours
daily for the length of your cruise, then a good autopilot has it
all over the windvane. It can be used in virtually all conditions
under sail or power and is worth its weight in gold.

Good foul-weather gear should be tested at home first,
before going to sea. Do not stint on quality here. If you don't
have dry pants, you will become chilled and suffer from hypo-
thermia. This can seriously impair your ability to function.
Immerse the seat of the pants in cold water in your bathtub.
Does the inside stay dry? If not, return them and get a different
brand.

A medical kit should cover all the usual illnesses that are possible and for which expert help is not available. At least cover the basics: seasickness, headaches, diarrhoea, constipation, urinary infections, vaginitis, respiratory infections, staph infections, allergies, cuts, eye injuries, and broken bones.

Finally, I know that in spite of all the precautions listed above, the outrageous expense involved, and the hazards and discomforts attendant on heading to sea, many reading these pages will do so some day. Read some of the excellent books on the subject. If you are a romantic who strives for new challenges, go out and slay your dragon; but take your time and care to ensure that there are no chinks in your armour.

A QUICK CHECKLIST FOR OFFSHORE SAFETY
Formal survey of your vessel
Three anchors with chain and rope
Tiedowns for the anchors/chain stopper
Double lifelines/netting forward
Secure stanchions/backing plates
Large cockpit drains
Jacklines in centreline of boat
Storm trysail on separate track
Reliable furling systems for sails
Locker security clasps and gaskets
Tiedown for companionway slides
Ventilator caps
Radar reflector
Autopilot/windvane
Canistered life raft/emergency supplies
Man-overboard pole(s) and horseshoes
Tiedowns or latches for drawers, refrigerator top,
    floorboards, books, pots, any loose items
Lee cloths for each crew member
Safety harnesses for each crew member
EPIRB (Emergency Position Indicating Radio Beacon)
Tapered plugs and underwater epoxy
Pumps (electric, engine driven, manual)

Check seacocks for function and deterioration
Gas detector/bilge–water alarm
Separate water supplies (at least two tanks/separate
    shutoffs)
Medications

from *North Atlantic Odyssey: Sailing to the Arctic Circle*.
Reprinted with permission from St. Martin's Press,
New York, 1989.

WOMAN ALONE

CLARE FRANCIS

Clare Francis left a successful business career to "travel before it's too late." She broke the women's speed record for crossing the Atlantic and has hosted three British television films about her exploits. Her bestselling novels include *The Night Sky* and *Wolf Winter*.

I

To sail the Atlantic singlehanded takes a great deal of physical effort and one should, ideally, be very fit indeed.

"Must get fit," I announced after a particularly greedy Christmas. "Running at dawn, visits to the gym, sensible food, no alcohol!"

"Great! I'll sit back and watch," said Jacques with the self-satisfied air of the working man. Tired of the vagaries of the boat fitting and delivery businesses, he had taken a job as a French teacher in Basingstoke for which, everyone was surprised to discover, he was fully qualified.

"Why don't you start properly and run around the valley at six tomorrow morning?" he smiled innocently. We had taken a rented farmhouse in Berkshire, the nearest place we could find to Jacques's new job. The lovely house had an unspoiled view of the Pang Valley, which was perfect running country with its many quiet country lanes.

"Splendid idea," I exclaimed. "Up at six and a quiet two-mile trot to start with. Don't want to overdo it."

At eight the next morning I jumped guiltily out of bed and trotted off into the mist thinking lots of healthy thoughts about clean, natural living and good exercise. Ten minutes later I lay flat on my back on the sofa, clutching my pounding head and wondering if my heart was up to the job.

Jacques viewed my panting form with interest. "That was quick," he remarked unnecessarily. "Perhaps you should have been a sprinter."

And that was the end of my special training except for a few quick darts around the marina when I was feeling especially overfed or unprepared. "The sailing'll get me fit," I kept saying in a confident voice, hoping desperately it would, for I only had to think of winching in the *Golly*'s headsails to make me feel decidedly nervous.

We started work again on the boat in February and there was no danger of getting any exercise out of it; I spent most of my time motionless, frozen by the cold. But the boat's bottom had to be painted and, with the aid of Ron and his helpers, we splashed on the anti-fouling as best we could, our arms stiff and our hands chilled. Luckily Ron had had the foresight to provide a flask of something fiery to thaw the stomach, and the working party frequently retired to the cabin for refreshments. It took a long time to get the boat painted but everyone enjoyed it immensely.

There were many other jobs to be done before the *Golly* would be ready for the new season. Ron kindly furnished more cabin windows to provide more light for the inside of the boat, only two ports having originally been fitted so as not to reduce the strength of the coach roof. But we all felt the boat was quite strong enough to take more windows and fitted the remainder without a qualm. And what a difference it made to the interior. It cheered me up enormously; the North Atlantic would be grey enough without trying to block out the light. A new forehatch was also fitted for the good reason that the old fibreglass hatch leaked like a sieve. Fibreglass hatches are almost impossible to make watertight. We had spent hours edging the rims with rubber gaskets but, the hatch being infinitely flexible, it would become watertight at one point, only to let in water at another. But the new Canpa hatch was a great improvement. Not only did it never let in a drop of water – and the *Golly* was a wet boat to windward – but I could open it from on deck, essential for a singlehander. It is frustrating to be on the foredeck and be unable to reach a sail except by trotting back along the deck to the main hatch, through the cabin, and into the sail locker to open the hatch from below. And you may be sure that, at the precise moment you open the hatch and stick your head out, some water will slip across the deck and hit you dead in the eye.

Another improvement was a folding propeller. This was part of Ron's go-fast strategy. "Should give you another quarter-knot," he announced proudly, "another five percent on your average speed. Bring you in ten days ahead of everyone else." Ron's optimism was boundless. One day I went down to the boat to find a black stripe had been painted along the hull just above the waterline. "Makes you go faster," said Ron, refusing to be drawn further, although he did wink in the direction of another competitor's boat and tap the side of his head several times, which I took to indicate that there was some psychological warfare going on.

In his desire to provide me with the fastest boat in the world Ron also became convinced that the *Golly* was too heavy. "All those teak fittings could come out, you know," he would say. "Could strip her out completely in a day." I thought of the stripped-out boats I had seen with canvas bunks, a bucket for a head, and a single gas ring on which to cook. Then I looked at the *Golly* with her teak-faced woodwork, comfortable bunks, and soft cushions to sleep on; her well-fitted galley with its gimballed stove with two burners, grill, and oven; her proper fixed head which could not be knocked over. There was no doubt in my mind. Life was too short and racing not important enough to take things to extremes; the trip would be uncomfortable enough without actually trying to make it miserable.

The last two weeks before the race were hectic, with more to be done than ever. With my list of provisions in hand I went off to the local supermarket and returned groaning with heavy boxes of food. Although I am a small eater, I find it very difficult not to set off on a voyage without enough food to feed six people for a month, or me alone for ten months. I decide on what to take by listing all the foods I like, estimating how much I'll eat in a week, and then multiplying that amount by the number of weeks I expect to be at sea – plus a bit more for greed.

This time I hoped to do the crossing in four weeks. For instance, in working out how much cheese to take, I reckoned one pound a week, which equalled four pounds of cheese, with a bit to spare, say five pounds in all. This system would have worked wonderfully except that my imagination is always larger than my stomach. I like many varieties of tinned fruit, but instead of taking a few of each, I applied my standard calculation to each variety. In this way the lower lockers filled up with 30 tins of plums, 40 tins of peaches, 20 tins of pears, two tins of prunes, and so on to a total of 120 tins of fruit. I do love fruit, but there was no possibility of eating my way through 120 tins in 28 days. But I could not decide which type of fruit to cut down. On my last crossing I had been possessed of a mad desire for peaches and it had proved to be such an obsession that I had been forced to ration myself to half a tin a day, a great hardship when one has little willpower and much appetite. If possible I wanted to avoid a similar shortage, but could not decide which fruit would prove to be my passion. Would it be peaches again? Or plums? There were strong indications it was going to be plums, but the matter was by no means certain so, rather than risk it, I left the 120 tins of fruit where they were, in the lockers already crammed with tins of vegetables, fruit juice, and savouries.

"Merde alors! What's all this?" exclaimed Jacques, on discovering the bulging lockers. And I was forced to explain that this large number of tins was essential to counterbalance the weight of the heavy new batteries to port.

Each tin had to have its label removed before the bilge water did the job instead and each had to be marked with its contents in waterproof ink. I never used a code in case I should lose the key, but made do with abbreviations instead. Thus apple-and-raspberry pie filling became "Ap & Rasp," while green peppers filled with rice and vegetables became "stffd peps."

In the midst of stowing the large quantities of food, Mother and Father arrived to give a helping hand. Since Mother never travelled to see the family without packing a sumptuous lunch into the trunk of the car, Jacques's eyes were alight with anticipation the whole morning and little work could be done until we had consumed a large feast washed down with a bottle of wine. After which an afternoon's work didn't seem very important anyway.

"Now," said Mother, "are you taking enough food? Well, however much you think you have, I've just brought along a few extras." Whereupon she disappeared in the direction of the parking lot.

"Where's Mother?" I asked a few minutes later. Jacques looked up and, turning pale, pointed behind me. An enormous cardboard box was making its way ponderously along the dock and under it were Mother's legs looking uncertain around the knees. Jacques leaped to the rescue and we were soon unloading tins of artichokes, asparagus, chestnuts, rich soups, and other delicacies.

"Just a few essentials," said Mother. "Now have you got enough warm clothes?" Ever since my sister and I had left home Mother had been sure that, if we weren't underfed, we were underclothed. Having once read an advertisement about some thermal underwear "that generates its own heat" and an article about the wonders of nuclear energy on the same day, Mother was a great believer in thermonuclear underwear. Indeed, in the winter resort where my parents went skiing every year, Mother was famous for her thermonuclear underwear, which she swore defied any number of sudden sittings in the snow.

Having given me a full set of her special underwear, Mother triumphantly held up a string of paper panties. "Much more practical," she declared. "Although I've brought a small bag of detergent and some clothespins as well, just in case you have time."

In the final week before we had to leave for Plymouth, I hurried off to the Meteorological Office at Bracknell to find out if the

North Atlantic promised any unusual conditions that year. I had phoned for an appointment with Arthur Blackham in the Ships Routeing Section and had been surprised to find my name produced an immediate response.

"I know you," he declared, "you're the one with the father who phones every day." At first I thought he had me confused with the daughter of a fanatical gardener, but Arthur's memory had stretched back three years to my previous crossing when, unknown to me, Father had phoned for weather news daily. Arthur quickly assured me that this had been no bother at all. On the contrary, he was glad to have been able to reassure Father as to the lack of gales, hurricanes, and other such unpleasant events.

"Glad to do it again this time," said Arthur as we pored over current and wind charts. "You shouldn't have any gales around the Azores."

"I'm not going that way," I mentioned.

"You're – " he stared at me aghast. "Not the northern route! Well, I hope your boat is capable of withstanding Force 8." He paused thoughtfully. "No, I'll rephrase that – Force 9."

I couldn't help thinking Arthur was being a bit pessimistic, but then I remembered that, as a master mariner, he had crossed the Atlantic a few more times than I had.

"But it's a very good year for icebergs," he continued, which I rightly took to mean that there weren't very many. On the last race, four years before, there had been many hundreds in the path of the direct route. But this year there were only 30 large bergs in thousands of square miles of ocean. "That's good?" I asked. "That's marvellous," affirmed Arthur. "It would need the luck of the devil to hit one this year!"

I was to remind him of that statement.

With a final check to make sure I hadn't forgotten the sextant, spare sextant, navigation tables, charts, ship's papers, passport with U.S. visa, medical kit, face cream, spare tin-opener, and the thousand and one other things to remember, Jacques and I set sail for Plymouth. It was a wonderful sail, but with only a week to go before the start I was beginning to feel nervous and I spent most of the time puttering about the boat wondering what I had forgotten to do. Jacques kept reassuring me that preparation was 90 percent of the Trans-Atlantic Race and that I would be one of the few to be fully prepared. "I mean, what have you got left on your list of things to do?" he asked. I looked down the list and read out a few items like "Buy small tin of face cream for Panic Bag." "There you are," said Jacques, "you're hardly prepared at all!"

Millbay Docks at Plymouth were already full of boats, and more were arriving by the hour. The final number of entries had dropped to about 120 but, seen in a mass, it still seemed an awful lot. The French had the most impressive fleet of boats. They had dominated the race for many years and were determined to be first again in Newport.

The race was divided into three classes: the Jester Class for small boats under 38 feet, the Gipsy Moth Class for intermediate sizes, and the Pen Duick Class for the giants more than 65 feet. Most of the very large boats were French because, theoretically at least, the larger the boat the faster it goes, and the French were determined to be the fastest. *Club Méditerranée* had arrived and was ready to start, although this was hard to believe from the many workers swarming over her decks. If anything, she was larger than I had imagined and I could only stare in awe at her four tall masts with their enormous sail area. If one person had to sail that ship singlehanded I was extremely grateful it wasn't going to be me.

Tucked away among the throng of boats were several I knew well from the Round Britain and Azores races. Significantly most of them were moored in a line together, and while other competitors scurried around looking worried, these boats echoed to the sound of laughter and clinking glasses. If there had been a prize for enjoying the pre-race week, the British would certainly have won it, followed closely by the Czech, Polish, and Dutch contingents whose days seemed to start at 11 p.m. As always, the attitude of the British left the French perplexed and confused. Was this the great British challenge, out to regain their lost trophies? Surely, in the wake of Francis Chichester and Geoffrey

Williams, previous British winners of the race, didn't we want to win again? But for most people the short answer was no, unless by some delightful stroke of fate one just happened to arrive first. It was the British attitude that the racing mustn't interfere with the main purpose of the adventure, which was to have an enjoyable time in Plymouth, make one's way across the Atlantic in a reasonably seamanlike manner without taking too long about it, and to have an even more delightful time in Newport by way of recovery. It was the getting there that was important rather than the time one took to do it. Not to say that everyone didn't have a passage time he was hoping to match or better. But then, if one had taken 60 or even 80 days on the previous race, this didn't take much doing. The secret of the British nonchallenge lay in their choice of boats. While the French glittered in an array of light, fast, and fantastic racing machines, the British glowed quietly in a jumbled collection of standard family cruising boats and unusual ocean craft designed for seaworthiness rather than speed.

There were exceptions, the most notable being Mike McMullen's *Three Cheers*, which was the only British entry with a chance of being first in Newport. Mike and his yellow trimaran had very nearly won the Round Britain Race, losing the 2,000-mile race by only one hour, and we were certain he could win the Trans-Atlantic. *Three Cheers* was only 46 feet long but she was very light and fast. With the help of his fabulous wife, Lizzie, Mike had worked immensely hard on the boat, always sailing and tuning her in search of more speed. Even in the first days of that week in Plymouth, Mike forwent the reunion parties to take *Three Cheers* sailing. But we were all behind him, not only because he was such a trier, but because he managed to combine determination with a tremendous sense of fun.

Sometimes it was nice to dream of speeding along at 20 knots in a boat like *Three Cheers*, but there were other boats that made us envious and for entirely different reasons. The craft that made us almost speechless with jealousy was Jock Macleod's *Ron Glas*. Jock was a chap who liked his sailing. But he also liked his comfort and failed to see why one should always preclude the other as seemed to be the rule. He had commissioned Angus

Primrose to design him a "gentleman's boat" that would sail adequately but not in such a manner as to get one wet. The result was the junk-rigged schooner *Ron Glas*.

The essence of the junk rig is that it can be entirely controlled from a remote position. In the case of *Ron Glas*, all sailhoisting, trimming, and reefing were "handled" from the cockpit. Since the cockpit could be completely enclosed and boasted a swivel armchair, this meant that Jock could sit back in the warm and dry, a glass of Scotch at his elbow, and sail for thousands of miles without venturing on deck. This bore such favourable comparison with sail changing on the heaving and very wet foredeck of a conventional yacht that *Ron Glas* was always full of visitors eyeing her design with wonder and delight. Even those of us who knew the boat well couldn't help feeling a renewed pang of envy at the sight of Jock's oilskins still as bright and unsalty as the day he had bought them, and there was a strong rumour that in all the years Jock had been sailing the boat, he had never once put them on.

The keen racing boys were always trying to find ways of saving weight in order to go faster, but Jock's priorities were somewhat different. "What's the boat's water capacity, Jock?" asked an interested visitor.

"A hundred gallons," replied Jock.

"And how much are you taking on the race?"

"A hundred gallons."

"But that's going to weigh you down, isn't it?"

"Well yes," agreed Jock, "but then I've got to have enough to use my shower. And of course, enough to get me back to Scotland after the race."

"But can't you fill up with water in Newport?"

"Why no!" exclaimed Jock, looking shocked. "It's full of chlorine and would quite ruin my Scotch and water."

Another Angus Primrose junk-rigged design was the famous *Galway Blazer* that Bill King had sailed around the world single-handed. It was now owned by Peter Crowther who held the trans-Atlantic record for the slowest crossing ever. In the last race Peter had sailed an old gaffer called *Golden Vanity* and taken

80 days to reach Newport. Luckily his food and water held out, although it had been touch and go for, unbeknown to him, his cat had also been attending a few parties in Plymouth and gave birth to a fine litter in the middle of the Atlantic. The kittens were in good health on arrival, though Peter was beginning to look decidedly skinny.

But the best-known junk-rigged boat of all was *Jester*. This fine little boat had taken part in every race so far, first belonging to the race's originator, Blondie Hasler, and then to the capable Mike Richey. Mike was an expert navigator and a director of the Institute of Navigation, but during the last race he had not been so expert in his provisioning and, so the story went, had begun to run short of whisky while still miles from Newport. He was understandably delighted therefore when a ship stopped and lowered a bottle attached to a life buoy. Anticipation mounting, Mike waited patiently for the bottle to float over. Then, catching it at last, he whipped it out of the water only to find the bottle was quite empty save for a scrap of paper with his position on it.

Few boat designers seem to take their own boats on long ocean crossings, but Angus Primrose was different. Having seen so many of his designs go around the world or across the Atlantic singlehanded, he had decided to take one of his standard production boats in both the Azores and the trans-Atlantic races. The boat Angus had chosen was a beamy family cruising boat that he affectionately referred to as "the block of flats" because of its high topsides and large amount of accommodation. Significantly, its cockpit could seat more people with drinks in their hands than boats of twice its size, and frequently did. Angus had done very well in the light airs of the Azores Race and took enormous delight in telling everyone what a relaxed race he had had.

"Three meals a day, eight hours sleep a night, and only changed sail twice. Nothing to this singlehanding," he said. That remark cost him a lot of drinks, but Angus never minded and would merely repeat it with undiminished glee.

Among other old friends in the race was Martin Wills who

held the record for the second slowest crossing of the Atlantic. Martin only bothered to keep his boat sailing if the wind was being what he described as "reasonable." If it blew anything remotely "unreasonable" he was inclined to lower all sail and read one of the many hundreds of comics with which he stocked the boat, getting under way again only when he remembered to, if then.

Two other old friends were Richard Clifford in *Shamaal* and Gustaf Versluys in *Tyfoon*, both of whom had been great friends and rivals in the Round Britain. Gustaf, who was the friendliest of teddy bears and quite the best thing to come out of Belgium since brussels sprouts, had the 35-foot *Ohlson*, younger sister to the *Golly*. But having the smaller boat was no problem to Gustaf; one look at the size of his shoulders and I knew he wouldn't be far behind me, not to say very far in front.

It was marvellous to see so many old friends, but as the week progressed I had to spend more and more time on the *Golly* trying to sort out the last-minute problems and panics. Luckily for me, it was Jacques's half-term holiday and he was able to stay down for the whole week. Without him nothing at all would have got done, for every time I started to do a job another reporter would appear for an interview. Most were very polite, offering to come back later if I was busy, but others always seemed to have a deadline they were about to miss and couldn't wait a second. Most of their questions were good but there were a fair number of, "Why does a nice girl like you . . . ?" By far the most popular was, "Are you expecting a rough trip?" which was a bit masochistic, I decided. After a lot of thought I came up with what I considered to be a reasonable but not unlucky reply, and it was really vital not to say anything unlucky. It's not that I'm superstitious, but I do think it must be tempting fate to say, "Rough trip? No, no, I'm expecting lovely weather." So I hit upon the reply "I'm expecting gales for the first half of the trip and fog for the second and then I won't be disappointed!" which I thought covered the situation quite nicely without being too pessimistic. At least, that was what I believed then.

The only question I found impossible to answer was, "But

how do you manage a large boat like this?" Quite clearly I could manage her, otherwise I wouldn't be there, but I was up against the image of the singlehanded lady sailor. If you were anything short of being a nautical lady wrestler, then you were too weak to handle anything more than a dinghy. I became a little tired of this and started to behave badly when the question came up. I would give a good imitation of Charles Atlas in one of his more amazing poses or stride up to the questioner and give him a hearty slap on the back while offering, in ringing tones, to show him my biceps if he could spare me a moment.

About one thing I was certain: on being asked when I hoped to arrive in Newport, I answered with great certainty, "July the fourth." This would mean making the crossing in 28 days, which was a fast time. "So you're out to win the lady's prize and beat the lady's record!" whistled a reporter, writing busily. Certainly both these things would be nice but I didn't bother to explain the more important reason for arriving then. If I arrived any later I would have less than a week to spend with Jacques and my parents before they had to return to England. Also the Fourth of July marked the 200th anniversary of American Independence and I didn't want to miss the celebrations. Besides, the whole point of taking the *Golly* was to get there in a faster time than my previous five and a half weeks, which had seemed far too long. Four weeks would be a great improvement and, although it would mean averaging 100 miles a day, I was sure the *Golly* could do it.

II

By her Halfway Day across the Atlantic *Golly* was making good time by the northern route, lying second in the Jester class and fourth overall in the race.

If I were to get the chores finished by midmorning I would have to get started straightaway. I lay in my bunk awhile and planned my strategy. I would get the unpleasant jobs over with first and work toward the enjoyable ones. That meant starting with the washing up, the filming, the cleaning, and going on to the cooking, the eating, the navigation, and the radio.

I read a chapter of Chichester's *Along the Clipper Way* to give my mind a rest, then rolled out of my bunk to have a look on deck. There was nothing but a white blanket as usual, although it looked a bit thinner than before. I switched on the black box, turned it through 360 degrees so that its sensor arm had a complete sweep of the horizon, and when it reported no ships, I turned it off. I then checked our course, the wind speed, and the trim of the sails. A quick look at the self-steering gear, always half-frightened of what I might see, and I had finished my routine checks. Now for the washing up, which sat in a small canvas bucket in the cockpit. It would take only a minute to do it with some fresh seawater and then it would be over for another two days, or even three if I re-used the same knives and forks and ate off paper plates.

When I was halfway through my long breakfast I suddenly decided to brave the cold and have a wash because I knew I wouldn't have the courage to face another for a long time. I had been inspired by one of the contents of the parcel my god-mother had given me. It was some Yves St. Laurent talcum powder and, when I sniffed it, it smelled so good that I longed to smell like that too. It was not that I smelled badly – it was just that I could not be put to the acid test of having people sit beside me. I was musty and salty, rather like an ancient sea relic. I longed to feel fresh and vaguely feminine again, although I wondered if I'd still recognize the feeling.

As I washed and powdered myself I was amazed to discover that I had a new body. There were bones and hollows where none had been before. I had always thought my hips were naturally wide, but they were really quite narrow. If I could manage to stay that way, my clothes would look marvellous on me. But, with a sigh, I had to admit that a bikini would not look as good because, along with my hips, my bosom had almost entirely disappeared. I hadn't been much of a Jayne Mansfield to start with but I was still a bit put out. It was the principle of the thing.

With so many sharp bones protruding, I was covered in a multitude of bruises that ranged through every colour from dirty orange to bright purple. On favourite spots like my knees and thighs they were arranged in clusters like exhibits at a flower show. I was well practised in moving around the boat carefully, but when every single object was sharp, jutting, or just plain hard, it was impossible to escape them all the time. The worst were the cleats. If they didn't get me on the ankle when I walked by, then they'd bang me on the knee as I crawled past. But it was my shins that had the most painful encounters and always with the sill of the main hatchway, which was both hard and sharp. In bad weather it was impossible not to receive bruises everywhere, for the motion of the boat was too wild to anticipate with any accuracy. It was a matter of clinging on and dodging the bits of boat as they came at you.

After my wash I felt better and even tackled the washing up, an achievement that gave me great satisfaction. Then, to my delight, I saw a watery sun behind the clouds and within two minutes I had taken a sun sight. It was a good feeling to know where I was, particularly when it put me right where I had estimated my position to be. I would have liked to have taken another sight to verify the first, but the cloud thickened again and I saw no more of the sun that day. Navigation was a thing I enjoyed doing so long as the weather was reasonable. If it was rough it took hours of balancing and terrible concentration to get the horizon, the sun, and the sextant to come together. Then I would find that peering through the eyepiece had made me cross-eyed and I was unable to focus on the chronometer. Having missed the precise time I would then have to start all over again. To make matters more difficult my hands had become stiff and swollen with a number of unhealed cuts in the creases of the fingers, so that I was unable to handle the sextant as well as I might.

Generally I went to sleep when it got dark, at about ten o'clock Atlantic time. Just before I turned in I would switch on the masthead light, have a quick look on deck and around the horizon, and set up the spare compass beside my bunk. I always slept on the leeward, or lower bunk of the two settee berths in the main cabin, so that I couldn't fall out. Although the quarter berth was nearer the companionway and the instruments, it was difficult to get in and out of it quickly, and I preferred the settee berths where I could roll out and be on my feet within moments. By leaning my head over the edge of the berth I could also see the spare compass and check that we were still on course without having to go on deck every time. In fog I worked the little black box from the bunk too so that, unless there was some sail changing or trimming to be done, I need not go on deck at all.

On clear nights I would wake every hour or so, roll out, stumble up on deck and look around. There were never any ships, but there was often sail trimming, or worse, sail changing to be done. Once back in my sleeping bag I would drop straight off to sleep again as if I'd never been up. I could never do it on land, but it was easy at sea. The physical tiredness blotted out any thoughts that might keep me awake and, after the initial complaints, my body got used to my strange nocturnal habits.

Not surprisingly, waking up and going on deck were never so easy as falling asleep again. Worry about ships was the greatest inducement to look around, followed shortly by anxiety about an indefinable something. I was never sure what this something might be, possibly a piece of jetsam or a whale or a giant squid with arms 50 feet long that was about to pull the boat down. But something always made me roll out, get up, and take a look until doing so became an automatic reflex. But I needed no help to wake myself up when the wind changed strength. With a sense that always stayed awake I could feel changes in the boat's motion and speed, and would slowly become aware that I needed to put up more or less sail. If the wind increased I would reduce sail in no time, but if it decreased I would have great debates as to whether I was going to ignore the fact or not. Sloth usually won the argument and I would make up the most elaborate excuses for putting it off – like "wind's bound to get up again," "won't make any difference over 3,000 miles," and "I don't care anyway!"

One of Ron's presents to the boat had been a kitchen timer, and it was this I used to wake me every hour, although I had a talent for sleeping through it when I really put my mind to it. There was also an off-course alarm attached to the off-course computer. This device was most ingenious. It could be set to ring at various degrees off course and with varying sensitivity and it was the only sure way of knowing that, led by the self-steering, the boat had followed a change in the wind direction. But there was one problem. My nerves couldn't stand all the ringing and pinging. There I'd be, just settling into my sleeping bag with the prospect of an hour's uninterrupted sleep, when I'd find that my eyes were staring at the woodwork. Jamming them shut, I'd then listen to my nerves jarring like chalk on a blackboard. "Now stop this," I'd say to myself, "of course that alarm isn't about to go off; just forget about it." Eventually I'd doze off into an uneasy sleep whereupon a halyard would slap against the mast. Suddenly I'd be wide awake and bolt upright listening for some dreaded sound above the racket of my heartbeat. Then I'd remember that sound I was dreading was only the alarm and, groaning, would lie back and try to sleep again. Five minutes later the alarm would sound. Bolt upright, heart pounding, nerves jangling like piano strings, I would stand up to find I had no knees, only jelly. Staggering to the alarm I would switch it off, put the boat back on course, and ooze back into my bunk like a runny cheese. "Haven't you forgotten something?" some voice would say. "Absolutely not," I would reply. "But the alarm – shouldn't you put it back on?" By that time I didn't need to reply, because, with nerves relaxed and eyes like weights, I had fallen into a deep sleep.

Although I became used to getting up every hour, there was one aspect of interrupted sleep that I never became accustomed to, and that was the vividness of my interrupted dreams. As my sleep became deeper through the night, so my dreams became even more graphic and technicoloured – epic dramas that had me on the edge of my seat. Between the instant of hearing the timer go off and waking, I would find myself hanging off cliffs, being chased by monsters or, worst of all, reliving my most embarrassing moment. So real were some of these dreams that they would reverberate around my brain for hours, even days, afterwards and I would have the unpleasant feeling I was living several lives at once . . .

As I approached the Grand Banks it became bitterly cold. It was as if the wind had blown out of an enormous refrigerator. I could almost feel the arctic ice in its breath. There was a different smell in the air too, a strong scent of fish and decaying sea life, carried down with the melting ice.

As always there was fog. Sometimes it would fade a little, but then it would swoop down as thick as ever, and we would be sailing into a white curtain again. I tried not to peer ahead too often because all I could see were the hundreds of icebergs my eyes conjured up and my nerves couldn't stand the strain.

The place had a terrible emptiness to it, a desolation that entered one's bones with every blast of icy wind. I had a strong impression of space and distance, and for once I was aware of how very far from land we were. Normally I never thought beyond the three miles of water I could see around me, a miniature world across which the *Golly* seemed to be sailing forever. But here, I was aware of what I was, a small person in the middle of a large ocean. And it was a cold and lonely feeling.

Loneliness was not something I often experienced at sea. I missed people, which is an entirely different thing, for it has the promise of reunion and plenty of human company in the future. Also, the boat and the sea were familiar old friends and, until either gave me cause to believe otherwise, I felt safe in their company. I have only felt real loneliness in big cities or other places where there are plenty of people about but no one to talk to. Normally I dislike being alone and if there are people around I will always seek them out. But here there was not much chance of finding someone to talk to, so I didn't feel I was missing anything. It was the difference between going for a walk on your own with the prospect of seeing the family for tea and coming home to a silent and empty house to find a note stuck on the door: "Gone to a party – you're invited too!" but no indication as to where the party might be.

Out here in the deathly quiet and dank fog, I suddenly wanted to be where I was sure everyone else must be – in the warm and sunny ocean to the south. For a moment I even imagined that I had been sucked hundreds of miles to the north, and it was only by frequent looks at the compass and chart that I convinced myself I was heading south of Newfoundland. The best remedy for loneliness and thoughts of the Arctic was to keep myself occupied, but even when busy down in the cabin, I felt an eerie atmosphere that made me shiver.

Once, as I was sitting on deck sucking and blowing on my fingers, waiting for them to thaw out and allow me to finish a sail change, it occurred to me that I was either on the wrong route or mad. It was midsummer and if I were only a few miles to the south I could be lying under a burning hot sun, frying my skin to a turn, and sipping a gin on the afterdeck. Instead, here I was, doing my best to impersonate a polar bear, not only in appearance, but also in habitat.

And what was more, I was tired and fed up. After 17 days of sail grappling, being thrown around, and not getting any sleep, I suddenly decided that I was very tired indeed and didn't feel prepared to face another of those killing sail changes. Far from getting more practised at dropping the genoas neatly, I seemed to throw them over the side all the time. And sitting on the lower sail didn't appear to impress the wind – it would blow into a fold of the canvas and form a balloon that grew and grew until the sail billowed up into a small spinnaker. When I jumped on it or grabbed at it or lay on it, the balloon would only reappear elsewhere. After much grappling I would eventually persuade the sail to bunch itself up and disappear down the forehatch, only to face the same kind of undisciplined behaviour from the next sail when I pulled that up on deck. There was one sail, the Number One genoa, that was particularly heavy and unbending and it took all my strength to move it about. I didn't bother to bag that sail because I could never have lifted it up in one piece. Instead I left it loose in the sailbin so that I could pull it up section by section. With hands that would hardly grip, this was a real struggle.

Neither was sail hoisting and winching any easier than it had been when I was afflicted by the Lurgy. My hands complained bitterly at contact with the ropes and I didn't seem to have the energy to wind on the winches. I had always winched in the large genoas in easy stages – getting some sail in, then resting, pulling a little more and another pause, and then, if the last few inches were impossible, I would head the *Golly* into the wind to take the pressure off the sail and quickly winch in the rest. But now it wasn't weakness that made it difficult, it was a deep tiredness and, I had to admit, a general lack of enthusiasm.

In the dense fog and cold, I stayed below as much as possible, huddling around the heater like a road-mender at his brazier. I would thaw my hands, then swivel around to scorch my feet and socks until they had stopped steaming. But I did not like to leave the heater on when I was asleep and unable to watch it, so I relied on two sleeping bags and my faithful hot-water bottle to keep me warm at night. Even so, I always felt cold, mainly as a result of my hourly excursions on deck. My body clock seemed to turn off my interior heating system at night and I shivered violently as soon as I got up. By the time I returned to my bunk, my teeth were rattling like castanets and I was shaking. It took several minutes to warm up again and fall asleep.

To keep myself company in the evenings I quite often listened to the BBC Overseas Service. The programs were a marvellous mixture of news, education, and items on obscure topics like "Hedge Trimming in Britain Today." They also broadcast fascinating plays with characters called Rodney, Cynthia, and Charles, who played polo when they weren't murdering each other. Sometimes I left the radio on without really listening to it because it was so nice to hear human voices.

One item of news that had me gasping was the announce-
ment that the weather in Britain was the hottest since they knew
not when. Temperatures of 90 degrees plus were being
recorded, cattle were being given sunshades, and most of London seemed to be jumping into the fountains at Trafalgar
Square. I went up into the cockpit and had a look around;
obviously I was on a different planet, probably Mars. It was
very odd to be freezing on a latitude 300 miles to the south of
Plymouth.

I was approaching iceberg country, but I wasn't too worried.
There were so few of them about that year, and the ten or 20 that
had been reported had drifted off to the south and east of me.
Admittedly there were more on their way down from the north,
but at the point where I was likely to meet them, they were in a
path that ran down the eastern edge of the banks from north to
south. This path was perhaps 60 miles wide, but compared to
the way the bergs spread out farther south, this really seemed
quite narrow when you were dashing across it with your eyes
closed. A mere half-day's sail.

Ridiculous to worry about it, I decided. Only a few icebergs.
Thousands of square miles of ocean. Can't do much about it
anyway. So, after a delicious supper of tomatoes and cheese on
toast, and an hour listening to Brahms, I gave a last shiver and
went to sleep.

The wind was up and down during the night and I had to
make a couple of difficult sail changes that lost me a lot of sleep.
At dawn I took a look on deck, my eyes opening out of habit
rather than desire, and at the sight of the usual white blanket
staggered back to my bunk for some more vivid dreams. An
hour later I awoke but did not bother to go up on deck, merely
checking the compass and swivelling my little black box in a
circle. I could see that the fog was still about and I could sense
that the boat was going well, so there didn't seem any point in
getting cold on deck. When I next awoke I was surprised to find
I had overslept and hurried up on deck, my eyes blinking from

the light. To my delight I found the fog had cleared and I could see as far as the horizon ahead. This was a nice surprise!

Then I looked behind.

At first my eyes didn't comprehend. There was so much dazzling whiteness, the craggy mountains were so brilliant in the morning light that they seemed to be part of the sky. But white they were and craggy too. Two large icebergs a mile astern. One probably a quarter of a mile long, flat and rectangular. The other very tall with a sharp point at one end. And then my eye caught a third, grey with shadow and jagged too.

I whimpered slightly and sat down before my knees did it for me. The *Golly* was as steady as a rock in the light wind and, guided by the indefatigable self-steering, was holding a perfect course. I knew that by her wake, which was as straight as a ruler. Following the course of that straight line I could see exactly where we had been a few minutes before. And that was between the two large bergs.

I am not a very religious person; at one point I was actually a nonbeliever, but there are times when one doesn't make an issue of these things. And I said a heartfelt prayer to the effect that if there was Someone Up There, I was really terribly grateful for the icebergs having been moved out of my path or for me having been moved out of theirs, whichever was the case. And, although I didn't merit it, and was very ungrateful, and absolutely the least deserving, would God awfully mind keeping an eye on me just a little bit longer? I obviously needed the assistance.

I sat looking at the bergs for half an hour, until they began to disappear over the horizon. I couldn't stop thinking about one thing. I must have passed within yards of those bergs, and if I'd been on a fractionally different course, I would have hit one. My sixth sense had really let me down – but then it had always functioned best in response to cruiseliners with their hot baths and five-course dinners.

Like someone delivered from the jaws of a lion, I thereafter decided that life was really quite wonderful. Winching in genoas became a positive and uplifting experience, particularly for my biceps, and the chores became just another part of the rich pageant of life. As if to purify my soul and make me feel that I had deserved my escape, I rushed around the boat cleaning, dusting, oiling, and rubbing. I took eight sun sights during the day, using the ordinary cabin clock, which I checked for accuracy at least ten times. I scrubbed the galley. I put a hand into the depth of the food lockers, a brave venture, because it was not unusual to have damp and moldy spaghetti coil itself around one's fingers. I bagged some sails lying loose in the sailbin. And of course, I did the washing up. Then the wind died. It seemed a good time to have a belated celebration and I had a very small glass of Scotch, which was delightful.

from *Woman Alone*,
David McKay Co., New York, 1977,
by permission of the author.

ENDURANCE

ALFRED LANSING

In the fall of 1915 Ernest Shackleton's 10-month attempt to lead an expedition on foot across Antarctica ended when his ship *Endurance* was crushed in the ice. The twenty-eight men made camp on an ice floe and drifted for six months, living on whatever they could catch. In April 1916 they were able to launch three lifeboats and after six nightmarish days landed on Elephant Island. Shackleton and five of the men then set out on what has been called one of history's greatest feats of navigation.

The wind had gradually swung around to the southeast, the perfect direction for driving them north. Shackleton ordered the sails set, and after they were up, he sent Crean, McNeish, Vincent, and McCarthy forward to get some sleep, saying that he and Worsley would stay on duty throughout the night to watch for ice.

When everything was squared away, Shackleton turned and looked astern. It was just possible to make out Elephant Island as a hulking, shadowy mass. For several minutes he stared without speaking.

A forbidding-looking place, certainly, but that only made it seem the more pitiful. It was the refuge of twenty-two men who, at that very moment, were camped on a precarious, storm-washed spit of beach, as helpless and isolated from the outside world as if they were on another planet. Their plight was known only to the six men in this ridiculously little boat, whose responsibility now was to prove that all the laws of chance were wrong – and return with help. It was a staggering trust.

As the darkness deepened, ten thousand stars pricked through the blue-black sky, and the little wisp of a pennant that fluttered from the *Caird*'s mainmast described an irregular circle across the sparkling heavens as the boat rolled before the quartering sea.

The two men sat side by side, Worsley steering and Shackleton huddled close up against him. Their primary concern was ice, and Shackleton and Worsley kept a sharp lookout. They passed an occasional lump early in the evening, but by ten o'clock the sea appeared to be clear.

From time to time Shackleton rolled cigarettes for both of them, and they spoke of many things. It was obvious that the burden of responsibility Shackleton had borne for sixteen months had nibbled away somewhat at his enormous self-confidence. He wanted to talk and to be assured that he had acted wisely.

He confided to Worsley that the decision to separate the party had been a desperately difficult one, and he abhorred having to make it. But somebody had to go for help, and this was not the sort of responsibility which could be delegated to another person.

As for the journey itself, he seemed strangely doubtful, and he asked Worsley's opinion of their chance. Worsley replied that he was sure that they would make it, but it was evident that Shackleton was far from convinced.

The truth was that he felt rather out of his element. He had proved himself on land. He had demonstrated there beyond all doubt his ability to pit his matchless tenacity against the elements – and win. But the sea is a different sort of enemy. Unlike the land, where courage and the simple will to endure can often see a man through, the struggle against the sea is an act of physical combat, and there is no escape. It is a battle against a tireless enemy in which man never actually wins; the most that he can hope for is not to be defeated.

It gave Shackleton a feeling of uneasiness. He now faced an adversary so formidable that his own strength was nothing in comparison, and he did not enjoy being in a position where boldness and determination count for almost nothing, and in which victory is measured only in survival.

But more than anything he was dreadfully tired, and he wanted simply for the journey to be over, and as quickly as possible. If only they could make Cape Horn, he said to Worsley, they would cut one-third off the distance they had to go. He knew it was impossible, but he asked Worsley whether he thought the southeast wind just might hold long enough for them to do so. Worsley looked at him sympathetically and shook his head. Not a chance, he replied.

Just before six o'clock, the first light of dawn crept across the sky, and as it grew brighter both men relaxed. Now if they came upon any ice, at least they could see it.

Shackleton waited until seven o'clock and then he called the other men. Crean rigged the Primus, and after a considerable amount of trouble getting it to light and keeping the hoosh pot in place, they finally had breakfast.

When they had finished, Shackleton announced that the watches would begin, four hours on and four hours off. Shackleton said he would take the first trick with Crean and McNeish, and Worsley would have the other with Vincent and McCarthy.

To classify the dangers they faced in order of magnitude would have been impossible, but of the known threats, the greatest undoubtedly was ice – especially at night. One single collision with an unseen fragment could have ended the journey in a moment. Thus Shackleton's plan was to get north with all possible speed before turning east toward South Georgia.

For the next two days they were lucky. The wind held steady out of the southwest – much of the time almost at gale force. By noon on April 26, they had logged a total of 128 miles from Elephant Island without encountering a sign of ice.

However, those two days were an ordeal during which they were introduced, one at a time, to the endless miseries which constituted life on board the boat. Always and forever there was the water – the all-pervading, inescapable water. Sometimes it was just a shower of spray thrown up from the bow and flung astern by the wind, which caused no real suffering except to the man at the helm. Much worse were the quieter, solid seas dipped up by the bow that poured aft and sloshed into the cockpit. And worst of all were the occasions when the boat plunged down just as a wave broke. Then green, foaming water rolled across the decking, splashed into the cockpit, and drained down into the boat in icy streams through a score of openings in the canvas decking, as rain might pour through the roof of some dilapidated shack. Within twenty-four hours after leaving Elephant Island, the decking had begun to sag so that there were a dozen pockets to hold the water.

The man at the helm, of course, suffered the most, and each of them took his turn at the yoke lines for an hour and twenty minutes during each watch. But the other two men on duty were better off only by comparison. When they weren't bailing or tending the sails or shifting ballast by moving the rocks in the bottom, they spent their time trying to avoid the streams coming from above. It was of little use, though. Invariably they wound up huddled over with the water pouring off their backs.

All of them were dressed more or less the same way – heavy wool underwear, woollen trousers, a thick, loose sweater, with a pair of light gabardine Burberry overalls on the outside. Their heads were covered with knitted, woollen helmets and Burberry outer helmets, tucked in at the neck. On their feet they wore two pairs of socks, a pair of ankle-high felt boots, and finneskoes – reindeer-skin boots with the hair side out, though every trace of hair had long since worn off, leaving them bald and limp. There was not a set of oilskins on board.

Such clothing was intended for wear in intense, dry cold – not on board a pitching, spray-drenched boat. Here it had almost wick like action, soaking up every icy drop until the saturation point was reached, then maintained.

The best that could be done was to live with this trial by water, as they had on the trip to Elephant Island – to sit as still as possible after each soaking so as to avoid contact with the newly drenched area of clothing. But to sit motionless in a 22-foot boat in a heavy sea can be difficult indeed.

The boat had to be pumped out at fairly frequent intervals, usually two or three times each watch, and the job required two men – one to operate the plunger while the other held the icy brass cylinder down into the water in the bottom of the boat. Even with mittens, the hands of the man gripping the cylinder would go numb within the space of five minutes, and they would trade places.

Nor was the discomfort on board limited to the men on watch. They realized from the very beginning that even sleeping had a special brand of unpleasantness all its own. The sleeping bags were located in the bow, nominally the driest part of the boat. To reach them involved a tortuous crawl on hands and knees over the rocks in the bottom. The closer a man got to the bow, the more restricted the space became, until finally he had to get down on his belly and slither forward, insinuating himself between the underside of the seats and the ballast.

When at last he had reached the bow, there was the job of getting into his bag, then finally the problem of going to sleep. Fatigue helped, of course, but even so, the action of the boat in the bow was more violent than anywhere else. At times they were heaved bodily upwards, only to fall down onto the rocks again, or perhaps to be slammed from beneath as the boat was pitched aloft by a new wave. The *Caird* had been equipped with six sleeping bags so that each man might have his own. But Shackleton soon suggested that they share three bags and use the others as mattresses, to protect them from the rocks. Everyone quickly agreed.

They discovered, too, that under the decking there was not quite enough room to sit upright. For the first couple of meals they tried to eat half bent over, with their chins pressed down against their chests. But this position greatly interfered with swallowing, and the only thing to do was to stretch out on the rocks in the bottom.

But no matter what position they assumed – sitting, reclining, or lying in their sleeping bags – the struggle against the motion of the boat was ceaseless. The 2,000 pounds of ballast in the bottom gave the *Caird* a particularly vicious action, and she jerked upright after every wave. Worsley thought she was over-ballasted and he urged Shackleton to throw some of the rocks overboard. But Shackleton took a characteristically cautious view of the matter. The only way to see if Worsley was right was to dump the ballast – and then it would be gone forever. It was better, Shackleton felt, to put up with the wicked motion of the boat than to risk being light.

They had sailed from Elephant Island in rather high spirits, knowing that they were embarked at last for civilization. As McNeish had recorded – "wet through, but happy through it all."

But after two days of uninterrupted misery, their cheeriness had worn away. And by noon on April 26, after Worsley had fixed the position at 128 miles from Elephant Island, the ordeal to which they were committed had become altogether too real. There was only the consolation that they were making progress – at the agonizingly slow rate of about 1 mile every half hour or so.

The actual position on April 26 was 59° 46' South, 52° 18' West, and it put the *Caird* a scant 14 miles north of the 60th parallel of latitude. Thus they had just crept over the line separating the "Raving Fifties" from the "Screaming Sixties," so called because of the weather that prevails there.

This, then, was the Drake Passage, the most dreaded bit of ocean on the globe – and rightly so. Here nature has been given a proving ground on which to demonstrate what she can do if left alone. The results are impressive.

It begins with the wind. There is an immense area of persistent low pressure in the vicinity of the Antarctic Circle, approximately 67° South latitude. It acts as a giant sump into which high pressure from farther north continually drains, accompanied by almost ceaseless, gale-force, westerly winds. In the prosaic, often studiously understated language of the U.S. Navy's Sailing Direction for Antarctica, these winds are described categorically: "They are often of hurricane intensity and with gust velocities sometimes attaining 150 to 200 miles per hour. Winds of such violence are not known elsewhere, save perhaps within a tropical cyclone."

Also in these latitudes, as nowhere else on earth, the sea girdles the globe, uninterrupted by any mass of land. Here, since the beginning of time, the winds have mercilessly driven the seas clockwise around the earth to return again to their birthplace where they reinforce themselves or one another.

The waves thus produced have become legendary among seafaring men. They are called Cape Horn Rollers or "greybeards." Their length has been estimated from crest to crest to exceed a mile, and the terrified reports of some mariners have placed their height at 200 feet, though scientists doubt that they very often exceed 80 or 90 feet. How fast they travel is largely a matter of speculation, but many sailormen have claimed their speed occasionally reaches 55 miles an hour. Thirty knots is probably a more accurate figure.

Charles Darwin, on first seeing these waves breaking on Tierra del Fuego in 1833, wrote in his diary: "The sight is enough to make a landsman dream for a week about death, peril and shipwreck."

As viewed from the *Caird*, the sight of these rollers constituted ample reason for such thoughts. In the rare moments when the sun shone, they were cobalt blue, which gave them the appearance of being infinitely deep – as indeed they were. But most of the time the sky was overcast, and then the whole surface of the sea turned a sombre, lifeless grey.

There was no sound to the relentless advance of these cliffs of water except the hiss of their foaming brows when they rose to such a height or charged forward so fast that they lost their balance and their crests tumbled to the force of gravity.

Once every ninety seconds or less the *Caird*'s sail would go slack as one of these gigantic waves loomed astern, possibly 50 feet above her, and threatening, surely, to bury her under a hundred-million tons of water. But then, by some phenomenon of buoyancy, she was lifted higher and higher up the face of the onrushing swell until she found herself, rather unexpectedly, caught in the turmoil of foam at the summit and hurtling forward.

Over and over again, a thousand times each day, this drama

was re-enacted. Before long, to the men on board the *Caird*, it lost all elements of awesomeness and they found it routine and commonplace instead, as a group of people may become inured to the perils of living in the shadow of an active volcano.

Only very occasionally did they think about South Georgia. It was so remote, so Utopian, that it was almost depressing to contemplate. No man could have endured with just that to keep him going.

Instead, life was reckoned in periods of a few hours, or possibly only a few minutes – an endless succession of trials leading to deliverance from the particular hell of the moment. When a man was awakened to go on watch, the focal point of his existence became that time, four hours away, when he could slither back into the cold, wet rockiness of the sleeping bag he was now leaving. And within each watch there were a number of subdivisions: the time at the helm – eighty eonic minutes, during which a man was forced to expose himself to the full wickedness of the spray and the cold; the ordeal of pumping, and the awful task of shifting ballast; and the lesser trials which lasted perhaps two minutes – like the interval after each numbing spray struck until a man's clothes warmed enough so that he could move once more.

Again and again the cycle was repeated until the body and the mind arrived at a state of numbness in which the frenzied antics of the boat, the perpetual cold and wet came to be accepted almost as normal.

On April 27, three days out from Elephant Island, their luck turned bad. About noon a raw and penetrating mistlike rain began to fall, and the wind slowly started to move around toward the north – dead ahead.

They were now perhaps 150 miles north of Elephant Island and still well within the zone where they might encounter ice. Thus they could not afford to be blown a single mile to the south. Shackleton and Worsley spent several minutes discussing the possibilities and finally decided there was no choice but to hold the *Caird* up into the wind as best they could.

And so the struggle began, swinging from one tack to the

other and taking a wearisome pounding in the process. It was all the more unpleasant because they were simply absorbing punishment while doing nothing more than holding their own. But about 11 p.m., to their great relief, the wind eased down and moved into the northwest. By the time Worsley's watch took over at midnight they were able to resume the course to the northeast.

At dawn on April 28, only a light northwest breeze was blowing; actually, it was the best weather they'd had since leaving Elephant Island, four days before. But there were dangerous signs of deterioration, both among the men and their equipment. Shackleton noticed with apprehension that the familiar pains of the sciatica he had suffered at Ocean Camp were coming back. And all of the men were bothered by an increasing sensation of discomfort in their feet and legs – a feeling of tightness.

About mid-morning, McNeish suddenly sat down in the centre of the cockpit and peeled off his boots. His legs, ankles, and feet were puffy and dead white, apparently from lack of exercise and from being continually soaked. When Shackleton saw the condition of McNeish's feet, he suggested that the other men remove their footgear – and they were all the same. Vincent was in far the worst condition, apparently suffering from rheumatism. Shackleton looked in the medicine chest and gave him the only remedy which seemed likely to help – a small bottle of witch hazel.

The damage to Worsley's navigational books by the constant soaking was an even more serious problem. The destruction of these books could mean losing the way across this forsaken waste of ocean. And though every effort was made to protect them, they had to be taken out whenever a sight was taken.

Both covers of the logarithm book were soggy, and the wet was beginning to spread to the inside pages. The *Nautical Almanac*, with its tables of sun and star positions, was in even worse shape. It was printed on cheaper paper and was fast approaching a state of pulpiness. Its pages had to be carefully peeled apart to separate them.

In the matter of taking sights, Worsley at first tried bracing himself inside the cockpit. But it was no good. To remain upright was difficult enough; to get an accurate reading was impossible. He found that it was best to kneel on the helmsman's seat, with Vincent and McCarthy holding him around the waist.

Early in the afternoon of April 28, the relatively good weather from the northwest came to an end as the wind slowly moved to the west and began to freshen. By dusk it had inched to the SSW and risen almost to gale force. Night came on and an overcast blotted out the stars. The only way to steer was by watching the pennant on the mainmast blow out before the wind and holding to a course which kept it pointed just off the port bow.

Only once in the night was a positive check on the direction permitted, and then a flaming match was lighted so they could see the compass for a moment to make certain that the wind was still out of the same quadrant. They had only two candles which were being strictly preserved for that time that now seemed so far away – the landfall at South Georgia.

The dawn on the fifth day, April 29, rose on a lumpy sea under a dull sky. Low, troubled clouds scudded past, almost touching the surface of the water. The wind was nearly dead astern, and the *Caird* laboured forward like a protesting old woman being hurried along faster than she cared to go.

Just before noon a rift appeared in the sky, and Worsley hurriedly got his sextant. He was just in time, for a few minutes later the sun smiled down for one wintry flicker and then was gone. But Worsley had his sight, and Shackleton had recorded the chronometer reading. When the position was worked out, it put the *Caird* at 58° 38' South, 50° 0' West – they had covered 238 miles since leaving Elephant Island, six days before.

They were almost one-third of the way.

One-third of the sentence had been served.

Throughout the day and into the night, the southwesterly wind continued, growing ever stronger. By the time the bleak grey sky grew light on the morning of April 30, the surface of the sea was torn into foam, and the frenzied screech of the gale through the rigging rose and fell hysterically as the *Caird* was lifted to each successive swell. The temperature had dropped very close to zero, and the bitterness of the wind suggested that it was blowing straight off pack ice that was not very far away.

As the morning hours passed, it became more and more of a struggle to steer the boat. The 60-knot gale drove her head down into the seas, and the huge waves that rolled up astern constantly threatened to slew her around broadside. By mid-morning she was wallowing more than sailing, running off to one side and then the other, and taking seas on board with almost every wave. The pump was not adequate to handle the water, and extra hands had to be called to bail. Toward noon the boat began to ice up.

The decision was inevitable, but Shackleton put it off as long as he dared. They pumped and bailed and beat the ice off her – all the while fighting to hold her stern up into the wind. Noon . . . one o'clock . . . two o'clock. Shackleton reluctantly gave the order to come about. The sails were dropped, and the sea anchor, a cone-shaped piece of canvas about 4 feet long, was put over on the end of a long bow line. It dragged through the water and thus brought the *Caird*'s bow up into the wind.

Almost at once conditions improved. At least less water came on board. The boat, however, behaved like a thing possessed. She staggered drunkenly upward over each new wave, then plunged sideways only to have her bow jerked violently around as she seized up on the sea anchor. There was never a moment – not even an instant of repose. The only thing to do was to hang on, and endure.

It was not long before the furled sails started to collect ice, and with each icy burst of spray their load grew heavier. Within an hour, they were frozen into a solid mass, and the action of the boat was growing sluggish as she began to get top-heavy. The sails had to be removed, so Crean and McCarthy were sent forward, and after knocking off the ice, they brought the sails below and stuffed them into the already crammed space under the decking.

But then a heavy coating began to accumulate on the oars. There were four of them lashed against the shrouds. As the ice built up, they became like miniature bulwarks which prevented the water from spilling overboard before it froze. Shackleton watched anxiously, hoping that the load of ice on deck might not grow too heavy. But in the failing light of dusk he saw that it would be dangerous to let it go until morning. He ordered Worsley, Crean, and McCarthy to go with him up onto the pitching deck.

With great effort they clubbed the ice off the oars, then pitched two of them over the side. The remaining pair was lashed to the shrouds about 18 inches above the deck so that the water would run off.

It took more than twenty minutes, and by the time they were finished it was dark and they were utterly drenched. They crept back into the cockpit – and the night began.

Each of the watches shivered through their four hideous hours, cringing beneath the decking, sodden and half-frozen, trying to remain upright against the wild lurching of the boat while perched on the despised rocks in the bottom.

For seven painful days the rocks had made eating difficult; they had interfered with bailing; they had vastly complicated the simple act of getting about, and they had made sleeping all but impossible. But it was moving them that was worst of all. Periodically they had to be shifted in order to ballast the boat properly, which meant lifting them while crouched over and kneeling, often painfully, on other rocks. By now, every sharp corner and every slippery surface was intimately known and utterly detested.

Then, too, there were the reindeer hairs. They moulted from the insides of the sleeping bags, and at first they had been only a petty annoyance. But no matter how much hair was shed, the supply seemed inexhaustible. And they were everywhere – the sides of the boat, the seats, the ballast. They clung in wet clumps to faces and hands. The men breathed them as they slept, and occasionally woke up choking on them. The hairs ran down into the bottom and clogged the pump, and little clusters of them were turning up more and more frequently in the food.

Gradually, as the long hours of the night crept by, a subtle change could be detected in the boat. For one thing, the trickles of water through the decking became smaller, then finally ceased altogether. At the same time her behaviour was growing noticeably less violent, and instead of pitching wildly, she rose to the seas with increasing restraint.

The first light of dawn told why. The entire boat above the waterline was encased in ice, half a foot thick in places, and the rope to the sea anchor had grown to the size of a man's thigh. Under the weight of it, she was riding at least 4 inches deeper, like a waterlogged derelict rather than a boat.

Worsley was on watch and he immediately sent McCarthy to awaken Shackleton, who hurried aft. When he saw the situation, he excitedly ordered all hands called. Then he himself took a small axe and cautiously crawled forward.

With extreme care so as not to puncture the decking, he began to knock the ice away with the back side of the axe. Periodically a wave burst against the boat and swept over him, but he kept at it for nearly ten minutes while the others anxiously looked on. By then he was so stiff with cold that he could no longer trust his grip or balance. He crawled back into the cockpit with the water dripping from his clothes and his beard frozen half-stiff. He was shivering noticeably as he handed the axe to Worsley to continue the job, cautioning him to use extreme care while he was on the decking.

And so each of them took his turn at chipping for as long as he could endure it, which was rarely more than five minutes. First they had to knock off enough ice to get a handhold and a place to put their knees. To stand up on that glassy, rolling deck would have been to commit suicide, for had a man fallen overboard, the others could never have got in the sea anchor and hoisted sail in time to rescue him.

Below, Shackleton discovered that ice was forming even inside the cockpit. Long icicles hung from under the decking, and the water in the bottom was very nearly frozen.

He called for Crean, and together they managed to get the Primus stove alight in the hope that it would give off enough heat to warm the cockpit above the freezing point. Unless the water in the bottom could be thawed enough so it could be pumped out, there was danger that it would simply sink the boat under them.

It took an hour of agonizing work on deck before they felt the *Caird* begin to regain her buoyancy. But they kept at it until they had succeeded in getting rid of most of the ice except a large chunk on the sea-anchor line which they simply could not risk attempting to reach.

Shackleton then called them below to have some milk. They gathered around the stove, almost sick with cold. It seemed inconceivable that their numbed bodies could have given off any warmth, but apparently they did, for after awhile the icicles under the decking began to melt and drip down onto them. Not long afterward the water in the bottom had thawed enough so they could pump it out.

Shackleton still had Crean keep the Primus stove alight, but toward noon the acrid fumes it gave off made the air almost unbreathable and it had to be extinguished. It took several minutes for the atmosphere to clear, and then they became aware of a new smell – a fetid, sweet-sour sort of odour, like spoiled meat. McNeish discovered it came from the sleeping bags, which in fact had begun to rot. A closer examination disclosed that two of them actually were slimy inside.

Throughout the afternoon the coating of ice steadily built up again. And late in the day Shackleton decided there was too much at stake to gamble on the chance that the *Caird* would survive until morning. Once more, he ordered that the boat be cleared. It took more than an hour, but finally it was done, and after a ration of hot milk they settled down to wait for morning.

The southwesterly gale screamed on, showing not the slightest sign of fatigue. The watches of that night were like a tally sheet of infinity. Every individual minute had to be noted, then lived through and finally checked off. There was not even a crisis to relieve the tortured monotony. When at last, about six o'clock, the sky to the east began to brighten they could see that once again the boat was carrying a dangerously heavy burden of ice. As soon as the light permitted she had to be chipped clear for the third time.

It was May 2, and the beginning of the third day of the gale. The weather throughout had been overcast so that no position could be obtained. Now the anxiety of not really knowing where they were was added to everything else.

Some time after nine o'clock, the wind eased ever so slightly, though nowhere near enough to get under way. A few minutes later the *Caird* rose to a particularly high sea, and just then she was struck by a breaking wave. The smallest quiver – a gentle shock – passed through her, and the wave rolled on. But this time she didn't swing back up into the wind. The sea anchor was gone.

There was a moment of confusion, then they felt her roll sickeningly to starboard as she fell off into the trough of the sea and they knew instinctively what had happened.

Both Shackleton and Worsley scrambled to their feet and looked forward. The frayed end of the buoy line was dragging through the water. The lump of ice was gone – and the sea anchor with it.

Shackleton thrust his head below and shouted for the others to get the jib. They hauled it out, frozen into a rumpled mass. Crean and McCarthy crept forward over the heavily rolling deck, dragging the sail with them. The rigging, too, was frozen and had to be beaten into compliance. But after a long minute or two they got enough ice off the halyards to hoist the jib to the mainmast as a storm trysail.

Slowly, grudgingly, the *Caird*'s bow once more swung around into the wind, and all of them felt the tension go out of their muscles.

The job of helmsman now was to hold her as close to the wind as she would go, swinging from one tack to the other. It required constant vigilance, and it could hardly have been more unpleasant, facing into the breaking seas and the piercing wind.

Fortunately the gale continued to diminish, and by eleven o'clock Shackleton decided to risk hoisting sail. The jib was removed from the mainmast, and the reefed lugsail and mizzen were run up. Then, for the first time in forty-four hours, the *Caird* was under way again toward the northeast, and the journey was resumed. But it was a slovenly course, with the boat running before the enormous following sea, her bow half buried by the force of the wind astern.

Shortly after noon, as if from nowhere, a magnificent wandering albatross appeared overhead. In contrast to the *Caird*, it soared with an ease and grace that was poetic, riding the gale on wings that never moved, sometimes dropping to within 10 feet of the boat, then rising almost vertically on the wind, a hundred, two hundred feet, only to plunge downward again in a beautifully effortless sweep.

It was perhaps one of nature's ironies. Here was her largest and most incomparable creature capable of flight, whose wingspread exceeded 11 feet from tip to tip, and to whom the most violent storm was meaningless, sent to accompany the *Caird*, as if in mockery of her painful struggles.

Hour after hour the albatross circled overhead, and there was an elegance of motion to the bird's flight that was very nearly hypnotic. The men could hardly avoid a feeling of envy. Worsley remarked that the albatross could probably have covered the distance to South Georgia in fifteen hours or less.

As if to emphasize their wretchedness, Worsley recorded: "Reindeer bags in such a hopeless sloppy slimy mess, smelling badly & weighing so heavily that we throw two of the worst overboard." Each of them weighed about 40 pounds.

Later he wrote: "Macty [McCarthy] is the most irrepressible optimist I've ever met. When I relieve him at the helm, boat iced & seas pourg: down yr neck he informs me with a happy grin 'It's a grand day sir' I was feeling a bit sour just before . . ."

Throughout the afternoon and evening the weather gradually grew less violent; and by dawn on May 3, the wind had fallen off to a moderate southwesterly breeze. As noon approached, the clouds started to thin out. Before long patches of blue sky appeared, and soon the sun was shining down.

Worsley took out his sextant, and it was no task at all to get a sight. When he had worked it out, the fix put their position at 56° 13' South, 45° 38' West – 403 miles from Elephant Island.

They were just more than halfway to South Georgia. Thus, in the space of only an hour, or maybe a little more, the outlook on board the *Caird* was completely altered. The battle was half won, and a warm sun was overhead. The off-duty watch no longer huddled in the dismal confines of the forecastle. Instead the sleeping bags were hauled out and run up the mast to dry. The men peeled off various articles of clothing, and boots, socks, and sweaters were tied onto the shrouds and backstay.

The sight that the *Caird* presented was one of the most incongruous imaginable. Here was a patched and battered 22-foot boat, daring to sail alone across the world's most tempestuous sea, her rigging festooned with a threadbare collection of clothing and half-rotten sleeping bags. Her crew consisted of six men whose faces were black with caked soot and half-hidden by matted beards, whose bodies were dead white from constant soaking in salt water. In addition, their faces, and particularly their fingers, were marked with ugly round patches of missing skin where frostbite had eaten into their flesh. Their legs from the knees down were chafed and raw from the countless punishing trips crawling across the rocks in the bottom. And all of them were afflicted with salt water boils on their wrists, ankles, and buttocks. But had someone unexpectedly come upon this bizarre scene, undoubtedly the most striking thing would have been the attitude of the men – relaxed, even faintly jovial – almost as if they were on an outing of some sort.

Worsley took out his log and wrote:

Moderate sea, Southerly swell.
Blue sky; passing clouds.
Fine. Clear weather.

> Able to reduce some parts of our clothing from wet
>   to damp.
> To Leith Harb. 347. m [miles]

By evening the sun had done a wonderful job of drying, and when they crawled into their sleeping bags that night the sensation was distinctly pleasant – at least by comparison.

The good weather held throughout the night and into the following day, May 4; and again the gear was distributed among the rigging. The wind was out of the southeast at no more than 15 knots. Only an occasional sea splashed on board so that they had to pump only twice during the day.

Worsley's sight at noon put the position at 55° 31' South, 44° 43' West, a run of 52 miles in twenty-four hours.

Two days of good weather had worked their magic, and among the entire crew there was a growing feeling of confidence, subtle but unmistakable. In the beginning, South Georgia had existed only as a name – infinitely distant and lacking in reality.

But no more. They were even at this moment less than 250 miles from the nearest point on South Georgia. And having already covered 450 miles, the distance that remained was at least conceivable. Three days more, or maybe four at the most, should see them there, and then it would all be over. And so that peculiar brand of anxiety, born of an impossible goal that somehow comes within reach, began to infect them. Nothing overt, really, just a sort of added awareness, a little more caution and more care to insure that nothing preventable should go wrong now.

The wind remained steady out of the southeast during the night, though it grew considerably stronger, with occasional squalls to almost 40 knots. With the coming of light on May 5 the weather had returned to its old familiar pattern – overcast sky with a nasty, lumpy sea running. The wind was on the starboard beam so that the spray broke over almost at will. By nine o'clock, everything was as wet as it had ever been.

Otherwise, it was a notably uneventful day, distinguished

only by the fact that toward evening the wind shifted slowly to the north and then the northwest. It increased in velocity too, and by dark was blowing a gale.

Steering was difficult that night. The sky was overcast, and the pennant on the mainmast by which the course had once been kept had blown away, bit by bit, in successive gales. Now they had to steer by the feel of the boat and by watching the shadowy white line of a breaking sea ahead.

At midnight, after a drink of hot milk, Shackleton's watch took over, and Shackleton himself assumed the helm while Crean and McNeish stayed below to pump. His eyes were just growing accustomed to the dark when he turned and saw a rift of brightness in the sky astern. He called to the others to tell them the good news that the weather was clearing to the southwest.

A moment later he heard a hiss, accompanied by a low, muddled roar, and he turned to look again. The rift in the clouds, actually the crest of an enormous wave, was advancing rapidly toward them. He spun around and instinctively pulled his head down.

"For God's sake, hold on!" he shouted. "It's got us!"

For a long instant nothing happened. The *Caird* simply rose higher and higher, and the dull thunder of this enormous breaking wave filled the air.

And then it hit – and she was caught in a mountain of seething water and catapulted bodily forward and sideways at the same time. She seemed actually to be thrown into the air, and Shackleton was nearly torn from his seat by the deluge of water that swept over him. The lines to the rudder went slack, then suddenly seized up again as the boat was viciously swung around like some contemptible plaything.

For an instant, nothing existed but water. They couldn't even tell whether she was upright. But then the instant was over; the wave had rolled on, and the *Caird*, though stunned and half dead under a load of water that rose nearly to the seats, was miraculously still afloat. Crean and McNeish seized the first implements that came to hand and began to bail furiously. A moment later, Worsley's watch fought their way out of the sleeping bags and joined the struggle, throwing water over the side with a wild urgency, knowing that the next wave would surely be the finish unless they could lighten her before it struck.

Shackleton at the helm kept looking astern for another tell-tale streak of brightness. But none appeared, and ever so slowly, as they frantically pumped and bailed and ladled the water overboard, the *Caird* lifted to the seas again.

The ballast had shifted and the glass on the compass was broken – but they apparently had won. It took more than two hours to get her emptied out, and much of the time they were working in icy water to their knees.

Crean started a search for the Primus stove. He found it at last, wedged up against the ribs of the boat, but it was completely clogged. For a half hour he worked over it in the dark, his patience slowly ebbing away. Finally, through clenched teeth, he swore at the stove. Then it lit and they had some hot milk.

The dawn of May 6 revealed an ugly scene. The wind was blowing nearly 50 knots from the northwest, and the *Caird* was straining into it, trying to hold to a northeasterly course. As every wave passed, some portion of it poured on board the boat.

But it seemed really not to matter too much. They had been pounded and bruised and drenched almost to the point of insensibility. Furthermore, the wave during the night had somehow changed their attitude. For thirteen days they had suffered through almost ceaseless gales, then finally a huge rogue sea. They had been the underdog, fit only to endure the punishment inflicted on them.

But sufficiently provoked, there is hardly a creature on God's earth that ultimately won't turn and attempt to fight, regardless of the odds. In an unspoken sense, that was much the way they felt now. They were possessed by an angry determination to see the journey through – no matter what. They felt that they had earned it. For thirteen days they had absorbed everything that the Drake Passage could throw at them – and now, by God, they deserved to make it.

Their resolve was strengthened when Worsley worked out the position. It put them at 54° 26' South, 40° 44' West. If this figure was accurate, they were a scant 91 miles from the western tip of South Georgia, and very soon there should be a sign of land – a bit of seaweed or a piece of driftwood.

As if to mock their determination, though, the sea rose menacingly throughout the morning. By noon it had grown so treacherous that Shackleton felt it was foolhardy to press on, though Worsley urged him to do so. At one o'clock Shackleton gave the order to heave to. They came about and dropped the sail. The jib was run up the mainmast and they began once again to tack back and forth into the wind.

All of them fell sullen – even Shackleton, who from the beginning had required of the men that they make every effort to remain cheerful in order to avoid antagonisms. But it seemed too much – to be so close, possibly only one good day's run, and to have to stop.

The strain on Shackleton was so great that he lost his temper over a trivial incident. A small, bob-tailed bird appeared over the boat and flew annoyingly about, like a mosquito intent on landing. Shackleton stood it for several minutes, then he leaped to his feet, swearing and batting furiously at the bird with his arms. But he realized at once the poor example he had set and dropped back down again with a chagrined expression on his face.

The rest of the afternoon passed without incident until almost dusk when Crean started to prepare the evening hoosh. A minute or two later, he called for Shackleton to come below. Crean handed him a mug of water to taste, and Shackleton took a small sip; then a grave expression came over his face. The second cask of water – the one that had got adrift during the launching of the *Caird* from Elephant Island – was foul. It had the unmistakable brackish taste of sea water that apparently had seeped into it. Not only that, but the cask was hardly half full, indicating that a great deal of the water had leaked out.

Crean asked Shackleton what he should do, and Shackleton, rather snappishly, replied that there was obviously nothing they could do – it was the only water they had, and they would have to use it.

Crean went ahead and made the hoosh. When it was ready the men sampled it cautiously, and found that it was disagreeably salty. For Shackleton, the discovery meant simply that the need for haste had now become acute. As soon as it was dark and Worsley was at the helm, he went aft and the two men discussed the situation. Their food, Shackleton said, should last two weeks. But they had less than a week's supply of water – and that was brackish. Thus a landing had to be made, and soon.

The inevitable question then became – would they hit South Georgia? Shackleton asked Worsley how accurate he thought their navigation had been. Worsley shook his head. With luck, he said, maybe within 10 miles, but it was always possible to make a mistake.

They both knew that except for one or two tiny islands, the Atlantic Ocean beyond South Georgia is a void all the way to South Africa, nearly 3,000 miles away. If, through a miscalculation or because of a southerly gale, they missed the island, there would be no second chance. The land would then lie to windward of them, and they could never beat back toward it. They dared not miss.

Fortunately, as the night wore on, the northwesterly gale diminished slightly, and the sky began to clear. At 1 a.m., Shackleton decided it was safe to get under way, and they again set their course for the northeast.

The all-important thing now was to learn the position, but soon after dawn a foglike mist moved in. They could see the sun, but only as a hazy outline. Worsley kept his sextant handy all morning, hoping that the fog would clear. After several hours, he took his notebook and, partly in desperation, he scribbled: "Most unfavourable conditions for Obs. Misty with boat jumping like a flea."

Normally, in taking a sight, the perimeter of the sun is brought down to the horizon with the sextant. Now the best that Worsley could do was to peer through the mists at the sun's blurred image and try to estimate its centre. Again and again he took sights on the theory that when he averaged them out he might come up with a reasonably accurate fix. He finally put the position at 54° 38' South, 39° 36' West, 68 miles from the tip of South Georgia. But he warned Shackleton not to put much stock in it.

The original plan had been to round the western tip of South Georgia, passing between Willis and Bird Islands, then swing east and run along the coast to the whaling station at Leith Harbour. But that had assumed reasonably decent navigating conditions, and had not taken into account the shortage of water. Now it no longer mattered where they landed, just so long as they did land. So they altered course to the east, hoping to hit anywhere on the west coast of the island, and it was of very little consequence where.

It turned out, too, that the water situation was considerably more serious than they had first imagined. Not only was the water brackish, but it was polluted with sediment and reindeer hairs which had somehow gotten into the cask. This noisome liquid, that had to be strained through gauze from the medicine chest, was drinkable – but just barely so, and it only aggravated their thirst. Furthermore, Shackleton had reduced each man's ration to about a half-cup per day, and the serving of hot milk at the beginning of each watch during the night had been eliminated. That afternoon, Shackleton informed them that for the rest of the voyage they could only afford to have hoosh twice a day.

Throughout the afternoon there had been a mounting air of expectancy that they would sight some indication that the land was close by – birds or kelp or something. But there was none. And with the approach of evening, the attitude of expectancy gave way to one of apprehension – of a strangely paradoxical sort.

By Worsley's estimate they should have been a little more than 50 miles off the coast. But Worsley's calculations were admittedly crude, and they could easily have been much closer.

On the west coast of South Georgia there was not the smallest settlement, much less a beacon light or even a buoy to guide them. In fact, even to this day, the west coast of South Georgia is only sketchily charted. Thus it was entirely conceivable that they might come upon the coast in the dark – suddenly and disastrously.

On the other hand, their fear of running onto the island was oddly counterbalanced by the dread awareness that they might just as easily miss it altogether – run by it in the night, and never know it was there. Indeed, they might already have done so. The darkness was now complete, and the *Caird* pounded forward on an ENE course with the wind on her port beam. The men peered ahead into the night with salt-rimmed eyes for the shadowy image of a headland; and they strained their ears for any unusual noise, perhaps the sound of surf pounding on a reef. But visibility could hardly have been worse – an overcast blotted out the stars, and the foggy mist still swept across the surface of the water. The only sounds that could be heard were the moaning of the wind through the stays and the surge of the heavy confused sea that was running.

Thirst, of course, heightened their expectation and prolonged each anxious minute. But in spite of the discomfort and uncertainty there was an undercurrent of suppressed excitement. Each of the watches made wild, speculative guesses about how soon they would reach the whaling station and what it would be like to bathe and have clean clothes and sleep in a real bed and actually eat food served on a table.

Gradually the hours crept by, though there was nothing to indicate that they were nearing the coast. At 4 a.m., when Worsley's watch came on, Shackleton remained with him at the helm to keep a lookout for the land. They were making about 3 knots, and by six o'clock they should have been less than 15 miles offshore – but there was not a sign of it – not the smallest bit of ice or shred of seaweed.

Seven o'clock came – 12 miles from the island, and yet no trace. The air of anticipation was slowly being replaced by a feeling of increasing tension. Some of the peaks on South Georgia were nearly 10,000 feet high. Surely they would be visible by now.

At eight o'clock, Shackleton's watch was due to take over. But nobody thought about watches. Instead all hands crowded into the cockpit, searching ahead and to each side in an atmosphere of competition, of hoping, of anxiety – all at once. But there was only the sea and sky, just the same as there had always been.

Toward nine o'clock, Shackleton sent Crean below to prepare some hoosh. When it was ready they ate it hurriedly in order to return to their lookout posts.

It was a strange time, a time of eagerness and expectation – underscored by grave, unspoken doubts. It was all so nearly over. An occasion for excitement, even jubilation. And yet, in the back of their minds was a nagging voice which refused to be silent – they might very well be looking in vain. If the island was there, they should have sighted it hours before.

Then, at just after ten-thirty, Vincent spotted a clump of seaweed, and a few minutes later a cormorant was sighted overhead. Hope flared anew. Cormorants rarely ventured farther than 15 miles from land.

Soon the foggy mists began to break up, though ever so slowly. Ragged clouds still scudded along close to the surface of the water. But the visibility was better. At noon the fog was almost gone. But the interminably heaving sea stretched in every direction.

"Land!"

It was McCarthy's voice, strong and confident. He was pointing dead ahead. And there it was. A black, frowning cliff with patches of snow clinging to its sides. It was just visible between the clouds, possibly 10 miles away. A moment later the clouds moved like a curtain across the water, shutting off the view.

But no matter. It was there, and they had all seen it.

from *Endurance: Shackleton's Incredible Voyage*,
McGraw-Hill, New York, 1959.
Reprinted by permission of Curtis Brown, Ltd.

THE HIGH SEAT OF ABUNDANCE

JACK LONDON

Jack London grew up on the waterfront and served in the San Francisco Bay fish patrol as a youth. After the 1906 earthquake he sailed from San Francisco in his ketch, the *Snark*, with his wife and a small crew; their perilous 2,000-mile voyage from Hawaii to the Marquesas had not been made before by a sailing ship.

London headed for Melville's paradisal Typee, the valley of Hapaa, only to find that diseases introduced by white visitors (including leprosy) had decimated the islanders. He spent twelve of the last eighteen months of his life in Hawaii, wracked by disease himself. In his last stories set on the islands, London moved away from harsh judgements about the savagery of mankind to study deeper bonds between people of all races.

On the arrival of strangers, every man endeavoured to obtain one as a friend and carry him off to his own habitation, where he is treated with the greatest kindness by the inhabitants of the district; they place him on a high seat and feed him with abundance of the finest food.

Polynesian Researches.

The *Snark* was lying at anchor at Raiatea, just off the village of Uturoa. She had arrived the night before, after dark, and we were preparing to pay our first visit ashore. Early in the morning I had noticed a tiny outrigger canoe, with an impossible sprit sail, skimming the surface of the lagoon. The canoe itself was coffin-shaped, a mere dugout, fourteen feet long, a scant twelve inches wide, and maybe twenty-four inches deep. It had no lines, except in so far that it was sharp at both ends. Its sides were perpendicular. Shorn of the outrigger, it would have capsized of itself inside a tenth of a second. It was the outrigger that kept it right-side-up.

I have said that the sail was impossible. It was. It was one of those things, not that you have to see to believe, but that you cannot believe after you have seen it. The hoist of it and the length of its boom were sufficiently appalling; but, not content with that, its artificer had given it a tremendous head. So large was the head that no common sprit could carry the strain of it in an ordinary breeze, so a spar had been lashed to the canoe, projecting aft over the water. To this had been made fast a sprit guy: thus, the foot of the sail was held by the mainsheet, and the peak by the guy to the sprit.

It was not a mere boat, not a mere canoe, but a sailing machine. And the man in it sailed it by his weight and his nerve – principally the latter. I watched the canoe beat up from leeward and run in toward the village, its sole occupant far out on the outrigger and luffing up and spilling the wind in the puffs.

"Well, I know one thing," I announced; "I don't leave Raiatea till I have a ride in that canoe."

A few minutes later Warren called down the companionway, "Here's that canoe you were talking about."

Promptly I dashed on deck and gave greeting to its owner, a tall, slender Polynesian, ingenuous of face, and with clear, sparkling, intelligent eyes. He was clad in a scarlet loin-cloth, and a straw hat. In his hands were presents – a fish, a bunch of greens, and several enormous yams. All of which acknowledged by smiles (which are coinage still in isolated spots of Polynesia) and by frequent repetitions of *mauruuru* (which is the Tahitian "thank you"), I proceeded to make signs that I desired to go for a sail in his canoe.

His face lighted with pleasure and he uttered the single word, "Tahaa," turning at the same time and pointing to the lofty, cloud-draped peaks of an island three miles away – the island of Tahaa. It was fair wind over, but a head-beat back. Now I did not want to go to Tahaa. I had letters to deliver in Raiatea, and officials to see, and there was Charmian down below getting ready to go ashore. By insistent signs I indicated that I desired no more than a short sail on the lagoon. Quick was the disappointment in his face, yet smiling was the acquiescence.

"Come on for a sail," I called below to Charmian. "But put on your swimming suit. It's going to be wet."

It wasn't real. It was a dream. That canoe slid over the water like a streak of silver. I climbed out on the outrigger and supplied the weight to hold her down, while Tehei (pronounced Tayhayee) supplied the nerve. He, too, in the puffs, climbed part way out on the outrigger, at the same time steering with both hands on a large paddle and holding the mainsheet with his foot.

"Ready about!" he called.

I carefully shifted my weight inboard in order to maintain the equilibrium as the sail emptied.

"Hard a-lee!" he called, shooting her into the wind.

I slid out on the opposite side over the water on a spar lashed across the canoe, and we were full and away on the other tack.

"All right," said Tehei.

Those three phrases, "Ready about," "Hard a-lee," and "All right," comprised Tehei's English vocabulary and led me to suspect that at some time he had been one of the Kanaka crew under an American captain. Between the puffs I made signs to him and repeatedly and interrogatively uttered the word *sailor*. Then I tried it in atrocious French. *Marin* conveyed no meaning to him; nor did *matelot*. Either my French was bad, or else he was not up in it. I have since concluded that both conjectures were correct. Finally, I began naming over the adjacent islands. He nodded that he had been to them. By the time my quest reached Tahiti, he caught my drift. His thought-processes were almost visible, and it was a joy to watch him think. He nodded his head vigorously. Yes, he had been to Tahiti, and he added himself names of islands such as Tikehau, Rangiroa, and Fakarava, thus proving that he had sailed as far as the Paumotus – undoubtedly one of the crew of a trading schooner.

After our short sail, when he had returned on board, he by signs inquired the destination of the *Snark*, and when I had mentioned Samoa, Fiji, New Guinea, France, England, and

California in their geographical sequence, he said "Samoa," and by gestures intimated that he wanted to go along. Whereupon I was hard put to explain that there was no room for him. "*Petit bateau*" finally solved it, and again the disappointment in his face was accompanied by smiling acquiescence, and promptly came the renewed invitation to accompany him to Tahaa.

Charmian and I looked at each other. The exhilaration of the ride we had taken was still upon us. Forgotten were the letters to Raiatea, the officials we had to visit. Shoes, a shirt, a pair of trousers, cigarettes, matches, and a book to read were hastily crammed into a biscuit tin and wrapped in a rubber blanket, and we were over the side and into the canoe.

"When shall we look for you?" Warren called, as the wind filled the sail and sent Tehei and me scurrying out on the outrigger.

"I don't know," I answered. "When we get back, as near as I can figure it."

And away we went. The wind had increased, and with slacked sheets we ran off before it. The freeboard of the canoe was no more than two and a half inches, and the little waves continually lapped over the side. This required bailing. Now bailing is one of the principal functions of the *vahine*. *Vahine* is the Tahitian for woman, and Charmian being the only *vahine* aboard, the bailing fell appropriately to her. Tehei and I could not very well do it, the both of us being perched part way out on the outrigger and busied with keeping the canoe bottom-side-down. So Charmian bailed, with a wooden scoop of primitive design, and so well did she do it that there were occasions when she could rest off almost half the time.

Raiatea and Tahaa are unique in that they lie inside the same encircling reef. Both are volcanic islands, ragged of sky-line, with heaven-aspiring peaks and minarets. Since Raiatea is thirty miles in circumference, and Tahaa fifteen miles, some idea may be gained of the magnitude of the reef that encloses them. Between them and the reef stretches from one to two miles of water, forming a beautiful lagoon. The huge Pacific seas, extending in unbroken lines sometimes a mile or half as much again in length, hurl themselves upon the reef, overtowering and falling upon it with tremendous crashes, and yet the fragile coral structure withstands the shock and protects the land. Outside lies destruction to the mightiest ship afloat. Inside reigns the calm of untroubled water, whereon a canoe like ours can sail with no more than a couple of inches of freeboard.

We flew over the water. And such water! – clear as the clearest spring-water, and crystalline in its clearness, all intershot with a maddening pageant of colours and rainbow ribbons more magnificently gorgeous than any rainbow. Jade green alternated with turquoise, peacock blue with emerald, while now the canoe skimmed over reddish-purple pools, and again over pools of dazzling, shimmering white where pounded coral sand lay beneath and upon which oozed monstrous sea-slugs. One moment we were above wonder-gardens of coral, wherein coloured fishes disported, fluttering like marine butterflies; the next moment we were dashing across the dark surface of deep channels, out of which schools of flying fish lifted their silvery flight; and a third moment we were above other gardens of living coral, each more wonderful than the last. And above all was the tropic, trade-wind sky with its fluffy clouds racing across the zenith and heaping the horizon with their soft masses.

Before we were aware, we were close in to Tahaa (pronounced Tah-hah-ah, with equal accents) and Tehei was grinning approval of the *vahine*'s proficiency at bailing. The canoe grounded on a shallow shore, twenty feet from land, and we waded out on a soft bottom where big slugs curled and writhed under our feet and where small octopuses advertised their existence by their superlative softness when stepped upon. Close to the beach, amid coconut palms and banana trees, erected on stilts, built of bamboo, with a grass-thatched roof, was Tehei's house. And out of the house came Tehei's *vahine*, a slender mite of a woman, kindly eyed and Mongolian of feature – when she was not North American Indian. "Bihaura," Tehei called her, but he didn't pronounce it according to English notions of spelling. Spelled "Bihaura," it sounded like Bee-ah-oo-rah, with every syllable sharply emphasized.

She took Charmian by the hand and led her into the house, leaving Tehei and me to follow. Here, by sign-language unmistakable, we were informed that all they possessed was ours. No hidalgo was ever more generous in the expression of giving, while I am sure that few hidalgos were ever as generous in the actual practice. We quickly discovered that we dare not admire their possessions, for whenever we did admire a particular object it was immediately presented to us. The two *vahines*, according to the way of *vahines*, got together in a discussion and examination of feminine fripperies, while Tehei and I, manlike, went over fishing tackle and wild-pig-hunting, to say nothing of the device whereby bonitas are caught on forty-foot poles from double canoes. Charmian admired a sewing basket – the best example she had seen of Polynesian basketry; it was hers. I admired a bonita hook, carved in one piece from a pearl-shell; it was mine. Charmian was attracted by a fancy braid of straw sennit, thirty feet of it in a roll, sufficient to make a hat of any design one wished; the roll of sennit was hers. My gaze lingered upon a poi-pounder that dated back to the old stone days; it was mine. Charmian dwelt a moment too long on a wooden poi-bowl, canoe-shaped, with four legs, all carved in one piece of wood; it was hers. I glanced a second time at a gigantic coconut calabash; it was mine. Then Charmian and I held a conference in which we resolved to admire no more – not because it did not pay well enough, but because it paid too well. Also, we were already racking our brains over the contents of the *Snark* for suitable return presents. Christmas is an easy problem compared with a Polynesian giving feast.

from *The Cruise of the Snark*,
Macmillan, New York, 1911.

Ancient Navigators of the South Seas

Stephen Thomas

A full account of Steven Thomas's years in the South Pacific is
given in his book *The Last Navigator,* published by Henry Holt.

In the opening metaphor of Joseph Conrad's classic *The Secret
Sharer*, a young captain finds himself poised between the clear, if
demanding, sea, and the land, which resembles a fish weir, a
"mysterious system of half-submerged bamboo fences, incomprehensible in its division, and crazy of aspect." Many of us are
drawn to the sea for the same reason; it is a place where the
elements of life are made clear by the awesome forces of nature.
It cannot have escaped us that the art of navigation is a way to
dance among those vast natural forces.

While I was sailing a boat from England to San Francisco via
the Marquesas and Hawaii, it became my dream to learn a vastly
different language of the sea – that of the indigenous Pacific
navigators, who use only stars, waves, birds, and the lore of their
fathers to make accurate landfalls on distant islands. These navigators once practised their arts throughout Oceania. Now only
a handful of them are active on the tiny atolls of Micronesia's
Central Caroline Islands. I had the privilege to be the student of
one of them: Mau Piailug, a master navigator from Satawal
Island. For various periods in 1983, 1984, and again in 1988, I
lived and voyaged with him; I was adopted into his family,
learned his language and his ways of finding land.

Piailug became famous when he guided the *Hakule'a*, a 60-
foot replica of a Polynesian voyaging canoe, on a voyage from
Hawaii to Tahiti. The voyage was an important demonstration
of the thesis that the Pacific Islands were populated by a race of

seafarers on intentional voyages of discovery. Long before Europeans had even ventured offshore, these seafarers had touched islands covering a quarter of the earth's surface. We cannot know the exact methods by which the ancients guided their canoes; they were never recorded. But we can reasonably assume that their techniques were similar to those used by the Micronesian navigators of today. Piailug and his colleagues are the keepers of a fully functioning non-instrumental navigation system that addresses the same set of problems as do our methods of navigation but with vastly different tools.

As I began my education I was impressed with the dedication required to learn these navigational arts. Carolinian languages are unwritten; all lessons must be committed to memory at the feet of a master.

Piailug began learning this "talk of the sea" from his grandfather at age five. When the old man died he continued learning from his father. At age 17 Piailug was initiated in the sacred Pwo ceremony to become a full-fledged *palu*. He continued to learn from his elders, as he does to this day.

The second thing that impressed me about his navigational system was its unity and beauty. The young student's first lesson is *paafu*, the "star structure." Thirty-two lumps of coral placed in a circle on a pandanus mat represent the rising and setting points of the 15 principal navigational stars. These stars rise in the east, arc through their "paths" overhead, and set in the west. Although the stars rise four minutes earlier each evening, making the night sky appear to change with the seasons, they always rise and set on the same azimuth. The "star structure" is a sidereal or star compass. It provides a means to organize all directional information about course, current, drift, wind, and swells, as does the 360-degree structure of our mariner's compass.

While the student learns the names of the navigational stars he also learns their "partners" or reciprocals. The partner of rising Altair, is setting Altair, the partner of rising Vega is setting Antares. The master will often construct a small canoe from coconut fronds and place it in the middle of the circle of coral lumps. He has each student name the stars over the bow, stern, outrigger, and lee platform as he turns the canoe through all points of the star compass.

The next series of lessons teach the star courses to and from all the islands in the Central Carolines. These directional instructions are called *Wofanu*, literally "to look at the island." While reciting the lore, the student mentally places himself on an island and in his mind's eye gazes along a star bearing to the island that lies beneath it. Wofanu is repeated in a long chant: "I sit on Satawal, I sail rising Altair on Truk. I sit on Truk, I sail setting Altair on Satawal. I sit on Satawal, I sail rising Gamma Aquila on Puluwat. I sit on Puluwat, I sail setting Beta Aquila on Satawal." He continues, naming each island and its guiding star.

While the student is learning Wofanu he will also begin to learn what is perhaps the most intriguing aspect of Micronesian navigation. *Pookof* is a system that posits certain sea creatures – noddies, terns, whales, dolphins, turtles and so on – in a ring around each island. As in Wofanu, the student recites the star course from an island to each creature and back to the island. These creatures are said to have been placed in the sea long ago, by Fanur and Wareyang, the two sons of Palulap, the great navigator. They are to aid the palu when he is lost. He will only perceive them when lost, it was stressed to me. There is a mystical aspect to this system. The navigator must be spiritually prepared in order to use it.

Individually the creatures are called *epar*, which means to "fix" or "aim." Pookof, the name of the system, means to tie a series of knots in something, typically a flower lei. Thus the system ties around each island a series of fixed points. Each creature has a name and certain markings unique to it alone. When one of these creatures dies, another with the same markings is said to take its place. Some of these epar, like the pod of killer whales said to lie under setting Pleiades from Satawal, might plausibly return to the same feeding grounds again and again. Others border on the fantastic, such as the whale with a dolphin swimming around its mid-section in the direction of rising Corvus from Satawal. Yet pookof is still considered an indispensable element of the "Talk of the Sea." It has endured even while many of the magical practices of former times have been discarded.

From the age of five to nine or 10, the student may concentrate on these lessons alone. Then, his father or master will begin to take him to sea to learn the "Talk of Sailing," a vast body of lore and skills necessary to navigate.

One of the key skills in the "Talk of Sailing" is to keep one's course without benefit of a compass. At night, one uses the stars. If sailing from Satawal to, say, Truk, one can use the star Altair as it rises in the east. If Altair has not yet risen or is too high, one must follow one of a number of substitute stars which travel the same "path" through the sky. Learning the substitute stars can only be done at sea. If the eastern horizon is obscured by clouds, one must steer by a star over the stern, the outrigger, or the lee platform – a practice which reaches back to the navigator's first lessons.

By day one steers by the swells. Typically in the area around Satawal the trade winds push up an east or northeast swell. A north, southeast, or southerly swell might be running as well. Since the swells come from afar, the vector of their approach is constant. Navigators check the swells' direction against the stars at morning and evening. They steer by them by keeping a constant angle between the canoe, the swells, and the *bwogabwogh*, or knots formed as the swell systems intersect.

As simple as this technique is to describe, it is difficult to put into practice. It is even more difficult on a dark, overcast night with no guiding stars visible and no moon to illuminate the surface of the sea. In these conditions the navigator must rely on his feel of the canoe's pitch and roll in the seaway. This technique, simply called "feeling," is the ultimate test of the navigator's skill. I have seen Piailug steer all night by "feeling" two very slight swells, from the north and east. In the morning, he made a perfect landfall on a tiny island.

While Wofanu gives the navigator the nominal course to steer, it provides him with no strategy for a voyage. Thus, another critical body of lore contained in "Sailing" gives the course corrections for all permutations of wind and current for all voyages commonly made from Satawal – in itself, a staggering amount of information. The speed of the current is estimated by watching the island of departure "move" one way or the other across the stars behind it. Depending on the number of star points it has "moved," a set of course corrections is invoked. Once at sea, the navigator must keep a sharp eye for a change of current, for he has no way to fix his position objectively.

Probably the most important technique contained in the "Talk of Sailing" is *Etak*, which means "Dragging." It is a plotting system that allows the navigator to mentally track the events of his voyage. For each voyage, a reference island lying athwart the rhumb line is specified. Although the reference island cannot be seen, imaginary "roads" from the picket of star points behind it are visualized as focusing through it and are projected onto the rhumb line, dividing it into segments, or drags. The grid gives the navigator a mental construct in which to reckon the events of his voyage.

The first and last segments of a voyage, called the "Etak of Sighting," span the distance between the island and the point at sea at which it disappears beneath the horizon. The second and second-to-last segments of a voyage, called the "Etak of Birds," encompass the typical fishing range of noddies and terns. Each dawn these birds fly out 18-20 miles from their island roosts, fish for the day, and return to their roosts at dusk. When closing an island, a navigator in doubt about his position will lie-to in order to observe the birds. The Etak of Birds and Etak of Sighting are the only Etak that are objectively fixed. The rest are purely theoretical.

One intriguing feature of the Etak plotting system is that the islands are pictured as moving while the canoe remains stationary. This feature allows the navigator to process all his time-speed-distance events through a single sea-level perspective instead of having to switch, as we do, to the bird's-eye perspective of the nautical chart. An increase of boatspeed is visualized as the reference island "moving" faster under the picket of stars behind it. An increase in current is visualized as the target and departure island "moving" away from the direction of the current.

Another important body of knowledge is the "Talk of the Skies," meteorological lore which allows the navigator to make forecasts by the shape, colour, and speed of the clouds at sunrise and sunset. Cloud shapes and colours are "read" within the context of a sidereal weather calendar called the "Fighting of Stars." Certain "fighting stars," when just beneath the horizon at dawn, are said to struggle for breath, causing inclement weather. Unfavourable cloud signs during the fighting of a star are an indication of bad weather. While a sidereal calendar marking the months is common knowledge, the "Fighting of Stars" is kept secret among navigators.

The seaways between islands are each uniquely named. Thus if one sails between Satawal and Lamotrek, one sails "Oairek." One must learn the names of all seaways, more than 60 in all. Pairs of seaways with similar alignments are called "Brother Seas." If a navigator forgets the alignment of one seaway, he can jog his memory by remembering its "brother." Yet another system, called "Star Channels," gives directions for finding channels through various atolls' reefs. A navigator possessing this knowledge can safely enter a channel at night. One without it must lie-to until day.

There are many other pieces of lore contained in the corpus of Micronesian navigation. Some spill into the metaphysical. "The Torch of the Lagoon of Anuufa," for instance, is a set of star directions like Wofanu, but one which takes the navigator from the mysterious lagoon of Anuufa to destinations like a two-headed whale, a man in a stone canoe, and a man in a canoe of ferns. Lore such as this is the navigator's literature. He recites it when drinking an alcoholic palm-sap, *tuba*. It gives him status and makes his students and crew proud of him. But it also indicates that navigation is not merely a set of utilitarian skills.

Another body of lore, "Itang," contains the wisdom and ethics of the culture in a set of allegorical poems. While instruction in Itang is not part of the navigator's routine training, a fully initiated navigator, a palu, is expected to know it. Itang is used only in grave situations. By uttering just a word of it to a chief, a navigator can protect himself or his crew from harm. "In the talk of the sea," Piailug told me, "the canoe is the mother and the palu is the father. The crew are the children." The navigator is bound by his ethics to serve his crew as their father and his island as its steward.

The more I learned about Piailug's navigation, the clearer it became that it was impossible to practise it outside the culture of Satawal. Navigational training equipped Piailug not merely with a set of skills enabling him to find distant islands and fishing grounds, but imbued him with a complete world view that was fed by and linked to the sea. On Satawal, seafaring and living are one and the same.

In my initial dream to go to Oceania and apprentice myself to a palu, I imagined that I, too, could become a navigator. By the end of my time with Piailug, I realized that he and his crew were welded into a single unit by blood and culture. I was a man from a different world. To join them, I would somehow have to reform myself as Satawalese. I could never be the secret sharer of Piailug's way of navigation.

from *Yachting Magazine*,
March 1990.

SUICIDE TACK

BERNARD MOITESSIER

In August 1968 Bernard Moitessier left Plymouth on a round-the-world solo race sponsored by the *Sunday Times*. Only two of his competitors cleared the Atlantic round the Cape of Good Hope, although Donald Crowhurst tried to steal the race by cruising in circles and sending back false reports on his position. Eventually Crowhurst was lost at sea; Nigel Tetley, believing Crowhurst was ahead of him on the homeward leg, pushed his battered boat too hard and sank; Robin Knox-Johnston, the eventual prizewinner, was swamped and had no radio contact. As far as Moitessier knew, he was in first place with clear sailing when he rounded Cape Horn, but he suddenly decided not to return to Europe. He continued on into the Southern Ocean and ended up in Tahiti, completing a voyage of one-and-a-half times around the world.

I

The wind's strength is unsteady, but sailing has become restful, with the barometer at its best for days. Drizzle alternates with blazing sun. I spend my time reading, sleeping, eating. The good, quiet life, with nothing to do. And little by little the water tank fills up.

Since I left Plymouth, I've been listening to as many English and French speaking radio stations as I can, hoping to get news of Nigel, Bill King, and Loïck. I haven't heard anything about them, but I have been listening to a lot of political talk from many different countries. What a laugh! Now I really understand why so many people just turn their backs and go away when political leaders open their mouths.

The Vietnamese radio programmes come in more and more clearly, but after twenty years away from my native land I hardly understand the language I used to speak fluently. At most I can make out a word or a simple sentence from time to time. Just the same, I leave the radio tuned to Saigon by the hour; it stirs old memories of Indochina, and my beautiful Chinese junk . . .

Everything hovering in the air of Asia at that time, the richest, most formative period of my life, comes back to me with incredible clarity. I smell the aroma of wood oil that permeated it, the smell of the sugar jars during the sail back to Rach-Gia, the slight noise of the sheet blocks, the creaking of the heavy battens. All that gave birth to *Snark*, my two *Marie-Thérèses*, and then *Joshua* and her search for a truth which I had perhaps lost, but which is gradually being reborn in the wake of the present trip.

II

In the days when I had my junk I was much too young to be my own taïcong, and had hired one known from Réam to Camao. The crew never spoke to him, because the taïcong needs all his peace to communicate with the gods and read on their faces. At mealtime, the crew would gather round the steaming rice kettle, forward if it was fine, amidships in a seaway. But always far from the taïcong, keeping their voices down so as not to disturb him in his communion. The young deckhand served him aft, respectfully giving him the rice bowl with both hands, without a word. Then he joined the others, slipping like a shadow on his bare feet.

When I was sailing with the fishermen of the Gulf of Siam the taïcong would tell me, "Keep the swell two fingers off the quarter, and you should always feel the wind behind your left ear, looking forward. When the moon is one big hand plus a small hand from the horizon, or when that star is one arm from the other side (in case the moon is hidden by a cloud), then the sea will become a little more phosphorescent, and we will almost be in the lee of the island to set the first lines."

There were no compasses on the Gulf of Siam junks, and I did not want one used during my sailing school cruises in the Mediterranean. Instead of bearing 110° from France to Corsica my crew had to steer with the mistral swell very slightly off the port quarter. At night it was the Pole Star, one small hand abaft the port beam. And if there was neither distinct swell nor star, we made do with whatever we had. I wanted it that way, because concentrating on a magnetized needle prevents one from participating in the real universe, seen and unseen, where a sailboat moves.

In the beginning they could not understand my insistence on getting away from the compass, that god of the West. But in exchange, they began to hear the sky and sea talking with the boat. And when blue-tinted land appeared on the horizon, looking as it did to the mariners of old, all nimbed with mystery, a few of them felt that our rigorous techniques should leave a door open to those gods which the modern world tries so hard to exclude.

The wind, the sea, the halo, the rainbow, the mares' tails amid the lapping, murmuring of the water, full of worried things and hopes. And I try to sense the secondary NW swell as the wake stretches ever eastward.

In a little Indonesian port, I followed the preparation of a Chinese junk that was to carry a shipment to Djakarta by way of the Thousand Island archipelago, strewn with reefs and rocks. The taïcong waited for three days after the loading, squatting without a word, without a gesture, contemplating the sky and the sea, in communion with the immaterial things that float all over the East. Then the junk weighed anchor in a nice beam breeze, with neither chart nor compass. I had the feeling she was protected by the gods of the Far East, and by the big eye carved on either side of her bow.

The moon rises later each night, changing her shape, becoming smaller and smaller. I can understand why people in the East prefer to tell time by the moon, who changes, disappears, and then returns. I cannot say exactly what it is she helps one feel, but I think all those who go to sea prefer the moon to the sun.

Nearly four months after we left Plymouth I knew my voyage would go far, but I had no idea it might go farther still, among the intangible wayposts of sea and time. Already four months of sky and stars, with fresh winds, calms, gales followed by calms, calms followed by light airs, then more calms and more fresh winds. And now I listen for the threat of a gale in the cirrus and the sounds of the sea.

The average has improved, the wake is much longer; Cape Leeuwin is far astern, Tasmania not too far ahead. If we continue at the rate we have for these last few days, we should be there in less than a week. And there may not be any gale, because the cirrus is beginning to lower and the stars are not twinkling much this evening, which tells me the wind is no longer angry up there.

Strong winds in the upper atmosphere cause large density gradients between layers of air at different temperatures. The stars then twinkle more than usual, because of the increased refraction bending the light. And when the high altitude winds blow very hard, this almost always tells of an approaching disturbance, or at least unsettled weather.

One very fine night, a taïcong fisherman told me why the stars announce the wind when they twinkle strongly. It is because there is wind up there, and it blows on the little flames of the stars, just as one would on a candle. So the stars flicker. The wind then blows with all its might, but can't blow them out, so it gets angry and comes down to the sea in revenge for being unable to blow out a single star, even the lowest ones close to the horizon. There, the stars could not resist the wind, which can blow very hard when it really gets angry. But there is a god close to the horizon to protect the low stars.

If it were not for the god of the horizon the wind would make them disappear one after the other. Then it would wait for the high stars to sink close to earth, to blow them out in turn. And men could not go on living, because there would be no more stars.

Years later, I learned that low stars always twinkle more than high ones because their light penetrates a thicker layer of air than at the zenith, making for greater light refraction.

I believe that science may someday permit men to reach the stars with their spaceships. I believe above all in the old East, which lets me go there any time I like with a candle and some wind. And I will paint a big black and white eye on *Joshua*'s bow when she finishes her journey, having found her way among the gods of my native Asia.

III

Taking advantage of the fine sun, and also of Christmas, I unwrap the smoked York ham specially prepared for Loïck and me by Marsh & Baxter, at the request of our friends Jim and Elizabeth Cooper. I had kept it in the hold under its original wrapping, saving it for these cooler latitudes, where it would be safe from heat waves.

The ham is perfect, without a trace of mould after four months in a humid atmosphere. Hey! What's happening to me? I suddenly start drooling like a dog with a choice bone under his nose. I must have had a long-standing ham deficiency – on the spot, I snap up a piece of fat the size of my wrist; it melts in my mouth.

Land in sight! I can't believe it. The mountains of New Zealand, a good 50 miles away, stand out very clearly on the horizon. Such visibility is amazing, but there is no mistake, the sextant confirms our position.

Joshua ghosts along at less than a knot on the flat sea, and passes 20 yards from a family of sleeping seals without waking them. They are already astern when one of them gives the alarm. I could see him tossing in his sleep, moving his flippers instead of keeping them across his chest. It looked as if he were dreaming. I wonder why the seals around here are so fearful, whereas the ones in the Galapagos treated us as equals. It may be because Galapagos seals are sea lions – their fur has no commercial value.

The sun sets. What little breeze there was today drops completely. Great peace all around, I will spend a nice quiet Christmas with the stars.

Calm . . . calm – I have the blues tonight. I think of my friends. I think of my family. I have everything I need here, all the calm, all the stars, all the peace. But I lack the warmth of men and I feel blue. For dinner, I added a can of corned beef to the remains of my noon concoction to make it edible. And I uncorked the bottle of champagne. I was not supposed to touch it before leaving the last dangers of New Zealand astern. I am not quite beyond the second cape, but tonight is Christmas, the calm is almost flat, the rocks are 50 miles off and not on my way. And above all, I feel blue, and that's why I opened Knocker's second bottle, the Cape Leeuwin one.

The shadow of the rat passes before my eyes. He looks at me gravely. I have seen him a few times since that old story. But those stories never grow old. They only change their shape.

It was the night before our Tahiti-Alicante sailing. The rat came in through the open porthole and dropped onto a plate in the galley. I jammed him against the floor with a book before he could hide in the hold.

We did not have a stick handy, so Françoise passed me the slingshot. I held the rat pinned with my foot on the book. But I aimed a little high to avoid hurting myself, and missed. When I pulled the slingshot again for another shot, the rat looked at me: he knew I was going to kill him. But his eyes said I still had the choice.

He was a big good-looking rat, probably fairly young, his brown fur glossy with health. A beautiful animal, healthy and alive, full of hope, full of life.

I felt like grabbing him by the tail and slinging him back to his coconut trees, saying "It's all right for this once, but don't let me ever catch you here again." And he would have never returned, because he was a coconut rat, not a sewer rat. But I think man carries hatred for rats in his heart. I shot at point-blank range, and killed him with a stone in the head. If there had not been that look, before, one rat more or less would not have made any difference. But the look was there, and it put me face to face with myself.

Midnight soon. The Cape Leeuwin bottle is almost empty. I think I've had it. The rat's shadow has become friendly – its look no longer carries the immense question to which I had failed to give the only answer.

IV

The descent toward the Horn has been under way for a week; a little hesitantly at first, to let a second gale pass by. Rain, hail, heavy breaking seas, occasionally impressive surfing. No damage done, no violent thrills except for the beauty of *Joshua* scudding along close-reefed in the light of the sky and sea as the wind swings around to SW.

No damage done – but I suspect my Beaulieu has died this time. It took a big blast of spray as I was filming breaking waves, and water entered the cable release opening on the side. I should have covered the hole with tape.

Without much faith, I stick a match wrapped with cotton in the hole to absorb the salt water. I do it five or six times, until the cotton comes out dry. Then I use cotton moistened with fresh water to dissolve any remaining salt, then more cotton warmed over a flame to dry everything out.

I press the shutter. It works! Sputtering a little, the camera comes back to life. I gingerly rewind the film. Now the film is safe: I'm lucky. Hope it will show the last breaking sea that I was filming. I take the reel out and gently warm the camera above the Primus stove, then stuff it with hot, dry newspapers.

In a saucepan, I heat the packets of moisture-absorbing silica gel. I warm some more newspapers on the stove, screw back the lenses, and wrap the Beaulieu in warm newspaper with the silica gel, after checking to see that it still works. A bad blow, if the camera had let me down. It has become a real friend. I believe it helped me to see things that I may not have seen as clearly on my own, during the voyage.

The wind has dropped and shifted to the NW, force 4 with drizzle. I don't like NW winds; they almost always bring some sort of trouble.

There is another bucket of rainwater under the mainsail boom. So far in the Pacific, I have collected 19 gallons of water, three-quarters of what I used in the last 35 days (at 2 1/2 quarts a day). During *Joshua*'s 56-day Indian Ocean crossing, she collected slightly more than my needs: 40 gallons, of which I used about 35.

All in all I am all right as far as the fresh water supply is concerned; the tank level is nearly the same as at the start. I think that a boat big enough to carry lots of food and spares could circle the globe several times, relying only on rain.

I used this morning's bucketful to wash the dish towel. A mistake, as it turns out. Last washed in the Atlantic doldrums, the dish towel helped me anticipate weather changes, now that I no longer have lumbago when the humidity increases.

When the dish towel could stand up it meant dry air and I

could expect regular SW winds for a while, with relatively nice weather and a generally blue sky aside from the normal cirrus and round cumulus. When it stood a little less stiffly, it was almost always the sign of a swing to the west, as the wind was already not so dry. And when my towel looked all droopy and clammy, as if it had wiped away all the sins of the world, I could expect northerly winds loaded with wet clouds.

I am seeking a smell, that of the glaciers and seaweed of Tierra del Fuego. I breathe in the night to the bottom of my being, and feel something like friendly presences seeking the smell with me. But the seaweed and glaciers are much too far, more than a hundred miles to the left.

A bit cool for a NW wind in this season. Must be blowing from the north across the channels of Patagonia, turning cold in contact with the frozen earth. Over the open sea the wind is probably deflected eastward by the belt of the westerlies, ending up as a NW wind, cold for no apparent reason. It would explain this gale that is not a real one, since the barometer is not too low. It would also explain the fairly regular sea, despite the exceptional height of the waves. They break in huge sheets, not in heavy cascades as they would in a real gale. That is why there is so little water on deck, apart from the freezing spray that jolts me out of my torpor.

A swell this high may portend a westerly gale for tomorrow or the day after, so we must run very fast, try to stay balanced at the limit. If it hits tomorrow, the Horn will protect us by breaking the swell, as *Joshua* will already be making for the Falklands in the Atlantic.

But if it hits tomorrow, on the 50-fathom shoal where the enormous swell can rear up as it does off a beach, then I hope there will at least be some sun and visibility before Diego Ramirez to aim true, not too far and not too close. Meanwhile – full speed ahead.

The lower part of the staysail is full of living pearls. They reach almost a third of the way up, then run off along the bunt of the reef. They come from the phosphorescent foam picked up by the bow and shattered by the whisker stay. If it were daylight, with the sun on the right side, there would be a big rainbow spread over fifteen yards on the lee of the bow. It would be no more beautiful than these thousands of little green stars glittering in the semi-dark of the astral night. The bowsprit is full of them too, brighter than those of the staysail because the black of the bowsprit stands out sharply against the clear background of the night.

Here and there, large flashes the size of a soccer ball appear in the sea, shining like giant glow worms. I have often seen them in the trades, and kept them in sight for sometimes thirty seconds before they went out. At first, I took them for the eyes of strange animals risen from the depths. I had even harpooned them, from the deck of my second *Marie-Thérèse*, both disappointed and relieved not to haul up a giant squid gnashing its beak at the end of my harpoon.

Nearly midnight. I am not sleepy. I wait at the foot of the mainmast. I can feel it quiver under my hand during the gusts. Things are still all right.

I am almost positive the wind will ease; it has gone to NNW, which proves conclusively that a low is not involved. Yet I know there is no such thing as conclusive proof here. Proof comes later, when you have gone through. And then it is still not proof.

I nevertheless decide to take the last reef in the mainsail. It is tiny now, with its big number "2" right next to the boom.

I feel better; my feet are warmer than a while ago. The mast has stopped quivering, except when the staysail pulls too hard in a gust. Talking in its second reef is out of the question. The second staysail reef is only for when it blows to death.

The clearing I am waiting for, without really daring to believe, for fear of the evil eye. The high latitude clearing! It appears like a great light. The sky clears to windward, and its brightness envelops the boat, driving SE the last banks of stratus and the fog beneath. In a few minutes the stars have reclaimed the sky. There is a lot of wind up there, they are twinkling very strongly. But there is little cirrus across the round moon. I hope she will be up when we pass the Horn, early tomorrow night if all goes well. The moon is low, even though she just crossed her meridian, because her declination is north, whereas we are in 56° south latitude. I have never seen the Southern Cross so high, nor so brilliant. The two little nebulae located in the extension of its long axis, straight above the Pole, remind me of two phosphorescent islands. Yet the sky looks like dawn. To the left the full moon, to the right the reflection of the ice-fields in the southern sky, and all around the silvery carpet of the sea breaking in long lengths.

The globes of fire that I saw in the waves earlier can be seen more than a hundred yards away now that the fog has lifted. They are plankton colonies, not the eyes of monster squids; I read the explanation somewhere. But I will probably never know why they shine so brightly, only to suddenly go out for no apparent reason. I would like *Joshua* to surf into one: at that speed, it would make fabulous fireworks in the staysail.

Past midnight. The wind is not easing. The seas are high, very high. The moon probably adds to the impression of height, by leaving the advancing wave faces in shadow, darker than all the white around. I ought to drop the main entirely, and perhaps the staysail. With only the storm jib and close-reefed mizzen, *Joshua* would still do very well, and stay this side of going too fast. But we are surfing; it is breathtaking at times, the log has already registered 48 miles in six hours. The hull speed has been exceeded. And – I don't know, shortening sail right now, no. Some sort of rhythm would be lost. The Horn is too close for shortening sail as long as things are all right, even if they are not quite what they should be.

During the last third of the advancing slope of each sea, the wind increases to force 9 for a few seconds. Then everything turns white, the boat luffs about 10° in the gust, and I grip the mainsail halyard tighter. The last third of the advancing face always provokes that little gust which draws forward 10° or so, fills the sails to the limit, and starts us surfing.

I feel a dangerous urge to go out on the bowsprit pulpit – I don't dare go beyond the staysail: it marks the farthest limit of good sense. In surfing, water is no longer water, but rock.

The swirls of foam raised by the bow fly in the lee of the hull for a few seconds, a light mist eddying behind the bellied stay-sail. The swirl goes on ahead and the boat tries to catch up. She sometimes makes it when surfing down a sea. A dangerous game, tremendously elating in this somewhat unreal world. My ears are burning. I put my inner hood back on, pull the hood of my foul-weather gear over it, and the sound of the ocean becomes a distant rumble as in a seashell.

I listen, I feel, I sift the invisible. A delicious warmth runs down my leg. I am vaguely surprised; it is already past. It saved me the complexities of zippers and trouser buttons, which might have prevented my perceiving something essential.

I try to sense the ice and seaweed that lie in the haze of distance. I know it is impossible, so far away, but I need to search to know what is beyond it.

A swirl of spray skims above the water along the windward side. Conical at first, it takes the shape of a little wave as an eddy from the bow sends it off to the right. The night is so clear I can see the little wave changing shape again. *Joshua* surfs after it, yawing far to starboard in pursuit of the phantom. Falling off – not luffing, as she should have.

A gust. This time *Joshua* luffs with more heel. The bowsprit buries itself and solid water roars across the deck. I grip the stay hard. The little wind-vane is still there. It must have dunked in the sea when we heeled, but did not break. I blow it a kiss.

Joshua drives toward the Horn under the light of the stars and the somewhat distant tenderness of the moon. Pearls run off the staysail; you want to hold them in your hand, they are real precious stones, that live only in the eyes. The wake spins out very far behind up the slopes of the seas like a tongue of fire and the close-reefed sails stand out against the clear sky, with the moon making the sea on the quarter glisten. White reflection of the southern ice. Broad greenish patches of foam on the water. Pointed tooth-like seas masking the horizon, dull rumbling of the bow struggling and playing with the sea.

The entire sea is white and the sky as well. I no longer quite know how far I have got, except that we long ago left the borders of too much behind. But never have I felt my boat like that; never has she given me so much.

I go below to fix my coffee and drink it slowly, both hands gripping the hot mug. God, that's good. I did not realize my hands were that cold. They are all swollen from soaking such a long time in wet gloves.

I just can't keep still. I go back on deck to have a look. Moving around the deck without a harness is possible, only a complete moron would be caught unawares – Don't be a fool, keep the harness! I'll keep it on, but with just one snap, and only when I sit still in the cockpit, not when I walk on deck between the bowsprit and the mizzen. You can start dreaming and then lose attention when sitting still, but not if you keep on moving around with eyes and ears wide.

One more look at the log before I plot our dead reckoning position on the chart and take a little nap. We have made very good time since yesterday noon, nearly 8 knots on average without counting the current which ought to give us another good knot. Nearly 2 a.m. and Cabo de Hornos is 130 miles away at the most. We will have to raise the mainsail again before long, to keep that nice average from dropping. If everything works out, the Horn should be right on the bow at sunset. I go below to sleep for a while.

The clear night is gone. Day is breaking. I didn't see the dawn, I slept through it. I hurry to raise the main and shake out the reefs, except the staysail's, which is a bit hard to take in when things get rough. The whole sky is full of joy and sunshine. I missed the dawn, but I know the day is going to be a beauty.

The entire sea is blue. It should be green, according to the Sailing Directions, because of a certain plankton which turns the Horn waters bottle green.

The sun climbs in the sky. The wind rises, and the mainsail is up close-reefed again. The wind rises further, backing gradually from NW to WSW. The mainsail has to be dropped, and the mizzen close-reefed.

The barometer has not fallen any more since last night's gale, and is not too low for the area. There is a terrific sun out. The noon sight is disappointing though, with only 171 miles covered in the last 24 hours. I had expected 20 miles more.

Diego Ramirez is still 47 miles away, so the Horn will not be rounded before night, which will come at 10 o'clock.

The sea becomes very heavy, very long, very high under a force 9 wind that has been blowing since the meridian sight. From the lower spreaders the scene is striking, with the tiny mizzen facing seas that look as if they are about to sweep over everything. Masses must have a hypnotic effect. You stare on and on – I am vaguely worried, but also feel there is no real danger thanks to the fairly strong current, 1.5 knots according to the chart, setting in the same direction as the wind, making the seas regular. Also, at 40 miles to port, the coast is too close for any secondary swell to come from here. Yet the sea is heavy, really heavy. It sweeps along in long, high, nearly horizontal crests, dotted with knolls and dips, but nothing like the sharp teeth and rough dunes of last night.

Occasionally a crest higher than the others becomes a wall of water, the sun slanting through its translucent peak giving it blue-green highlights. The sea then seems ready to change dress. But the rest remains deep blue, with hues melting every second into other shades of blue, like a great musical wave of endless vibrations. And the white streams down, iridescent with countless blues, green sparkling now and then. Once in a while part of the wall splits off, topples forward, and comes cascading down with a thunderous roar.

The wind is blowing as hard as before, still from the WSW. The sun slowly moves astern. The green highlights disappear, the blues turn almost violet. Heavy pink-lined clouds to the north tell me where land is, but I feel glad not to see it just now.

The sea continues to build. I drop the mizzen to keep the surfing within safe limits. One can never tell exactly what is going to happen while surfing in the high latitudes. The boat seems so happy, you're afraid she will try something new. I wonder how I dared go so far last night.

Standing on the pulpit, I search for Diego Ramirez, a bluish spot among the white patches sparkling on the horizon. I cannot see it yet. The storm jib bolt rope caresses my gloved fist gripping the stay. It gives me a warm feeling. I so badgered the sailmaker about reinforcements that he gave me his competitor's address to get me off his back. I felt then that it was like something sacred; I took my storm jib back and reinforced the clew myself so that the thimble would never rip out, whatever wind it met. And here it is, gathering all the passing wind, and caressing my fist as it pulls with all its tiny might.

I have set course for the Pacific again. I really felt sick at the thought of getting back to Europe, back to the snake-pit. I was physically tired by the Horn and my spirits sagged, then collapsed, after I decided to give up.

Sure, there were good, sensible reasons. But does it make sense to head for a place knowing you will have to leave your peace behind? Saint Helena or Ascension, yes ... and I wouldn't have stopped; I would have pushed on in the trade winds, telling myself, "Don't be a fool – you may as well just put in a little effort, try to pick up the *Sunday Times* prize, and leave again right away . . ." I know how it goes!

Trying to reach Tahiti nonstop is risky, I know. But the risk would be much greater to the north. The closer I got, the more disgusted I would be. If I can't hold on until the Pacific there will always be an island somewhere.

Mauritius . . . an island full of friends in the Indian Ocean, just after Good Hope. But I feel I can hold on until the Pacific – and that it is worth it.

I am really fed up with false gods, always lying in wait, spider-like, eating our liver, sucking our marrow. I charge the modern world – the Monster. It is destroying our earth, and trampling the soul of men.

"Yet it is thanks to the modern world that you have a good boat, with winches, Tergal sails, and a solid metal hull that doesn't give you any worries."

"That's true, but it is because of the modern world, because of its so-called 'civilization' and its so-called 'progress' that I take off with my beautiful boat."

"Well, you're free to split, no one is stopping you; everyone is free here, so long as it doesn't interfere with others."

"Free for the moment – but before long no one will be free if things go on; they have already become inhuman. So there are those who go to sea and hit the road to seek the lost truth. And those who can't, or won't anymore, who have lost even hope. 'Western civilization' is almost completely technocratic now, it isn't a civilization any more."

"If we listened to people like you, vagabonds more or less and barefoot tramps, we would not have got beyond the bicycle."

"That's just it; we would ride bikes in the cities, there wouldn't be those thousands of cars with hard, closed people all alone in them, we would see youngsters arm in arm, hear laughter and singing, see nice things in people's faces; joy and love would be reborn everywhere, birds would return to the few trees left in our streets, and we would replant the trees the Monster killed. Then we would feel real shadows and real colours and real sounds; our cities would get their souls back, and people too."

Everything beautiful and good that men have done they built with their dreams. When they set out, it was on a long voyage of exploration. The men wanted to find out where they came from, and where they were going. But they completely forgot why they were on the boat. And little by little they get fat, they become demanding passengers. They are not interested in the life of the boat and the sea any more; what interests them are their little comforts. They have accepted mediocrity, and each time they say "Well, that's life," they are resigning themselves to ugliness.

The captain has become resigned too, because he is afraid of antagonizing his passengers by coming about, to avoid the unknown reefs that he perceives from the depths of his instinct. Visibility worsens, the wind increases, but the beautiful sailboat stays on the same course. The captain hopes a miracle will calm the sea and let them come about without disturbing anyone.

If *Joshua*, who measures 40 ft, were racing a boat of the same design but 10 ft longer and with a proportionately larger sail area, she would lose every time, because a 50-foot boat sails faster than a 40-foot one.

Still, *Joshua* would have a chance of finishing ahead of the big boat in an ocean race, if she tried what is called the "suicide tack": seeking a different wind somewhere else. It either works or it doesn't, but there is no other way out. And if *Joshua* finds a fair wind 200 miles to the right of the bigger boat, for example, while the latter struggles with calms or headwinds, she can finish first. But if *Joshua* does not take the suicide tack, if she stays in the wake of the 50-foot boat, she'll be beaten flat.

That is where we are right now – and the big boat is far ahead. She has not yet finished the race, but if we do not take the suicide tack, she will win for sure. And when she does, the planet will explode, or else man will have become a brainless robot. Or both: robot-man will swarm over the earth, and our planet will rid herself of him like so much scum. A few Tibetan lamas may be left, and perhaps a handful of survivors in the mountains and at sea. And the whole cycle will have to start over again. The Monster will have won, and humanity lost.

The violent things rumbling within me vanished in the night. I look to the sea, and it answers that I escaped a great danger. I do not want to believe in miracles too much – yet there are miracles in life. If the weather had stayed bad for a few days longer, with easterly winds, I would be far to the north by now; I would have continued north, sincerely believing it was my destiny, letting myself be carried by the trades like an easy current with no whirlpools or snares, believing it was true – and being wrong. The essential sometimes hangs by a thread. Here I am, at peace, the bow pointed toward the East, when I could be heading north with an unsuspected drama deep inside.

from *The Long Way*,
Librairie Arthaud, Paris, 1970.